The COUNTESS and the NAZIS

The COUNTESS and the NAZIS

AN AMERICAN FAMILY'S PRIVATE WAR

RICHARD JAY HUTTO

LYONS
PRESS

Essex, Connecticut

An imprint of The Globe Pequot Publishing Group, Inc.
64 South Main Street
Essex, CT 06426
www.globepequot.com

Distributed by NATIONAL BOOK NETWORK

British Library Cataloguing in Publication Information available

Library of Congress Cataloging-in-Publication Data available

ISBN 9781493086566 (cloth)
ISBN 9781493086573 (electronic)

∞™ The paper used in this publication meets the minimum requirements of American National Standard for Information Sciences—Permanence of Paper for Printed Library Materials, ANSI/NISO Z39.48-1992.

For
Katy & Matt
Martin & Emily

CONTENTS

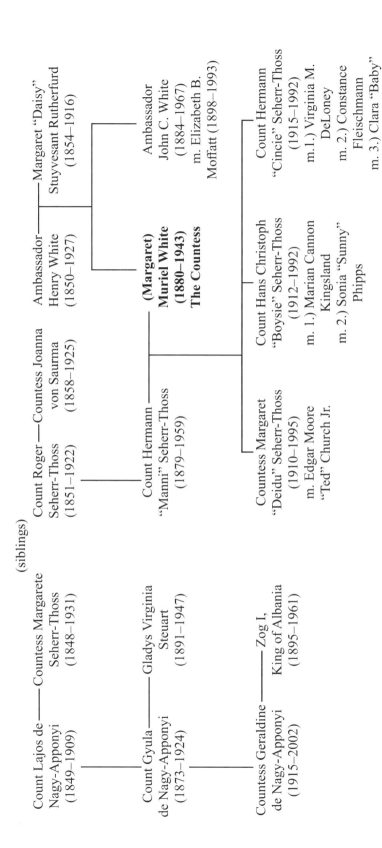

(siblings)

Margaret "Daisy" Stuyvesant Rutherfurd (1854–1916)

Ambassador Henry White (1850–1927)

Ambassador John C. White (1884–1967) m. Elizabeth B. Moffatt (1898–1993)

Count Roger Seherr-Thoss (1851–1922) — Countess Joanna von Saurma (1858–1925)

(Margaret) Muriel White (1880–1943) The Countess

Count Hermann "Manni" Seherr-Thoss (1879–1959)

Count Hermann "Cincie" Seherr-Thoss (1915–1992) m. 1.) Virginia M. DeLoney m. 2.) Constance Fleischmann m. 3.) Clara "Baby" von Gontard

Count Hans Christoph "Boysie" Seherr-Thoss (1912–1992) m. 1.) Marian Cannon Kingsland m. 2.) Sonia "Sunny" Phipps

Countess Margaret "Deidu" Seherr-Thoss (1910–1995) m. Edgar Moore "Ted" Church Jr.

Count Lajos de Nagy-Apponyi (1849–1909) — Countess Margarete Seherr-Thoss (1848–1931)

Count Gyula de Nagy-Apponyi (1873–1924) — Gladys Virginia Steuart (1891–1947)

Countess Geraldine de Nagy-Apponyi (1915–2002) — Zog I, King of Albania (1895–1961)

INTRODUCTION
March 13, 1943

THE GESTAPO OFFICERS WERE COMING FOR MURIEL, THE COUNTESS Seherr-Thoss. She had been repeatedly warned and threatened with arrest, and thus it was no surprise when she saw them walking up the drive to her home, Dobrau Castle, early one morning. Her cousin, Henry James White, was the naval attaché at the American embassy in Berlin and was interned by the Nazis. He wrote of Muriel's efforts to visit him, "She had consulted some old acquaintance who was pretty well up in the Nazi hierarchy and he had told her that if she and her husband wished to continue living in relative comfort, they would in no way bestir themselves to do more than write to me."[1] Yet Muriel was undeterred. Her cousin found her letters to him "often amazingly frank in their condemnation of all that was Nazi, and I have but little doubt that they were read during their transmission and that they may have played a part in her eventual violent death. Thinking they might be seized as evidence during our repatriation, I destroyed them."[2] Several generations later, Muriel's grandson recalls of her opposition to the Nazis, "She was always bucking their system, refusing to fly the flag or give the raised salute."[3]

She would be killed for her defiance.

(Margaret) Muriel White was the daughter of famous parents. Her father ran the US embassy in London for seven years before becoming the ambassador to Italy and then to France, where Muriel was born on October 12, 1880. His friend, President Theodore Roosevelt, called Henry White "the most useful man in the entire diplomatic service, during my Presidency and for many years before."[4] Her mother, known as Daisy, was a famous beauty born to wealth and privilege. Daisy's childhood friend, writer Edith Wharton, wrote of her, "It is hard to picture nowadays the shell-like transparence, the luminous red-and-white, of those young cheeks untouched by paint or powder, in which the blood came and went like the lights of an aurora."[5] Even her great-grandson recalls Daisy as "a remarkable beauty and force. Her personal ambitions would lead to much unhappiness in her daughter's life."[6] It is difficult to grow up as the daughter of a celebrated beauty, and Muriel's relationship with her mother was complex and fraught with tension. Beauty can be as cold as the marble that captures it.

Having been thwarted in several advantageous marriages, in 1909, at the relatively advanced age of twenty-nine, Muriel married Count Hermann Seherr-Thoss, oldest son and heir to his father's title and Silesian estates as well as a hereditary seat in the Prussian House of Lords.[7] It was not a happy marriage, especially when set against the backdrop of rising international tensions. Muriel was beset by financial and personal challenges, particularly after the US Congress shut off access to the bank accounts of American heiresses wed to titled husbands whose adopted countries fought on opposing sides during the First World War. Yet even with those financial restrictions, with financial support from her father and stepmother, Muriel was still able to pay for major renovations to two castles owned by her husband's family. As Adolf Hitler rose to power and Nazism spread rapidly, she also secured the funds and arranged visas for a Jewish family to escape from Vienna to Australia and begin a new life.

Muriel began her marriage loyal to her husband and his country. He even insisted that their son's first fiancée provide "proofs of her pure Aryan descent,"[8] and there is no evidence that she opposed his views initially. Yet Muriel evolved to such a degree that, at a 1937 dinner at the Hotel Adlon in Berlin, she went too far (particularly since her brother was then stationed at the US embassy in Berlin). With a Nazi district leader seated at her table, Muriel asked, "'Is it true the Party sometimes rewards deserving Jews by making them honorary Aryans?' . . . When the gauleiter [district leader] conceded that this happened on occasion, the countess followed up with a line that she must have been mulling over for quite some time: 'Can you tell me then how I could become an honorary Jew?'"[9]

From 1941, a German Army forced labor prisoner-of-war subsidiary camp, "Arbeitskommandos E115,"[10] and a full ammunition depot were operated in the village in view of her family's castle. There were widespread rumors that Muriel had hidden and helped two British pilots escape from the camp in 1941. They were never found, nor was the escape solved. Muriel's sons, "Boysie" (born in 1912) and "Cincie" (born in 1915), were German citizens and should have been in military service but had been sent to the United States for their safety. "In 1943, under threat of being sent to the Auschwitz concentration camp, the Gestapo demanded that she bring both of her sons back."[11] She told a friend she was being hounded by the Gestapo, who "during the war visited her very often in the palace. Officers of the secret police demanded that she bring her children back to the Third Reich. The Countess claimed that she was being followed and that there were strangers in the garden—that's why she spent most of her time in the palace chambers. Her biggest fear was being deported to a concentration camp."[12]

Fearing torture and believing that she might be forced to reveal the location of her sons, Muriel acted immediately when she saw the car full of Gestapo officers turn into the entrance of Dobrau Castle on the morning of March 13, 1943. She quickly climbed two flights of stairs inside the castle's tower. Knowing what she was about to do, her thoughts must have turned to what she perceived as her personal triumphs and failures. She had given her husband a daughter, as well as an heir and a spare, and then had depleted a large portion of her inheritance restoring and furnishing two of his family's castles. She escaped her home more than once—in one instance, she fled in a horse cart, barely dodging bullets while women around her were shot dead—and personally experienced three wars: World War I, the Silesian Uprisings, and World War II.[13]

Her first duty now was to protect her children—a duty in which for much of her life she believed that her mother had failed her. It had long been made clear to Muriel, who spoke six languages fluently, by her mother that intellectual pursuits by women would never be as valued as their physical beauty.

Muriel had never been able to confront her mother about Daisy's treachery in thwarting several fortunate marriages for her only daughter. She was long dead by the time Muriel became aware of what she had done. It seemed the knowledge came too late. Muriel's one comfort was that her own children were safe in America. In that endeavor, she had succeeded, and no one could take that away from her.

There, on the upper floors of the castle's tower, as she watched the Gestapo officers walk up the drive to arrest her, her duty done, Muriel leaped from the window to the gravel below.

Schloss Dobrau, where Muriel leapt from the tower. CREDIT: PAUL CHURCH

Chapter One

Henry ("Harry") White established the model of the State Department diplomat, in top hat and striped pants, who does his most effective business at weekends in historic country houses or in the corners of drawing rooms or even on the hunting field, who knows how to catch the right ear at just the right moment, and whose extensive acquaintance among the socially and politically great assures him of a private audience with any monarch, prime minister, or pope. There are two important lessons to be learned from Harry White's remarkable career: one, that it seems to have fitted almost no American legate but himself, and two, that it has been blindly followed by generations of diplomats who have confused dinner parties and weekends with power.[1]

—LOUIS AUCHINCLOSS,
THE VANDERBILT ERA: PROFILES OF A GILDED AGE

HAMPTON, BY 1790 THE LARGEST PRIVATE HOME IN AMERICA, ONCE reigned over twenty-five thousand acres at the height of its glory. Its founder, Colonel Charles Ridgely, was already a third-generation Marylander when, in 1745, he purchased 1,500 acres in northern Baltimore County. The eventual Georgian-style mansion, at twenty-four thousand square feet, overlooked formal gardens and landscaped grounds tended by enslaved laborers. Muriel's father, Henry White, who grew up there, recalled,

> I still remember the younger ones, who at that time were beginning to hear of freedom and of the possibilities of education, coming to me at times privately with little primers, and asking me to explain the spelling of certain words, or the meaning of certain combinations of letters,

which they could not understand; begging me at the same time not to let any of the elders know that they had done so, as it was one of the principles of slavery that they should not be taught to read or write. . . . I well remember having seen my grandfather Ridgley lose his temper on one or two occasions, and box the ears of one of the grooms for reasons which seemed to me entirely inadequate, and the incident left a most disagreeable impression on my mind.[2]

Henry White was born in Baltimore on March 29, 1850, the son of John Campbell White and Eliza Ridgely, and the grandson of another Eliza Ridgely, an heiress, fashion arbiter, and friend of the Marquis de Lafayette. Painted by Thomas Sully at only fifteen, she brought a large inheritance to her marriage to John Carnan Ridgely, combining for the first time two lines of the same family name. Their oldest daughter, Eliza, would be the mother of Henry White. Henry's father, John Campbell White, died in 1853, only six weeks before the birth of a second son, Julian LeRoy White, and the boys were brought up chiefly at Hampton by their grandfather and numerous relatives. As Henry recalled,

By far the happiest recollections of my childhood up to the age of fifteen were long annual sojourns from April or May to October or November at Hampton. The older I become, the more do I realize how valuable a background to a man in after life is the country home of his childhood and youth—especially when as in my case it was a large estate of 5000 acres over which the boys of the family were allowed to roam at will, with picnics in the woods, swimming in the Gunpowder River, tobogganing down the terraces of the garden, riding on horseback with one's grandfather, uncles, cousins, and any guest who might happen to be staying at the house.[3]

Their mother, Eliza "Didy" Ridgely White, was a wealthy and still-vibrant widow at thirty-seven when she married in Baltimore, in 1865, Dr. Thomas Hepburn Buckler, a physician who had treated President Buchanan, Chief Justice Taney, and General Robert E. Lee. Buckler was sixteen years older than Eliza and shared her pro-South views about the Civil War. Even though they lived in Maryland, a

Henry White and his grandfather in France. COURTESY OF THE WILLIAM TAPLEY BENNETT, JR. PAPERS, RICHARD B. RUSSELL LIBRARY FOR POLITICAL RESEARCH AND STUDIES, UNIVERSITY OF GEORGIA LIBRARIES, ATHENS, GEORGIA, 30602-1641

border state, "if the Ridgelys spent their summers in Newport it was because that resort had a sufficient number of warm-weather colonists from below the Mason-Dixon line."[4]

Although Henry White was just a child during the war years, he later wrote, "I have on the whole painful recollections of the Civil War and have had a horror of war in general throughout my life. It brings out all that is worst in human nature, causes friends of a lifetime to become enemies, to be suspicious of each other's patriotism, and I have never been able to see its advantage from any point of view."[5] His impressions greatly informed his diplomatic work and his efforts as one of five US peace commissioners at the Treaty of Paris negotiations in Versailles at the close of the First World War.

Henry and his brother were given an excellent education. His mother learned Latin when he did and then taught herself Greek so she could teach it to her sons. In the aftermath of the war and ensuing Reconstruction, it seemed a propitious time for the family to leave the United States. With only a brief interlude when he came home in 1869, Henry White lived chiefly in Europe until his paternal grandfather's death in Paris at the end of 1882. His half-brother, William Hepburn Buckler (always called Willie), was born in Paris in 1867. As Henry wrote, "In the year 1867, although only a little over seventeen years of age, but being as tall as I have been ever since, I began to go into society."[6] Although admitted to Cambridge, his health was deemed not hardy enough to undertake strenuous studies, having been educated privately by tutors his entire life.

As his granddaughter recalled,

His mother, Eliza Ridgely White Buckler, when left a widow with two small sons, took them to Italy and had them learn Italian. They corresponded almost entirely in Italian the rest of their lives. When she married Dr. Buckler, she moved the entire family, including her former father-in-law, Henry White, Sr., to Paris. HW [Henry White] and Uncle Willy almost always corresponded in French![7]

There were no financial issues to be considered, as he was born "of two old, honorable, and rich Maryland families."[8] As White's biographer wrote, "The family was one of considerable wealth; better, it was also a family of standards and breeding, which had held a recognized place in Maryland for generations."[9]

> It may be as well stated here that I had reached the age of nineteen years, without giving the slightest thought to any future career, or being as far as I can remember, in any way interested in myself, except with a view to getting as much enjoyment out of life as possible, which I did then, and I think have done ever since, more or less. In those days the idea of "service" was not generally entertained, and I had been brought up by my grandfather and my mother to feel that if a man were a "gentleman" and was fortunate enough to have the prospect of inheriting an income sufficiently large to enable him to live comfortably, even if not luxuriously in any country, he need not concern himself with any public work, or any other kind of work. And my brother and I were always told that such would be our condition.[10]

Henry proudly wrote that their grandfather White, who was with them during their years in Europe, "was the most devoted of grandparents, even going to the extent of giving us unlimited credit at the banks at which he kept an account. I am glad to add that neither of us abused his confidence in that or any other respect."[11]

The brothers were trained by their mother to "maintain regular hours, keep to their books, and learn the chief modern tongues. Harry grew up as a rarity in Parisian society, a man of the world without any of its vices."[12] The Franco-Prussian War forced them, along with many American families who had been enjoying the French court, to escape to London in 1870. For the next nine years, Henry White devoted himself to society, travel, and, most important, fox hunting. He explained,

> The hunting field, as I soon realized, is a wonderful place of training of character, good manners, good temper, and coolness of judgment, and it has played a very important part in the development of those qualities in the statesmen and military—not infrequently also even the Naval men of England. In any case, the nine winters of fox hunting were the best preparation which I could have had for the twenty-one years of Diplomacy of which I was subsequently (although I little knew it at the time) to have experience in England.[13]

It was the perfect time for White to enter British society. "A handsome and agreeable unattached young man of ample means, who excelled at all popular sports, was welcome, although American, at the very grandest country houses, and England was still ruled by the men who owned or leased them. . . . Society was fluid, although money was the ticket."[14]

Perhaps Henry White learned a great deal about bloodlines in his years of racing, as he could not have chosen a more distinguished wife than his, who descended from most of the eminent colonial families of the United States. Margaret "Daisy" Stuyvesant Rutherfurd was born on October 7, 1854, in New York City. Her father, Lewis Morris Rutherfurd, was an attorney best known as an astronomer and pioneering astrophotographer. His hobby turned into a vocation, and he left the law to pursue his passion. Using instruments of his own invention, he produced photographs of the sun, the moon, planets, and star clusters down to the fifth magnitude. One of the original members of the National Academy of Sciences and called "the greatest lunar photographer of the age," the lunar Rutherfurd crater on our moon is named for him. He invited guests to his home on Second Avenue to marvel at his observatory, boasting a thirteen-inch refracting telescope. The diarist George Templeton Strong recalled a bit unkindly his visit in 1859, to observe "a little miserable, loafing comet. . . . It looked like a distant street lamp dimly seen through a fog by a near-sighted man, a small, amorphous, hazy blotch of faint light."[15]

Born at "Morrisania," the family estate that once encompassed most of the Bronx and much of New Jersey, Rutherfurd was a grandson of US senator John Rutherfurd and a great-grandson of Lewis Morris, a signer of the Declaration of Independence. Major General William Alexander, the last Earl of Stirling[16] and third-in-command of General Washington's troops, was the uncle of Rutherfurd's grandfather.

If any founding families were not represented by Lewis Morris Rutherfurd, then his wife remedied that deficiency. The famously beautiful Margaret Chanler was born in South Carolina to Reverand John White Chanler and his wife Elizabeth Winthrop (from the colonial Boston family), who was a daughter of Judith Stuyvesant. Margaret Chanler was adopted by her childless aunt and uncle, Helena Rutherfurd Stuyvesant and Peter Gerard Stuyvesant, and interchanged her last names of Chanler and Stuyvesant. All those marriages added the Livingston, Beekman, Van Cortlandt, Jay, and Fish families (and fortunes) to the genealogy. In due course, Margaret's oldest son would, at the age of four, legally change his name from Stuyvesant Rutherfurd to Rutherfurd Stuyvesant in order to inherit one-third of a family fortune, which presently would be estimated at more than $73 million. It would be the daughter of that grand union and sister of that fortunate little boy, Margaret "Daisy" Stuyvesant Rutherfurd, who married Henry White in 1879. The Rutherfurds were famously attractive. One social arbiter of the day said of them, "The pair presented the unusual combination of an uncommonly beautiful woman married to an uncommonly handsome and distinguished man."[17]

One of little Daisy's next-door neighbors and childhood friends, Edith Jones, would become celebrated as the writer Edith Wharton. She fondly remembered Daisy and her family and their time in Newport:

> Best of all I liked our weekly walks with Mr. Rutherfurd over what we called the Rocks—the rough moorland country, at that time without roads or houses, extending from the placid blue expanse of Narragansett Bay to the gray rollers of the Atlantic. Every Sunday he used to collect the children of the few friends living near us, and take them, with his own, for a tramp across this rugged country to the sea.[18]

"After the Rutherfurd sisters [Daisy and Louisa] had outgrown their governess [Anna Bahlmann], she was transferred to the Jones residence, where she tutored young Edith."[19] Years later, Wharton recalled, "The intimacy between the two families had never relaxed, and during the years when Henry White was first Secretary at our London Embassy he and his wife were the means of my meeting many interesting people whenever I went to England."[20] Edith Wharton's most vivid memory of the couple, however, was how attractive they were:

> The Whites, in their youth, and even in their middle age, were one of the handsomest couples I have ever seen, and on the Rutherfurd side the beauty of the whole family was proverbial. The story was told of an Englishman and an American who were strolling down Piccadilly

together, and discussing the relative degree of good looks of their respective compatriots. "I grant you," the Englishman said, "that your women are lovely; perhaps not as regularly beautiful as ours, but often prettier and more graceful. But your men—yes, of course, I've seen very good-looking American men; but nothing—if you'll excuse my saying so—to compare with our young Englishmen of the Public School and University type, our splendid young athletes: there, like these two who are just coming toward us—" and the two in question were Margaret White's brothers, the young Rutherfurds.[21]

Henry White met Daisy Rutherfurd on one of his trips back to the United States. A bit lame from a hunting accident, he and his brother Julian went to Baltimore to view the Maryland Building from the first World's Fair—the Centennial Exhibition—in Philadelphia. At the close of the exhibition, Maryland's entry had been disassembled and brought home for display. While visiting the reconstruction, Henry White was shown "a photograph of Miss Margaret Stuyvesant Rutherfurd, of a well-known New Jersey and New York family, and was greatly struck by it."[22]

The next summer he was visiting Newport, where he

met her and fell immediately and completely in love. It was not strange that he did so. "Daisy" Rutherfurd was a young woman of really remarkable beauty and poise. She was the sort of girl at whom not only men but other women turned around to look. Forty years after this time, when White was in Paris with President Wilson, an Englishwoman recalled how she had first seen Miss Rutherfurd across a crowded theatre and had sat up with a gasp of delight at her loveli-ness. She was one of those few women whom it gives a man a kind of public distinction to marry.[23]

They wed on December 3, 1879, at Manhattan's St. Mark's in the Bowery, where Daisy's mother, grandmother, and great-grandmother had all been married. The minister, Reverend Dr. Henry C. Potter, a future bishop who was himself the son and nephew of bishops, was then the minister at Manhattan's Grace Church. He would become the "fashion-able" clergyman who officiated at the marriage of many society weddings,

Mora   707 BROADWAY, N. Y.

Daisy Rutherfurd White as a young woman. COURTESY OF HAMPTON
NATIONAL HISTORIC SITE, NATIONAL PARK SERVICE

including Consuelo Vanderbilt's to the ninth Duke of Marlborough and Cornelia Bradley Martin's to the fourth Earl of Craven.

One attendee, Margaret Livingston Chanler Aldrich, a first cousin of the bride, was only nine years old at the time but vividly recalled the wedding party: "Joy came down the aisles after the solemnization of matrimony had made them man and wife. The handsomest of couples? Not quite; the bride's parents following the four bridesmaids were even handsomer, though not equal in height."[24] Daisy was intimately involved in the life of that young cousin, and those of her ten siblings, who lost both their parents to pneumonia within two years of one another. The children were usually called "the Astor orphans," and Daisy was appointed one of their legal and financial guardians because she was nearer their age than the other trustees. She would take her duties very seriously over the years and was accused of acting "like a bossy elder sister"[25] to her younger Astor cousins.

> "Daisy" White sent a long list of dos and don'ts for Elizabeth [one of her Astor wards] while she was in France. It was imperative that Elizabeth be a good guest, "so that when you leave I shall hear what a pleasure your visit has been & not what a trouble." She should be sure to give "good liberal tips" to the servants in the households where she was staying—though Elizabeth should also be wary about the help ("I never trust maids to look after jewelry"). . . . Don't stay up late. To bed by a quarter to ten at the least. You are not strong now & all these things are of the greatest importance, as I am sure you do not wish to grow up to be a delicate woman.[26]

Daisy still invested time and effort in her marriage while attending to her young cousins while her husband found a renewed purpose. He wrote,

> Shortly after our marriage my wife, who had an exceptionally interesting mind and a strong sense of public duty, began to talk to me about doing something useful in the world, a matter of which we thereupon began to discuss from time to time. Eventually we came to the conclusion that Diplomacy would be on the whole the best way in which I could serve our Country, especially as she would be able to be of great assistance to me in the pursuit of that profession.[27]

707 BROADWAY, N.Y.

Daisy White in her wedding dress. COURTESY OF HAMPTON NATIONAL HIS-
TORIC SITE, NATIONAL PARK SERVICE

Armed with a newfound clarity, White began to let friends know of his interest in diplomatic service. By making such a consequential decision, "he converted all his previous training—his travels, his knowledge of different countries, his acquaintance with the English and French character, which otherwise might have been a mere luxury—into an admirable preparation for his future career."[28] Daisy White was crucial to her husband's success: "His wife was perfectly fitted . . . to give him domestic happiness. But in addition, she was a woman of ambition . . . she had the American feeling that everyone should have some useful employment."[29]

The Whites spent much of the next several years traveling and making contacts that would be enormously helpful to his career. They stayed in Ottawa for several days and were guests at Government House presided over by the Marquess of Lorne, then governor general of Canada and the future Duke of Argyll, and his wife, Princess Louise, the fourth (and most artistically talented) daughter of Queen Victoria. In Washington, they befriended Levi P. Morton. Then a congressman representing Manhattan, Morton would later become minister to France, vice president of the United States, and governor of New York. Not only would he be vital in setting White on his diplomatic career, but the two families would also eventually be united by marriage.[30]

In France, the Whites became friends with Countess Melanie de Pourtalès, who was a lady-in-waiting to the Empress Eugenie. At her Château de la Robertsau,[31] where the Whites made further beneficial contacts, she entertained Franz Liszt, Napoleon III and Empress Eugenie, Ludwig I of Bavaria, the Grand Duke of Baden, and Princess Metternich. Another important advocate for them in France was Daisy's cousin, Countess de Montsaulnin. Born Anna Elliott Morris Zborowska, her husband, Count Charles de Montsaulnin, was a deputy in the French Parliament. Although Anna's branch of the Morris family had lived in France for two generations, at her death in 1913, she still owned much of the east side of Broadway between 87th and 88th Streets in Manhattan. Anna would name her daughter Marguerite and call her Daisy in her cousin's honor.

The Whites were overjoyed when their daughter, Muriel, was born on October 12, 1880, in Paris while they were living at 2 Avenue Hoche.

Baby Muriel and her grandmother, Margaret Stuyvesant Rutherfurd. COURTESY
OF THE WILLIAM TAPLEY BENNETT, JR. PAPERS, RICHARD B. RUSSELL LIBRARY FOR POLITICAL
RESEARCH AND STUDIES, UNIVERSITY OF GEORGIA LIBRARIES, ATHENS, GEORGIA, 30602-1641

33333

They would return to Paris when her father became the US ambassador, and it would also be the site of her wedding in 1909.

In 1881, Henry White made an important visit to Washington and met President Garfield at a White House reception. Then his friend, Levi P. Morton, secured and accompanied him to a meeting with Secretary of State James G. Blaine to ask officially for a diplomatic posting. Blaine committed to an appointment for White and asked him to be patient while waiting for the appropriate machinations to take place.[32] Meanwhile, on Christmas Day 1882, Henry's beloved grandfather White died in Paris, leaving him for the first time with an independent income of $30,000–$35,000 per year (approximately $1 million per year in today's equivalency).[33]

Secretary Blaine proved true to his word. It is instructive to learn how Henry White was notified of his first appointment. He had become friends with several members of the very wealthy Rothschild banking family. On the weekend of July 14, 1883,[34] the Whites were guests at Ferdinand de Rothschild's new home, Waddesdon Manor, in Buckinghamshire, along with the Prince of Wales (later Edward VII) and the Duchess of Manchester, as well as "many persons of importance, politically or otherwise as could be gotten into the house."[35]

White's biographer described what happened at Waddesdon as part of the elaborate festivities:

He and other guests, one afternoon when fireworks had been announced, played tennis on the lawn till nearly eight o'clock; when they retired to dress for dinner there had been no apparent preparation for the coming display; but happening to look out of the window of his room, White suddenly saw a perfect army of workmen creeping out of the bushes in all directions, and beginning to erect frameworks for the various set pieces. They had been kept in hiding in the shrubberies since lunch-time in order to do their work inauspiciously and without delay.[36]

During the weekend, White was handed a telegram from Alphonso Taft, the US minister to Austria-Hungary.[37] White had been appointed as secretary of the legation at Vienna, which was not a position he sought, and Taft asked him in the telegram not to refuse until he received correspondence with an explanation. White learned that the position would be useful until another could be found, and several of his friends counseled him to accept. "To his friends and acquaintances this step seemed merely to provide a temporary employment, elegant rather than onerous, to a young man of wealth whose chief interest would always be in society."[38]

The climate in Vienna was not beneficial for Daisy's declining health, so Henry went alone, leaving behind his wife and young Muriel, and reported for duty in July 1883. He took rooms at the Imperial Hotel, and Alphonso Taft proved to be

> a blunt, common-sense gentleman of real cultivation, at seventy-two rounding out a vigorous and varied career in this rather ornamental office. . . . White found his first berth decidedly pleasant. To be sure, there were drawbacks—the unimportance of the American legation in the Austrian eyes, the snobbishness of the social life of Vienna, and the enforced absence of Mrs. White. . . . Had it not been for Mrs. White's absence he might have grown fairly content.[39]

Also, in 1883, Daisy made a shrewd decision. She wished to have her portrait painted by John Singer Sargent, who was "not yet the darling of the upper class."[40] It would be one of her earliest victories, since

> before he became a brand name, Daisy sought out the up-and-coming artist in his disheveled fifth-floor walkup studio in Paris. She wanted Sargent to paint her portrait. . . . Sargent's imposing portrayal of Daisy, over seven feet tall and every inch of it stately, became the focal point of the Whites' dining room in their London home. The aristocrats and members of Parliament who dined around their table marveled at the elegance of the composition. Word spread and Sargent's reputation soared in England. A star was born, helped in part by Daisy.[41]

Daisy's granddaughter recalled, years after her grandmother's death, the regal portrait staring down at them in their home in Washington. It was a daunting reminder of how they were expected to behave. In her later years, on a visit with her great-nephew to their former home, she remembered, "We children often felt as if she was zooming in and criticizing us even from the painting. It was very overwhelming."[42] One

Daisy Rutherfurd White painted by John Singer Sargent, 1883. NATIONAL GALLERY OF ART, PUBLIC DOMAIN

observer found Daisy's portrait "stately and arrogant. . . . She has an icy, determined stare; this was a woman of ferocious ambition. A few years after the original painting had been made, Daisy insisted that Sargent alter the tilt of her head to give her a more formal and imposing appearance."[43] While Sargent was working on the portrait, Daisy "left Paris for obligations in the south of France after only a few sittings."[44] He then turned to his portrait of Virginia Amélie Gautreau, which would shock society when it was exhibited as *Madame X*. One can only speculate what would have happened if Daisy's portrait had been completed first and exhibited instead of Madame X.

Henry James wrote to his sister from London, "The best portrait at the Academy is in my opinion one of Mrs. Henry White (Miss Rutherford [*sic*] of N.Y.) by Sargent, whom I told you I lately had here, from Paris, & like so much."[45] In 1902, Senator Henry Cabot Lodge wrote to Henry White, by then the first secretary in London, informing him that everyone wanted to have President Teddy Roosevelt's official White House portrait painted by Sargent, but Congress had appropriated only $800 for the commission. White spoke with Sargent, who replied that he would be happy to paint the president for that amount or, in fact, for nothing at all. In the event, $2,500 was then obtained from Congress.[46] The portrait of Roosevelt remains one of the most popular for White House visitors and the only one painted by Sargent.

The Whites learned they were expecting a second child after Henry had been in Vienna for several months, so he wrote to the State Department asking for another posting. Fortunately, Taft wrote a complimentary letter seconding the request (although he told White that he "ought really to go home and run for Congress, for in politics the opportunities would be far better than in diplomacy"[47]). On November 26, 1883, only five months into his Vienna assignment, Taft handed him a telegram offering the second secretaryship at London under the Romantic poet and academician James Russell Lowell as US minister. Queen Victoria said she had never seen an ambassador who "created so much interest and won so much regard as Mr. Lowell."[48] He was highly respected by the British academic community and befriended the author and critic Leslie Stephen, becoming godfather to his daughter, the writer

Virginia Woolf. At Lowell's recall, when Grover Cleveland was elected, he was offered a professorship at Oxford, but he declined and returned to the United States instead.

On December 20, 1883, Henry White left Vienna to spend the holidays in Paris with Daisy and Muriel, and at the new year of 1884, he began his coveted assignment in London. It would prove to be an excellent posting for both professional and personal reasons, and Lowell was a generous mentor who "was attracted, not merely by the open-hearted, high-spirited young man, but by his wife; he liked having the 'handsome young couple' about him; and it happily fell within White's power to do him personal as well as official service in their year and a half (1884–85) of association."[49] Within a year, White was promoted to first secretary. "He served there until 1892, under James Russell Lowell, Edward Phelps, and Robert Todd Lincoln, and it was widely recognized that he ably and tactfully ran the embassy for these ministers."[50]

The Whites gave up their home in Paris and moved into 22 Hertford Street in Mayfair near Green Park and Hyde Park. They were delighted when their son, John "Jack" Campbell White, was born there on March 17, 1884. He would graduate from Eton and from Harvard College and Law School and eventually join the family vocation, serving in several diplomatic posts, ending as US ambassador to Haiti and Peru.

White and Lowell worked well together even though their personalities were far from similar. While Lowell's interests were chiefly in literature,

> Henry White was soon cultivating a distinctly younger and gayer set, led by George Curzon, Arthur Balfour, Henry Cust, Lord and Lady Elcho, and St. John Brodrick. Their paths thus completely diverged. . . . White was happiest on some week-end devoted to riding, tennis, or yachting. Yet they not infrequently met in drawing-rooms as well as the legation office.[51]

He also joined the most popular men's clubs—the Marlborough, the St. James Club, and the Bachelors' Club—and the Prince of Wales joined the Whites for dinner at the Bachelors' Club, where he stayed until midnight. Dinners and balls followed, with Henry dancing with the Princess of Wales and both Whites attending a concert at Buckingham Palace.[52] Despite valid

Daisy White with son, Jack. COURTESY OF THE WILLIAM TAPLEY BENNETT, JR. PAPERS, RICHARD B. RUSSELL LIBRARY FOR POLITICAL RESEARCH AND STUDIES, UNIVERSITY OF GEORGIA LIBRARIES, ATHENS, GEORGIA, 30602-1641

worries, White was retained in London even when Cleveland, a Democrat, was elected president and the new minister was to be Edward J. Phelps. Valued and supportive friends ensured that Henry White, a Republican, was not only retained but also promoted to first secretary.

Daisy, meanwhile, joined the fight to save Florence Maybrick, an American woman who had been sentenced to death for murdering her English husband; the guilty sentence was commuted to life in prison. Hardly anyone thought she was guilty of murder, and there was a prolonged effort to free her. Daisy White visited her in prison and found "her face and hands pale and waxy like those of a person who has lost much blood," and her face "denoting absolute calmness, determination, self-control, with manners remarkably quiet and subdued."[53] She was finally released only after the death of Queen Victoria, who thought any woman who admitted having committed adultery, as Mrs. Maybrick had (and as her late husband had done repeatedly), was capable of murder.[54]

Daisy and Henry White became the only American members of the Souls. Daisy "was then at the height of her beauty and charm. Everyone admired her. It was not merely that she was lovely to look at; she talked well, with animation and distinction, and she had grace and poise."[55] The group seemed tailor-made for their gifts,

> for along with money and impeccable social credentials (for Americans anyway), they could boast Daisy's impeccable taste. The Souls prided themselves on their avant-garde preferences in art—John Singer Sargent became a favorite (thanks in part to Daisy) as did Burne-Jones and Whistler. And they shared a passion for literature and ideas. Oscar Wilde, Henry James, and Edith Wharton were "occasional Souls"—admired deeply for their work and on the fringes of the group, but not quite accepted as insiders.[56]

Although some viewed the Souls as suffering from "the insidious dry rot of mutual admiration,"[57] the Whites enjoyed the group's conversation and mutual support. It was natural that, as children, Muriel and Jack would play with children of the other Souls, and they were particularly drawn to the Wemyss children.

Hugo Charteris, Lord Elcho, was heir to his father, the tenth Earl of Wemyss. He and his beautiful wife, Mary Wyndham, were original members of the Souls. Two of their sons would be killed in World War I, and their daughter would marry the son of Prime Minister H. H. Asquith. Those events were still in the future, though, when the Whites were close friends. Lady Wemyss wrote her memoirs in 1932. She recalled,

> On January first, 1894, we went to a grand fancy-dress ball given by the Bruces at Norton. Daisy White did up and powdered her hair most beautifully, and I wore a Watteau evening-gown. . . . Jack White, Ego and Guy [her own two oldest sons] were zany and clowns, they acted their parts so literally that I fear they never could have been willingly invited to that house again: they ran wild, turning somersaults, and almost sacked the place.[58]

According to his mother, as the oldest son and heir,

> Ego's sense of ironical enjoyment developed early. One day at Pau he and I were driving home together in Nelly's brougham, returning from a visit to Mrs. Naylor Leyland (Miss Chamberlain, the famous beauty of 1881) who had gushed a good deal over him and praised his looks. . . . He [Ego] used to play with Jack White, who was at Pau with his mother (my great friend Daisy White). Jack talked of fighting for his country and going back to America.
>
> EGO: "What's America?"
>
> JACK: "Oh, why don't you know? America is my country, the biggest in the world."
>
> EGO: "Bigger than Pallis?" (Paris).

The conversation became acutely controversial and ended with Ego pushing Jack into the gutter. Jack gave a piteous account to his mother of his walk home with his sailor coat all splashed with mud. His mother asked him why Ego had done it and whether he was sorry afterward. "No," said the affronted Jack, "by no means, he did it to amuse himself and it did amuse him."[59]

Young Muriel also displayed an early independent streak. When she was around six, she walked into a tea party her mother was giving for a rather austere group of women and asked, "Can I please go to Hell with you and Papa instead of going to Heaven with the nurse?"[60] When she was twelve, she wrote to her mother, "I wonder if you are yet in Paris, how horrid the bull fights must be. I should like to *exterminate* those Spaniards for going to them. Do you know since when they existed? I should think that it would be likely that Philippe, the husband of Bloody Mary, invented them."[61]

The Whites moved to 9 Grosvenor Crescent in Belgravia in 1886. They also took a country place, Ramslade House, at Bracknell, near Windsor in Berkshire. When professional thieves broke in during a dinner party there in 1889 and stole jewelry worth $35,000,[62] their friends the Duke and Duchess of Westminster sent one of their jewels to the Whites from their own collection to help make up for the loss.[63] Daisy wrote to their American cousins that the house was modest, containing "not only room for themselves, the children, the governess, and twelve servants, but two extra bedrooms," and then had to explain that this was normal in England.[64] They were very near to Ascot, and during Ascot Week, "they more than once sublet the house furnished for as much as their whole annual rental unfurnished."[65]

Their first visitors were Henry James and George W. Smalley, the London correspondent of the *New York Tribune*.[66] The Duchess of Marlborough (née Consuelo Vanderbilt) recalled her first introduction to Edith Wharton during a visit to Ramslade. "We met in an English country house where I had arrived rather late. My hostess, the beautiful Daisy White, first wife of Harry White, then attached to the American embassy, took me to the window and, pointing to two distant figures walking on the lawn, said, 'Do you know those famous compatriots of ours?' They were Edith Wharton and Henry James in deep conversation."[67] Larz Anderson, having recently been appointed second secretary at the US embassy in London, recalled spending the holidays with his friends: "I was exceedingly glad to get down to Ramslade at Bracknell for Christmas with the Whites. . . . Christmas Day was characteristic. I was awakened at seven by Master Jack and Miss Muriel singing greetings of the morning, peace and good will, outside my door."[68] He described how effortlessly the Whites entertained on another occasion:

> We were met at the station, and drove down lanes, past a little lodge, through fields and a park to the door where servants came out to receive us. Then I was left entirely to my own devices. My bags and portmanteaux mysteriously disappeared but reached my own room somehow. When I went up after tea, my clothes were laid out and ready. Here the service makes living luxurious.[69]

The Whites later took the lease on Wilton Park near Beaconsfield in Buckinghamshire, where they entertained such guests as Lord Kitchener in July 1902 and Sir Alfred Lyall the next year. "The White residence was one of the places where the wealthiest and most attractive Americans mingled with the most intelligent and influential Britishers."[70] Daisy made sure that her brother, "Lewy," could meet the recently widowed Anne Sands "in a setting that did not compromise her."[71] They would marry in 1890, with Daisy as matron of honor, and the wedding breakfast was given by the Whites at 9 Grosvenor Crescent. After Lewy's death in 1901, having had two daughters, Anne Harriman Sands Rutherfurd was given away by Henry White when she married Willie K. Vanderbilt, becoming stepmother to Consuelo, Duchess of Marlborough, whose first love had been Lewy's brother, Winthrop.

Anne was

> intrigued by the breed of attractive Englishmen whom she met through Daisy and Harry White. . . . These men used their wealth and connections to become the powers that ran an empire rather than, like her compatriots, merely to accumulate more money. The English exercised their power in influential positions in the government, while, for the most part, Americans used their money to acquire the whole government.[72]

Daisy's health, never strong, continued to cause her absence from her official duties. George Curzon, eventually to be viceroy of India, wrote from London to her in 1891, in Paris, where she had gone for her health:

"Get better quickly, Daisy; it is slow without you."[73] She "was frequently ailing after the birth of her son, her ill-health keeping her out of society for months at a stretch. Within a short time, White was valued quite as much as his wife, and much more universally and unreservedly loved."[74] Henry's letters to his wife were loving and informative, keeping her abreast of news and information about their friends. He wrote to her from Ramslade, relaying a conversation with one man in their group who "thinks you very remarkable in having associated with all these people who have lovers without either having your head turned or changing in any way, and yet retaining the respect and admiration of the aforesaid people."[75]

In 1892, Grover Cleveland, a Democrat, was elected president of the United States. For a while it looked as if Henry White would be safe in his position as first secretary in London. But in October 1893, he was dismissed. Before he was replaced, because Ambassador Robert Lincoln (son of the late president) was away, Henry White served in his place as a pallbearer at the funeral of Alfred, Lord Tennyson, at Westminster Abbey. He recalled that he had "never witnessed a more impressive scene than when the coffin was lowered into the grave, which by the bye adjoins that of Browning at whose funeral I was also present in 1889—close by where I stood was the bust of Longfellow, at the unveiling of which by Mr. Lowell I was present."[76] In the same entry, White wrote, "I am over forty-two and . . . the best years of my diplomatic experiences are probably over."[77] Fortunately, he was decidedly wrong.

Former senator Thomas F. Bayard, who had served as Cleveland's secretary of state in his first administration, was appointed the US ambassador to Great Britain. Bayard would not be as successful as some of his predecessors, perhaps because he "was often peppery, would seldom take advice from anyone, and had some irritating mannerisms, such as a way of snatching papers from his assistants' hands."[78] Although Henry White returned to Washington, hoping he could still salvage his post, he was not successful.

His journey back to the United States was made far more pleasant by finding George Curzon on the same ship. "They shared the state apartment on the upper deck of the Hamburg-American liner *Fürst Bismarck*, which happened to be vacant and was given them at no extra charge.

They jested about the misspelling of Curzon's name on the seating list at table."[79] Characteristically, Curzon was unimpressed with the passengers and the food. There were many Germans onboard, and he wrote of them, "What a people! How coarse! How hideous! How utterly wanting in the least external element of distinction!"[80] Americans fared no better, as he called them "the least attractive species of the human genus."[81] His greatest complaint, though, was that the ship's officers had no knowledge and little appreciation for who he was. White's daughter, Muriel, then only twelve and already a diplomat, wrote to her father after his voyage (calling him "Most Honoured and Beloved Parent"), "I attribute your being taken for Mr. Curzon's father, not to your looking old, but to Mr. Curzon's youthful appearance."[82]

White remained in Washington and solidified his alliances, secure in the belief that a Republican would return to power in 1897. On a visit back to England, he heard in March of his mother's death in Baltimore. He sailed for home and was pleased to find that Mark Twain was a fellow passenger. He wrote to Daisy, "Mark Twain seems to have taken quite a fancy to me, having changed his seat from the captain's table to sit next to me. . . . He is a quaint, rough, and rather uncouth sort of person in manner, very frank and open in expressing his opinions. Today he hooked his arm into mine and took a long walk."[83]

Back at Hampton, he, his brother, and their half-brother carried their mother's remains to rest beside her first husband (her second husband, Dr. Buckler, although sixteen years older than she, lived until 1901 and was buried at St. Thomas Episcopal Church Cemetery). Eliza was joined in 1908 in Hampton's cemetery by Nancy Davis, a former slave who was freed before the war and remained with the family. She is the only African American buried at Hampton. Her tombstone inscription reads, "Thy people shall be my people, and thy God my God."[84] At his mother's death, Henry White was heir to one-third of her estate, then conservatively estimated at $1.6 million (more than $51 million in today's equivalent).[85]

Henry White had been correct about 1897. The Republican candidate, William McKinley, won the presidency the previous November and offered White either minister to Spain, which he urged him to accept, or his old post as first secretary in London. White "knew the Spanish climate would wreck his wife's health. He feared that it would be difficult to educate his children in Spain. His heart was in England,"[86] and that was where he chose to return.

The year would be auspicious for the Whites. In February, Henry was still in Washington and went to New York City to attend the famous Bradley Martin costume ball on February 10, during a heavy snowstorm. As he recorded in his daybook, "I left by morning train [from Washington, DC] to attend fancy ball at NY given by Bradley Martins. Went there with [Charles] McKim & had a very successful evening. Mrs. Morton & her daughters & the Brice daughters of Senator Brice the most successfully dressed, a really wonderful sight. Willie Buckler's costume particularly successful also."[87]

Henry was costumed as a cavalier in the days of Louis XIII, while his half-brother, Willie Buckler, may have worn a coat that had belonged to an ancestor. As noted, Henry attended with his friend Charles McKim, "the dean of American architects," costumed as Louis XIII, so it was appropriate that their costumes were complementary. McKim's partner in their hugely successful architectural firm, Stanford White, also attended with his wife, as did Henry's future wife, Emily Vanderbilt Sloane, and her husband. Henry might also have met one of the younger attendees, Alice Sands, who attended with her then-fiancé Vail Stebbins. She would later break that engagement and, in 1905, marry Edgar M. Church, eventually becoming the mother-in-law of Henry White's granddaughter and Muriel's daughter, Countess Margaret Seherr-Thoss.

Later that same year, in July, the Duchess of Devonshire, who had befriended the Whites at the Rothschilds' weekend party at Waddesdon Manor, invited them to her elaborate fancy dress ball held at Devonshire House in Piccadilly to celebrate Queen Victoria's diamond jubilee. Henry became one of only a handful of people who attended both of that year's famous costume balls. For the Devonshire event, Henry was costumed as Henri de Lorraine, Duc de Guise, and Daisy was Morosina Morosini, Dogaressa of Venice (perhaps as a nod to her Morris ancestors).

Daisy was delighted to accompany her husband when Queen Victoria invited them to dinner at Balmoral Castle in October 1897. As

Daisy and Henry White at the Duchess of Devonshire's costume ball, 1897.
COURTESY OF HAMPTON NATIONAL HISTORIC SITE, NATIONAL PARK SERVICE

a home privately owned by the monarch, rather than an official crown estate, invitations there were considered more personal and thus more highly prized. They were invited for dinner at 8:45 p.m. and were driven over from Braemar, about ten miles away. Daisy wore a black brocade dress by Worth with an aigrette in her hair as well as "a diamond and pearl chain, and diamond collar with a row of pearls."[88]

Other guests included the queen's youngest daughter, Princess Beatrice, who had been widowed the year before, and her sister, Princess Helena. In light of future discussions about the marriage of Muriel, it is particularly relevant that Daisy was seated at Queen Victoria's dinner next to Joseph Chamberlain, known as "Radical Joe," who was at that time secretary of state for the colonies. The former mayor of Birmingham and a radical member of the Liberal Party, Chamberlain eventually became a leading imperialist in coalition with the Conservatives. He made his fortune as a manufacturer of screws and was known as a champion for the working man. Having been widowed twice, in 1888 Chamberlain married, in New York City, Mary Crowninshield Endicott, daughter of the US secretary of war. With her guidance, he finally began to be accepted into upper-class society. His two sons (by the first and second marriages) would become, respectively, a Nobel Peace Prize laureate and a British prime minister. Yet, judging by what would eventually take place, Daisy must have acquired a negative opinion of her dinner partner that evening.

At an appropriate moment, Daisy was summoned to talk with Her Majesty for almost half an hour. Her only difficulty was standing over a seated (and already short) queen, and thus she had to lean down in order to hear and be heard. The queen knew of her health challenges and said, "I understand that you have been a sufferer for some time and you came here for your health five years ago; I hope this place is doing you some good." They also spoke of the "kind personal feelings" Americans had exhibited for the queen during her jubilee celebrations. Daisy explained to her,

> The President had wanted to send Harry to Spain as minister, but that I had rather prevented this because I wished to stay in England and I asked her if she thought I had done wrong. She said, "Oh, no. Where one is happy one is best." . . . And by and by the Queen gave a little

bow and smile which means dismissal, and I retired to talk to Princess Beatrice and the others.[89]

Daisy was pleased to learn later that Her Majesty "thought I had such a pleasant voice and speech . . . and that she thinks me very pretty!"[90]

Henry White continued to enjoy his posting in London and performed superbly, achieving diplomatic victories that were often not publicly credited to him. His powers of observation were acute. After a dinner party in April 1898, which included his friend Teddy Roosevelt, White wrote in his diary, "I was very glad to see Mrs. Beale, née Hattie Blaine, at dinner, looking really handsome in a particularly becoming black dress and having apparently entirely regained her spirits, which she had lost not unnaturally at the time of her divorce."[91]

Queen Victoria, the "Widow of Windsor," died on January 22, 1901. Henry White wrote to his friend, Senator Henry Cabot Lodge,

> All England is deeply touched at the innumerable tributes of affection and respect which have emanulated [sic] from our country in connection with the Queen's death. Mr. Choate [American ambassador] and I walked in the procession at Windsor after her body and then at the service in the Chapel after which we lunched at the Castle and were subsequently received by the King and Queen, both of whom, and the other members of the Royal family, who were all, except the Yorks, present, expressed their appreciation and seemed deeply touched.[92]

One year later, Daisy and Henry hosted King Edward VII and Queen Alexandra for a particularly successful dinner. Henry wrote to President Teddy Roosevelt's wife and suggested she share his letter with her husband, "if he should have a moment to spare for the consideration of frivolous topics."[93] White thought the evening "a great success and quite the least formal royal entertainment that I have ever been to; as they stayed till nearly one, having ordered their carriages at eleven thirty, I rather think."[94] He passed along the king's request to tell the president "that he was particularly glad that his first dinner at an Embassy since his succession should have been at ours."[95] It marked yet another royal success for the Whites.

Chapter Two

Miss [Muriel] White is a beauty of half a dozen seasons and has moved in the most brilliant circles of British and French society since her debut seven years ago. Her first appearance in London society was when she acted as a bridesmaid at Lady Peggy Primrose's marriage in Westminster Abbey, which King Edward and Queen Alexandra attended. She is very tall and graceful and has been described as the most charming listener in society.[1]

— THE EVENING WORLD, MARCH 8, 1909

In December 1904, during Teddy Roosevelt's third year as president, he wrote to Henry White. Having asked for the resignation of all his ministers and ambassadors, the president wrote, "As you of course know, I intend to appoint you ambassador to Italy after March 4th. I need hardly tell you, my dear fellow, how glad I am to be able to do this."[2] On March 6, 1904, Roosevelt nominated five ambassadors and eleven ministers to new posts. The plum assignment White would have preferred, ambassador to Great Britain, was given to Whitelaw Reid, owner and editor of the *New York Tribune*. Reid's sister-in-law, Ruth Livingston Mills, was a cousin of Daisy.[3]

The *London Times* was full of praise for White, proclaiming that "to lose White from London is to lose much. . . . We have few, if any, better diplomatists."[4] Nevertheless, by February, the Whites were preparing for their move to Rome. Henry went ahead of his family to get acquainted with the office and was received by King Victor Emmanuel III only two days after he arrived.

As a special mark of respect, Henry White wrote to President Roosevelt that he was asked by the king of Italy to spend a week with him

Muriel White as a debutante, 1898. CREDIT: ELIZABETH SEHERR-THOSS

"in the mountains, during which I had many long talks with him, and we spoke very frankly."[5] Not only did White's tenure in Rome begin with royal approval, but at his departure the dowager Queen Margherita gave an elegant farewell dinner at her palace in his honor.[6]

Rome would be the city where Muriel began to be noticed. While her family was still posted to London, she was reported as having inherited "her mother's social facilities and is the intimate friend of several almost royal ladies."[7] By serving as her father's second-in-command while her mother was frequently ill, Muriel enjoyed all the benefits of family background and financial advantage but didn't follow the usual social path taken by her fellow American heiresses.

After much effort, White was able to find a suitable home for his family. The Palazzo del Drago, in the Via Quattro Fontane, was built in the 1500s by Cardinal Tiberio Crispo, a close friend of Pope Paul III and of the Farnese family. Daisy had been quite ill with Bright's disease since 1899, but she was able to begin entertaining there again as long as she had Muriel to assist her. "To [Daisy's] efforts was due no small part of the impression the new ambassador made upon the critical Roman world. Though her hair was now silver gray, her commanding beauty was as striking as ever, and her gentle charm as appealing."[8]

Muriel's letters confirm that she had acute powers of observation even if her comments were not always in harmony with one another. She wrote from Rome an undated letter,

> Mother's friend the Duchess d'Aosta has been very kind to us here and yesterday we went to the Palace of Capodimonte to tea and she and the Duke took us all over the stables which are beautifully mounted and for a drive in their coach afterwards. The ship *Celtic* has just arrived from America laden with Mr. Pierpont Morgan and Mrs. Vanderbilt and lots of other millionaires. Italy seems to me to belong to the gilded compatriot whose well-dressed society I generally find most unsympathetic.[9]

She could, on one hand, appreciate the hospitality of senior members of the royal family while at the same time disparage the very society of which she was a now prominent member.

As their entry into Roman society, the Whites held a grand ball just before Ash Wednesday in the winter of 1907.

> Up the rose-red carpeted stairs the guests walked, the statues looking silently on. . . . In the antechamber each guest was asked to write his name in the large autograph books kept for that purpose, and then, passing on, was received by the Ambassador and Ambassadress in the first of the splendid series of salons thrown open for the occasion. . . . Mr. and Mrs. Henry White who represented the United States, and won the hearts of all Rome as well, and assisted by their charming daughter, Miss Muriel White, they made this ball an affair to leave its lovely pictures in memory. The scenic setting of an old Roman Palace captivates the stranger.[10]

Unfortunately, the Whites would later learn that not everyone who believed themselves worthy of an invitation received one.

Ambassador White had been urged to accept the appointment to Rome by Archbishop John Ireland, the first Roman Catholic archbishop of Saint Paul, Minnesota, and a close friend of Presidents William McKinley and Teddy Roosevelt. Since the 1870s, when the Papal States were defeated and most of the Italian peninsula was unified, the Holy See and the Italian government had continued to battle one another. Roman society was divided between "the blacks" who adhered to papal authority and "the whites" who obeyed the Italian civil head of state. No ambassador to Italy was then recognized by the pope, and all church officials were prohibited from having any contact with those accredited diplomats. Using official embassy stationery, White invited four cardinals to a dinner recognizing the American archbishop's visit. Not only was the Italian government pleased, but the more liberal faction at the Vatican was as well. The pope let his unofficial approval be known. One reactionary cardinal was vocal in his opposition, but White wrote to President Roosevelt,

> The longer I remain here the more convinced I feel that whoever occupies the place which I now fill, being the representative of the best and most enlightened Roman Catholics in the world, who contribute a very large portion of the Holy See's income, should be received at

the Vatican, and I have no doubt that in the course of time—not mine here possibly, but before very long—this will come to pass. We are unconnected with European complications and cannot be expected . . . to pretend to believe in "the prisoner of the Vatican."[11]

Muriel White was attracting many compliments and taking on more of her mother's role in the ambassador's entertaining. Born in 1880, and thus twenty-seven when the Whites moved to Rome, some already considered Muriel a bit long in the tooth to be unmarried. She was attractive and wealthy, and it was normal to speculate about her marital prospects. The Whites and Muriel were invited to a dinner in Rome given by Count Heinrich von Lützow, the Austro-Hungarian ambassador to the Royal Italian Court.[12] From Muriel's point of view, perhaps the most interesting attendee was Viscount Lascelles (1882–1947). Heir to his father, the fifth Earl of Harewood, Lascelles graduated from Eton and Sandhurst and then served as an officer in the Grenadier Guards from 1902 until 1905. At the time of the dinner he attended in Rome, Lascelles was an honorary attaché at the British embassy in Paris. He would play a role in Muriel's life before marrying the only daughter of Britain's future King George V.

There was another American woman who alternately fascinated and horrified Roman society and who would have her own part to play in Muriel's love life: the Princess Jane, as everyone called her. "Of the younger generation of American nobility, the Princess di San Faustino (née Campbell of New York) takes a prominent place. She lives in the Barberini Palace, dresses magnificently, plays bridge, and is the bosom friend of the Duchess Nicoletta Grazioli."[13] *Time* magazine referred to her as "the undisputed leader of the Anglo–US set in Italy."[14] "When Jane spoke it was like firecrackers exploding. She interrupted Kings and Ambassadors, took charge of the conversation in any group she entered, and leapt nimbly from subject to subject . . . abandoning a topic instantly when the talk began to be dull."[15]

In 1897, the same year the Whites were hitting their stride in London, Jane married Carlo, third Prince di San Faustino and Marquis del Monte Santa Maria, and quickly became known for her entertainment. Sir Oswald Mosley called her salon "a university of charm, where a young

A cameo portrait of Muriel given by the Marchioness of Crewe for serving as one of her bridesmaids. CREDIT: ELIZABETH SEHERR-THOSS

man could encounter a refinement of sophistication whose acquisition could be a permanent passport in a varied and variable world. If he could stand up to the salon of Princess Jane, he could face much."[16] The Duchess of Sermoneta wrote that Jane

collects human beings as others collect postage stamps or moths. . . . She is genuinely interested in them, and wants to know everything that concerns her friends. When she has learnt all she wanted she talks about it with light-hearted freedom, and as there is no detail of her private life or the workings of her own soul which she minds discussing quite openly over the bridge table, she can never imagine that anyone else minds being talked about either.[17]

Unfortunately Princess Jane and her accomplice, Duchess Nicoletta Grazioli, certainly did not look after Muriel White. In fact, they almost destroyed her marital possibilities.

It is not clear when Muriel first became aware of the barriers that had been placed in the way of her marriage prospects—but she would discover that some came from within her own family. Long after her marriage in 1909 and the death of her mother in 1916, Muriel wrote a lengthy and heartbreaking letter to her father in 1926, listing all the disappointments that had befallen her, the most important of which she had just learned the day before and came about at the hand of her mother.

Princess Jane told Muriel terrible things that another close friend, the Duchess Grazioli, had said about Muriel years before. She explained to Muriel that because Daisy White did not invite her or Donna Nicoletta, the Duchess Grazioli, to the grand reception at which all Roman society was present, they exacted their revenge. She confirmed that Viscount Lascelles, whom Muriel first met at the small dinner party at the home of the Austro-Hungarian ambassador in Rome, had indeed been in love with her and wished to marry her, but the Duchess Grazioli

was so furious with your mother for not inviting her that the moment she found out that Lascelles had come out here to marry you (which the boy made no secret of even to me when I asked him) she moved Heaven on earth to stop it. Cheatham at the British Embassy was in love with her and gave her presents, so she got him to laugh at Lascelles day in and day out about his affection for you & as you know ridicule kills most things in the very young. . . . Jane went on to say that it was a shame I had had a Mother who had always been my worst enemy & had not only spoilt what chances of my marrying well but many other chances I had had by her inconceivable lack of common sense & savoir faire.[18]

Muriel may have dodged a bullet, as Lascelles "had quite a reputation as a sort of serial suitor, albeit rather a failure! He was certainly under a great deal of pressure to marry and produce an heir. He did the Grand Tour as a young man and possibly used it as an opportunity to look for a suitable wife."[19] Thwarted in his first love, Henry, Viscount Lascelles, married at Westminster Abbey, in 1922 (when he was thirty-nine), Her Royal Highness Mary, the Princess Royal, only daughter of King George V and Queen Mary.

Princess Jane could not resist pointing out to Muriel what she had missed.

She went on to say that all the best that was in Lascelles would have been brought out if he had married me, that she heard he wasn't at all in love with Princess Mary & that he had come to Rome then with only one idea in his head (i.e., to propose to me as soon as possible.). "Of course," she continued, "no young man of his age was any match for such a practiced hand as Nicoletta in dealing with men & who had so many strings to pull here in Rome as she had so your happiness and Lascelles' was just sacrificed to Nicoletta's vengeance. If your mother had had the sense to let her alone you would have been Lascelles' wife now instead of Princess Mary."

Muriel tried to retain what dignity she could at hearing such devastating news with friends present. She assured her father,

I told her that I had begged Mother at the time to invite Donna Nicoletta to the Ricevimento [reception] (which was true) & was only told not to mix myself up with matters which didn't concern girls of my age. "How often the innocent have to suffer for the guilty" was her reply. I think she is disposed to be amiable & to make amends as she addressed me at parting as her "dear child." There wld. have been no good whatever in my antagonising her & it was much cleverer to smooth her down. She could do Margaret [Muriel's daughter] harm all over European society as she has great influence so it is much better to get on the right side of her. I naturally pretended to her that I was the happiest woman on earth but I couldn't help having a good cry afterwards.

Muriel noted to her father that Lascelles "is now one of the richest men in Europe and I now have in black and white (what I always suspected) that Mother ruined that!" Harewood House, where she would have been chatelaine, became "something of an establishment for meeting all the requirements necessary for royal occasions and regal living. In short, a royal palace."[20] Her friend Ella Matushcka also lamented Muriel's loss, as Lascelles "loved reading and art" and his "intellectual companionship" would have been a great comfort. The news was devastating to Muriel, who already was aware of several lost husbands. Muriel wrote to her father, "Think what a different life I would have had married to Marshall Roberts, Austen Chamberlain, Lord Beauchamp, or Lascelles."

Marshall Owen Roberts Jr. (1879–1931) was an American-born millionaire who became a British citizen. His father made his fortune leasing steamships to the US government during the Civil War, and at the father's death when the son was only one year old, he left an estate of $10 million.[21] Muriel wrote to her father, "Mother told me Marshall Roberts drank & that she would never have me inside of the house again if I married him."[22]

Then there was William Lygon, seventh Earl Beauchamp (1872–1938), who was the model for the character Lord Marchmain in Evelyn Waugh's *Brideshead Revisited*. He was governor of New South Wales and leader of the Liberal Party in the House of Lords. Muriel told her father, "I well remember that when Peggy Crewe[23] wanted to invite me for a week to stay with her to meet Beauchamp so that he could propose when he was making up to me Mother refused to let me go because she said she was sure he would never have any children! He has about 6!" In that instance, Daisy had excellent sources, as she was aware that Beauchamp was bisexual, a fact that was not widely known until he was publicly outed in 1931, long after this correspondence between Muriel and her father. Beauchamp married in 1902 Lady Lettice Grosvenor, granddaughter of the first Duke of Westminster, and fathered children, but the secret of his lifestyle was revealed by his brother-in-law, the second Duke of Westminster, to King George V. When the duke exposed Beauchamp's secret to King George V, the king responded, "I thought men like that shot themselves."[24] Beauchamp then resigned all his posts and was allowed to leave the country; he lived in well-known gay havens for the remainder of his life. His brother-in-law, the Duke of Westminster, sent him a note that read, "Dear Bugger-in-law, you got what you deserved."[25]

Austen Chamberlain was a different experience entirely, as his extended courtship with Muriel was avidly reported in both the American and the British press. Austen Chamberlain (1863–1937) was a British statesman, son of businessman and politician Joseph Chamberlain, and half-brother of future prime minister Neville Chamberlain. His marriage to Muriel, which would have been enormously beneficial to them both, never happened.

In July 1903, Muriel's engagement to Austen Chamberlain was publicly reported, although there was no announcement forthcoming. At the time, he was chancellor of the exchequer. American newspapers reported the engagement, albeit in terms that were not altogether complimentary to Muriel:

> It is a standing joke that Muriel White has played the part of bridesmaid so often she should know well what to do at her own wedding. Ambassador Choate said to her one day: "Now, Muriel, what, a bridesmaid again? When are we to see you attended rather than attending?" Miss White answered: "I may not be married yet, but that is my own fault, Mr. Choate." Mr. White naturally is ambitious for his daughter, and it is regarded here as a matter of course that she will marry an Englishman.... There is every reason to believe that the latest report is true, as two weeks ago Mr. and Mrs. White, with their daughter, were at a week-end house party invited by the Chamberlains to Highbury, where only intimate friends and relatives were of the family circle. Since then it is said that Austen Chamberlain has been paying frequent visits to Whitehall Place, where the Whites live in town, and that he has gone this week-end again to Wilton.[26]

One month later, in August 1903, their supposed engagement was widely reported:

> No event has caused such a stir in London society as the report that Austen Chamberlain, son of the Colonial Secretary, had become engaged to Miss Muriel White, daughter of the secretary of the United States embassy. Many of the English girls have sighed for young Mr. Chamberlain, as he is still called, though he is now forty years old, and rumor has had him engaged several times. This time, however, he does not deny it. While Joseph Chamberlain is said to be very much opposed to the match, Austen Chamberlain claims that he cannot see why he should not follow his father's example in marrying an American girl and Mrs. Chamberlain, who was Miss Endicott of Massachusetts, is said to be inclined to take her stepson's part. If this is so, then the chances of Mr. Austen Chamberlain are quite promising, for while "our Joe" is known to be exceedingly stubborn, it is also well known that he invariably follows his wife's advice in domestic affairs, though it has always been his wish that his son should marry into one of the great and wealthy English families. Mr. Chamberlain's attitude in the matter, however, is said to be more than mere conjecture and is regarded with some amusement. Mr. White is very fond of Austen Chamberlain and is said to be willing to use his diplomatic training in reconciling the elder Chamberlain to the arrangement. Miss White, the reported fiancée of Mr. Chamberlain, is one of the favorites of London society. She is a charming young girl of genuine American type, and since her coming out, two years ago, has been greatly admired. Mr. Chamberlain, it is claimed, lost his heart, hitherto considered invulnerable, to the American belle at their very first meeting.[27]

When no official announcement was made, perhaps her father wanted to protect her reputation, as Henry White then wrote to US Secretary of State John Hay, whom he addressed as "Chief," on American embassy letterhead:

> I do not suppose you and Mrs. Hay have believed or taken any stock in the report which appears to have gone the round of our papers of Muriel's engagement to Austen Chamberlain, followed shortly afterwards by a statement of the "bitter opposition of Chamberlain *père* to

Austen's marrying an American" as he wishes him to marry "a Countess." She is not engaged nor is Chamberlain *père* in the smallest degree opposed to Austen's doing so. On the contrary, he expressed to me not long ago his earnest wish that the son should marry. But Austen is 40 and Muriel 22 and the former seems to the latter party patriarchal! For further particulars of which there are many amusing ones and I must defer you to our next meeting. But the way in which Muriel's name has been sent around the country three times in the last year as engaged to three different individuals without the faintest shred of truth is quite disgraceful & must be the work of some unknown enemy of ours here.[28]

Ever the diplomat, White reported Austen Chamberlain's father's "earnest wish that his son should marry," but there is no mention of whether the bride should be Muriel. Newspapers reported that his father's opposition to a marriage with Muriel was because he "feels that the eldest son could more materially assist his prospects by marrying into one of the great and wealthy English families."[29]

What happened, then, to a marriage that seemed to be long desired? In Muriel's letter to her father, she wrote, "If mother had coaxed me a little and asked Austen Chamberlain to wait (which is what a Mother is there for instead of telling me that she wouldn't have me marry that common man from Birmingham) I probably in time would have accepted him." Perhaps Queen Victoria's dinner party at Balmoral Castle sealed Muriel's fate. Daisy White sat next to him for the evening and must have formed a negative opinion of "Radical Joe." She would already have been predisposed against him because of his working-class background and the business practices he utilized to make his money. The Whites would also have heard a great deal of criticism of him from their good friend and fellow Soul, Arthur Balfour. Henry White, in his letter to Secretary of State Hay, mentions the age difference (forty and twenty-two). It seems likely that an ever-ambitious Daisy decided that Muriel's marriage to a nontitled, nonwealthy son of a political radical who was "in trade" was not to be allowed. In her mind, he had too many strikes against him.

As Muriel's great-grandson recalled, "Daisy was rigid and deeply attentive to her own ambitions. Joseph Chamberlain and Daisy may have been very similar in character and personality, their son and daughter, respectively, caught in the dynamic of their own aims."[30] Chamberlain's family was not "notable enough for Daisy. I wager her ostentatious presence at Balmoral was meant to intimidate Chamberlin and, I bet, was highly offputting to him. It worked."[31]

Henry White had always been considered kinder than his beautiful wife, who was accurately called "a woman of steely social ambition."[32] Although he mentioned the age difference between his daughter and the prospective bridegroom as a possible reason for opposition to the marriage, it is likely that he deferred to Daisy in the issue.

Princess Jane's revelations to Muriel, even after all those years, would have been extremely difficult for her to hear. Muriel told her brother, Jack, of the revelation and then wrote to their father:

> Jack warned me not to tell anyone this & of course he is right so I am only letting you know how I feel because after what Princess Jane told me I must confide in someone or I shall choke! It is enduring for years absolutely unsympathetic surroundings combined with terrible loneliness & perpetual nagging that has broken down my nerves. . . . I was quite happy & contented here [Rome] till Princess Jane raked up all my feelings yesterday.

It is to their credit that Muriel and Austen Chamberlain remained on friendly terms for years. When he married in 1906, Muriel wrote to her Aunt Sophie (Mrs. Julian White), referencing a prediction made by another aunt, Georgina (Mrs. William Buckler), "I am delighted to see that Mr. Austen Chamberlain is engaged to be married so that at any rate Aunt Georgie's aimiable [sic] prophecy that I would end by marrying him will never be fulfilled."[33] In 1921, long after Muriel was married, she wrote to Austen Chamberlain, who was then Lord Privy Seal and leader of the House of Commons, about the political situation in Silesia and the anti-German attitude of French officials.[34] She wrote to her father from Rome in 1926, "I have had a very nice letter from Austen Chamberlain from Rapallo in reply to one I wrote him asking how he was (as he has been quite ill) & congratulating him on all he has done."[35] By then he was foreign secretary. He was eventually knighted with the Order of the

Garter and was awarded the Nobel Peace Prize. No one can deny his talents or his family's commitment to public service. Daisy's assessment of his lack of wealth, at least, turned out to be correct. When he died in 1937, his estate was valued for probate at £45,044.[36]

Evidently, Daisy's hopes for her daughter's fortunate marriage contained some selective blind spots. Muriel wrote to her brother, Jack, during ruminations about the possible choices of a bride for her own daughter, Margaret, "When I think what I escaped in the miscarriage of Mother's plans with regard to Lord Percy, I realize that marrying a miser is mild and a merciful fate compared to what she had in store for me. I hope she didn't know [he may have been gay] but with her crazy ambition, as revealed in her letters to Papa she might have swallowed even that in a Duke!"[37] Perhaps a gay duke as a son-in-law would have been more acceptable than a gay earl.

When Muriel's actual engagement finally *did* take place in March 1909, one news wire story that was widely printed even got the groom's name wrong.

> Paris—A report was circulated in diplomatic circles today that Miss Muriel White, the only daughter of Henry White, the American Ambassador to France, is engaged to wed Count Serth Josch, a wealthy Silesian nobleman and Roman Catholic. Miss White has been reported engaged many times before. When her father was secretary of the American Embassy in London gossip on different occasions had her betrothed to Lord Willoughby de Eresby, Lord Howard de Walden, the Hon. Reginald Ward, son of the Earl of Dudley, and Austen Chamberlain, son of Joseph Chamberlain. Miss White is a beauty of half a dozen seasons and has moved in the most brilliant circles of British and French society since her debut seven years ago.[38]

The inference was clear—Muriel was not in the first blush of youth at twenty-eight, having enjoyed "half a dozen seasons."

Other publications got the name right. The groom was Hermann, Count Seherr-Thoss (1879–1959). Called "Manni" within the family, he was the oldest of five sons and heir to his father's titles and extensive properties, as well as his hereditary seat in the Prussian House of Lords.

Hermann "Manni," Count Seherr-Thoss, in uniform. He wears the pickelhaube (spiked helmet) distinctive of Prussian officers. CREDIT: BAIN COLLECTION, LIBRARY OF CONGRESS

According to their oldest son, at the time his parents met, Manni was "a young secretary at the German embassy in Vienna. That was his job. It was an honorable profession and it didn't require tremendous educational background."[39] He and Muriel met at the home of Mr. and Mrs. R. S. Reynolds Hitt, who was then secretary of the US embassy in Berlin,[40] where Muriel had gone to attend some functions at the Kaiser's court. Hitt had served in several posts with Henry White and was a family friend. "The couple saw much of each other during Miss White's short visit in Berlin, and the count followed her back to Paris, where he pressed his suit with such ardor that the engagement was announced today."[41] At the time of the announcement, Muriel's parents were in Nice, "entertaining the officers of the American fleet. . . . In spite of the suddenness of the count's wooing, Ambassador and Mrs. White appear to be completely reconciled to the match."[42]

Although the announcement stated that the bride was twenty-five and the groom twenty-nine, Muriel was actually twenty-eight. The groom was serving as a lieutenant in the Cuirassier Life Guards of Potsdam and was formerly the military attaché at the German embassy in Vienna. He was reported to have an allowance of $3,000 per year from his father.[43] The Seherr-Thoss family descends from a branch of the line of Anhalt-Dessau, a member of the royal house of Ascania that also produced Catherine the Great. They were created barons in Bohemia in 1734 and counts in Prussia in 1775.

One publication noted, "Ambassador White will lose his office and his daughter almost the same time. . . . It is said [the groom] is very rich, popular, and that the match is purely a love affair. Miss White . . . ought to know her own mind and men pretty well. She has been abroad so much that she is half-foreign, anyhow, so it doesn't much matter."[44] Not surprisingly, the White family made discreet inquiries about the groom and his family. Reynolds Hitt, at whose home the couple met, wrote to Barclay Rives, a diplomat who had been secretary of the US embassy at Berlin.[45] Rives responded that he doubted whether an American girl brought up as Muriel was "could be happy in a family so economical as the Seherr-Thosses."[46] This reply should have served as a warning.

The day after the engagement announcement, the Whites were sent a letter from their close friend, Joseph H. Choate, under whom Henry White served when Choate was the US ambassador to Great Britain. Choate knew Muriel well and was quoted in an earlier article about her. He wrote,

> I have just read in the afternoon paper of the announcement of Muriel's engagement to "Count Herman Seherr-Thoss," an officer of the Royal Prussian Cuirassiers—and I hasten to add my congratulations if indeed this is true and is acceptable to you all. Tell dear Muriel that I congratulate her with all my heart and am very anxious to hear all about the happy man—for happy he must be, for he is one of the luckiest men in the world to get such a prize. But what will you and Mrs. White do without Muriel? And how will you ever be willing to come back to America to live leaving her in the heart of Germany? Do write quickly and tell me all about it.

A few weeks later, the Whites gave a dinner party at the embassy in Paris to honor the couple. The guests included several clergymen as well as Daisy's cousin, the Countess de Montsaulnin, and Mr. and Mrs. Thomas Nelson Page.[47] He was a well-known writer who would become the US ambassador to Italy. His wife, Florence, was the widow of Henry Field, heir with his brother to the Marshall Field fortune.

Muriel wrote to her aunt Sophie (Mrs. Julian White) on her monogramed stationery,

> I am the happiest person in the whole world as I became engaged to Manni Seherr-Thoss yesterday morning. He is far far too nice for me & I am longing for you to know him as he is good-looking & charming & amusing & brave & besides all this he is very religious & full of tender beautiful poetic thoughts which touch one's heart. I am glad now that I left Berlin so soon as it enabled me to receive his beautiful letters. He has been here a week & he told me that he loved me yesterday morning in my little blue sitting room. I love him dearly too & I can never thank God enough for having brought us together.[48]

Muriel noted that she would not yet send the letter she was writing until Manni heard from his father (presumably for his approval). She also wrote that her brother, Jack, had asked her not to announce the engagement "until after he has landed as he will be bombarded by reporters otherwise."[49] Muriel continued to her aunt that Manni's father "will give him one of his country places in Silesia where we shall live most of the year when we are married & where I hope you will both stay with us. I have always longed for a country life so everything is perfect & everyone tells us how charming his family is."[50] The young couple discussed their future plans as she wrote to her aunt, "Manni wants to study agricultural machinery in America as he will one day inherit very large estates. . . . When the date [of the wedding] is settled of course I shall write again & I will send you a photo of him as soon as I can."[51]

The mention of her fiancé as "religious" raised a complicating issue. Manni's family was Catholic, and Muriel was expected to commit their children to the Catholic faith (she would eventually convert). Her father, particularly as the current ambassador, had every reason to believe there would be two religious ceremonies—one Roman Catholic at the fashionable St. Joseph's Church on Avenue Hoche and another Anglican one at the American Episcopal Church (now the American Cathedral Church of the Holy Trinity). But the Roman Catholic authorities announced they would "only give a dispensation for Count Seherr-Thoss's marriage to a Protestant on the condition that there was only one religious ceremony, and that at the Catholic church."[52] Later it was asserted that the "the real opposition came more from Cardinal Kopp, bishop of Breslau [the groom's home diocese], than from Monsignor Amiette, archbishop of Paris."[53] However, "the archbishop of Paris, it is understood, declared the Catholics in America were too liberal and the opportunity to make an example in the case of the American ambassador should not be neglected."[54] The *New York Times* opined that the archbishop of Paris "thought it a good time to teach liberal American Catholics a lesson through the person of their ambassador."[55] Perhaps there was also lingering resentment from the church's conservative contingent about Ambassador White's dinner party for cardinals while posted to Rome.

On April 28, a small civil marriage ceremony with only a few close friends was held at the offices of the Eighth Arrondissement, presided over by the mayor. The groom was supported by his father and by Prince Radolin, the German ambassador to France. Witnesses for the bride were her father and her father's half-brother, William H. Buckler, then the secretary of the American legation at Madrid. For the civil ceremony, Muriel wore a blue voile dress and a large black hat. The wedding register listed Muriel's age as twenty-nine and the groom's as thirty. Many newspapers published an article headlined "German Count Weds Gifted Daughter of Ambassador White."[56] Additional signatures on the wedding certificate included Count Laszlo Karolyi, husband of Manni's first cousin, Fanny de Nagy-Apponyi, and Muriel's uncle, Rutherfurd Stuyvesant.

Muriel and Manni leaving their wedding. CREDIT: PAUL CHURCH

The next day, the religious ceremony was held at St. Joseph's Roman Catholic Church in the Avenue Hoche. The bride's father, Ambassador White, did not attend in order to register his displeasure at the single religious service. As a show of solidarity, the US ambassador to Great Britain stayed away as well. The ceremony, "while not what it would have been in the stately American Episcopal Church in the Avenue de l'Alma, was the occasion of a display of beauty and considerable pomp, while the reception at the embassy assembled a company which could hardly have been exceeded in brilliancy and distinction," reported the *New York Times*, noting that Paris was "being easily agitated over religious disagreements . . . somewhat exercised over the Catholic action in this case."[57] The groom's mother was absent, reportedly due to ill health, although all of the groom's brothers attended.[58] Muriel wore a white satin wedding dress with long lace train and was given away by her brother, Jack. The groom wore the white uniform of his regiment, as did many of his fellow officers and his brothers. Two young bridesmaids were Muriel's first cousins, Margaret Rutherfurd (named for the bride's mother) and Lucy Buckler.[59] After the service, Ambassador and Mrs. White gave a reception at the embassy for approximately one hundred guests. Attendees included several ministers of France and their wives; the American ambassador to the Court of St. James, Whitelaw Reid, and Mrs. Reid; secretaries at the American embassies in London and Paris; Mrs. W. K. Vanderbilt; Mr. and Mrs. William D. Sloane (she would become Henry White's second wife); and many titled guests. The *New York Times* noted that the "reception was brilliant," "four nations were represented," and there were tables "bearing costly gifts, with cards attached which formed a regular directory of the social world of America, France, England, and Germany."[60]

The groom gave his wife a cabochon sapphire and diamond bracelet and a ring. His parents gave her a diamond crescent, table silverware, a piano, and furniture. The Whites gave their son-in-law a new car and a silver-mounted dressing case, while their daughter received a diamond tiara and earrings, a dinner service, and a dressing case.[61] One family friend who attended the wedding, J. P. "Jack" Morgan Jr. (whose wife, Jane Norton Grew, was a childhood friend of the bride), gave her a yard-long necklace of pearls "with handsome diamond pendant."[62] Other gifts

Muriel and Manni Seherr-Thoss at their wedding reception at the American embassy in Paris. (Note the bust of her mother on the mantel.) CREDIT: ELIZABETH SEHERR-THOSS included a George III candelabra from Whitelaw Reid, the US ambassador in London; two silver trays from the Whites' old friend, Lord Curzon; and an heirloom ruby and diamond brooch from Lord Rosebery.[63] French President Armand Falliéres gave a Sèvres porcelain service.[64]

There was a general expectation that Muriel's fortune was not a target since the groom's family held "extensive estates," he received a generous allowance from his father, and he was expected eventually to inherit most of the family properties.[65] Nevertheless, "the marriage contract of Miss White and Count Seherr-Thoss contains no dowry provision. It expressly stipulates that the couple shall live under what is known as the 'regime of separation of property.'"[66] It would prove to be a wise but insufficient decision.

Yet even long after her marriage disintegrated, Muriel would return to the subject of her thwarted suitors. She wrote to her brother,

> I do not blame our parents for the step I took in Paris in 1909 as the result of a visit to Berlin. What I blame them for is having prevented my best chance of happiness, i.e., marrying a very rich man whom I was in love with whereby I cld. have lived in the only country I like without a material care in the world. Mother I blame less than Papa because she wasn't properly balanced. But Papa was. He admits himself that he mistrusted her plans & her judgement as far as I was concerned & that he told her so but why in God's name didn't he tell me? . . . all London knew how hard & ambitious mother was & how she tyrannized [*sic*] over me & how hopelessly weak Papa was to her. . . . I was the victim of Mother's ambition & Papa's weakness & indifference to *my* future as long as he cld. please Mother.[67]

The issue would cause one of Muriel's few criticisms of her brother. She wrote to him in the same letter, "There is no use your denying plain facts which everybody else who has known my life's history admits. You may think you are helping to brace me up by telling me to blame myself but there you are wrong. . . . I am not likely to get much sympathy from you."[68]

Chapter Three

I always believed that the French were a chivalrous people and I would not have believed them capable of the treason they committed against an unarmed population which they had promised in the Treaty of Versailles to protect with their troops.... [During the Silesian Uprising] the German schoolmaster was slowly tortured in the most barbarous way before death delivered him from his atrocious suffering.... In a nearby village the four daughters of the schoolmaster were stripped naked, raped, then forced by their inhuman rapists to serve them naked while they ate.[1]

—MURIEL, COUNTESS SEHERR-THOSS

A FTER A SUITABLE HONEYMOON IN THE SOUTH OF FRANCE, THE couple returned "to Breslau where the count is stationed at present, spending part of the time at one of the count's country places in Silesia."[2] Manni's parents lived at their principal home at Dobrau Castle. The estate was purchased in 1780 by Count Heinrich Leopold Seherr-Thoss, officially chief cupbearer to King Frederick the Great, who elevated him to the rank of count in 1775. With eighty thousand hectares of fields and forests, he was one of the richest landowners in Silesia. Poland's King Stanislaus I awarded him the Order of the White Eagle.[3]

In 1857, Count Hermann Seherr-Thoss rebuilt the baroque palace into the family's neo-Gothic residence. The gardens were designed by Gustav von Meyer, who created the green spaces at Sans Souci Palace in Potsdam. The local Catholic church at Dobrau, Saint John the Baptist, was built in 1867, with a generous gift from Countess Olga Seherr-Thoss, the groom's grandmother, who wrote six prayer books and died at Dobrau

Interior of the Great Hall at Schloss Dobrau, the principal Seherr-Thoss castle where Muriel and Boysie would eventually live and Muriel would die.

only two months after her grandson's wedding to Muriel. The family had been Protestant until her marriage. As Manni was the oldest son, Dobrau would eventually pass to him and, though she couldn't know it at the time, would be the site of Muriel's tragic death.[4]

For the time being, the young couple moved to another family home, Rosnochau Castle (Rozkochow after 1945), about eleven miles from Dobrau. Rosnochau, formerly a Harrach family property, was a three-wing complex in the baroque style built in 1734, located in Upper Silesia. It did not boast the level of comfort and staffing to which Muriel was accustomed, and she would expend a great deal of money and personal effort to bring it up to modern standards. One article about their early marriage noted that "Countess Muriel personally designed the plans for

Rosnochau, the first home of Muriel and Manni, where Muriel made and paid for extensive modernizations. CREDIT: PAUL CHURCH

renovating the castle, and transformed it into one of the most beautiful abodes in the province."[5]

The Seherr-Thoss family later owned another castle, Klagenfurt, at the foot of the Alps in Austria, as well as Grüben Palace, where Manni's father and the grandmother of his cousin, the future Queen Geraldine of Albania, were born. During their years at Rosnochau, before inheriting Dobrau, Manni was the founder of the local volunteer fire brigade while Muriel was known as "sensitive to others' harm and poverty. . . . The count's American wife turned out to be an interesting personality."[6]

The Seherr-Thoss family had long ties to the Prussian and German royal family. In June 1892, when Manni was only thirteen, the Dowager Empress Friedrich ("Vicky"), oldest child of Queen Victoria, stayed at Rosnochau for two nights while attending the wedding of the Imperial Countess Johanna von Oppersdorff to Hugo, Prince von Radolin.[7] Her son, Kaiser Wilhelm, stayed nearby with the bride's family. As a particular mark of appreciation to her hosts, the empress gave them a portrait of the Empress Maria Theresa of Austria that hung at Dobrau until it was destroyed by fire, along with a smaller John Singer Sargent portrait of Muriel, in 1945.

Muriel and Manni's only daughter, Margaret Muriel (always called by her first name and nicknamed "Deidu" within the family), was born at Rosnochau on April 4, 1910. No doubt in anticipation of their grandchild's arrival, Daisy and Henry White arrived at Bremen on the *Kronprinzessin Cecilie* on April 1. Muriel's father was in semiretirement after President Taft did not reappoint him when he took office in 1909, and he looked forward to meeting his first grandchild. After a stop in Berlin, the Whites made their way to Rosnochau Castle. It was a time of great rejoicing, as newly born Margaret was named for her grandmother, Daisy. After their visit, the Whites "went on to Wilhelmshöhe where on the following day they were the Kaiser's guests at luncheon with the prime minister."[8] They remained in Germany for several weeks, and then Henry left for Argentina, where he would be chief of the American delegation to the Pan-American Conference in Buenos Aires.[9]

Later in 1910, White accompanied former president Teddy Roosevelt on a tour of Europe, acting as his de facto chief of staff. They met

Henry White (far left) talking with Kaiser Wilhelm II and Teddy Roosevelt (on right, in hat), 1910, in Döberitz, Germany. CREDIT: BAIN COLLECTION, LIBRARY OF CONGRESS

every major European head of state except Tsar Nicholas II and officially attended the funeral of King Edward VII. Back in Washington, the noted architect John Russell Pope, who designed the Jefferson Memorial in Washington, the National Archives, and the West Building of the National Gallery of Art, was hired by the Whites to design a house for them. It was located at 1624 Crescent Place, a mile and a half north of the White House, near many embassies whose representatives were eager to enjoy a friendship with White and to benefit from his experience. Daisy's health continued to decline, and her husband turned down several diplomatic assignments, including a request to serve as ambassador to Haiti, a post that would one day be filled by his son.

In the summer of 1911, the Whites again visited Muriel and her family at Rosnochau. Earlier that same year Muriel had been the target of a bizarre attempt at blackmail. She was "pestered for weeks by letters from a man living in the neighborhood named Fiedler,"[10] who insisted upon large amounts of money from her. If she didn't pay, "he would blow up her castle with a dynamite bomb." Using a decoy letter, the Whites had Fiedler arrested; he was found guilty and sentenced to two years of hard labor.[11] Obviously, she was recognized by locals as a great heiress.

Muriel and Manni welcomed their first son, Hans Christoph (always called "Boysie" within the family), on February 6, 1912. On November 16, 1912, Muriel and Manni sailed from Bremen on the S.S. *George Washington* along with little Margaret, baby Boysie, a nurse, a valet, and a maid. After New York City, they listed their final destination as Washington, DC.

The Whites repeated their summer visit in 1914 and were there at the time of the brutal assassination in Sarajevo, Bosnia-Herzegovina, of Archduke Franz Ferdinand, heir presumptive to the Austro-Hungarian throne, and his wife, Sophie, Duchess of Hohenberg, on June 28. The deed set into motion the machinations that would incite World War I.

Henry White had gone to Breslau, about sixty-five miles from Rosnochau, to cash checks that day. "There was not the slightest symptom of apprehension or of unusual troop movements. A number of German officers were expected that night at the castle on their way to manoeuvres in the neighborhood. During the day telegrams arrived saying that the

Muriel Seherr-Thoss with her first two children, Margaret and Boysie.
CREDIT: PAUL CHURCH

manoeuvres had been postponed and the officers would not arrive—the first notice that trouble was imminent."[12]

On Saturday, August 3, Silesian officials announced that war had been declared and ordered all foreign nationals to leave immediately for Berlin. The Whites, accompanied by Muriel and her two children (Margaret was four and Boysie was two), went to Berlin and had to wait two weeks at the overcrowded Adlon Hotel until the American embassy could secure special trains to evacuate Americans to Holland. Henry White remembered the public reaction to the announcement that German troops had entered Belgium and Great Britain had declared war: "It was as though a thunderclap had fallen upon them."[13] In a terrible bit of timing, Manni, who had accepted a commission and was on the Russian front, had to be sent home just at that moment for a serious operation (probably kidney stones). At Muriel's request, the Whites took their two grandchildren with them to The Hague, while

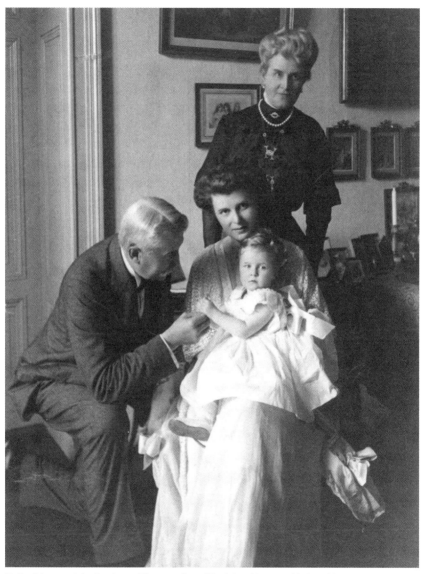

Baby Margaret in the lap of her mother, Muriel, with grandfather Henry looking on and grandmother Daisy standing behind. CREDIT: PAUL CHURCH

she remained behind with her husband. The Whites, with their two grandchildren in tow, sailed to the United States and then watched in horror as Europe descended into war.

Not surprisingly, Muriel sided with her adopted Germany. In January 1915, she wrote to family friend and former US first lady Edith Roosevelt, sending "papers by which the Germans seek to justify themselves for the invasion of Belgium."[14] Mrs. Roosevelt gave the correspondence to her husband, who then wrote to Henry White saying, "I gather from her letter that she was requested by those higher in authority to send these papers." He asked whether his draft of a reply was acceptable or whether White thought he should make changes.[15]

Later that same year, Muriel's second son, Hermann (always called "Cincie"), was born on August 7, 1915, in Berlin. Though Daisy retained her beauty, her health was continuing to deteriorate, and she would never see her newest grandchild.

The Whites enjoyed having their two older grandchildren with them and spent time at their new home in Washington, with "[Daisy's] health now being increasingly bad and at times almost alarming."[16] They retreated to their summer home, "the Poplars," in Lenox, Massachusetts, and summoned their daughter and son to return home. Muriel wrote to her brother, Jack,

> I have had very bad news of poor Mother's health which I presume has reach [sic] you also by now . . . poor Mother all but died in the train between New York and Stockbridge and she has acute Breit's [Bright's] disease[17] as well as enlargement of the heart. Papa says her condition is very critical & that she cries often & says that if you & I don't come soon she will not see us again. . . . Mother does not know that she is dangerously ill & Papa told me not to allude to this fact in my letters to him & to express sympathy with her illness . . . nothing but the fear of not seeing Mother again if I don't go soon is inducing me to make the trip.[18]

Although Muriel was apprehensive at leaving her ill husband and one-year-old baby, she sailed from Copenhagen on August 17. Margaret "Daisy" Stuyvesant Rutherfurd White died on September 2, 1916.

Ambassador White and both their children were with her as well as her brother, Winty.[19] Jack White had recently been transferred from Petrograd (St. Petersburg) to Athens and was with his parents for several weeks while Muriel was there for her mother's last week of life.

One obituary with a subhead reading "Was Friend of Queen Victoria" noted, "Mrs. White lived so long in Europe that she and the members of her family were much more closely identified with society there than in this country."[20] The *New York Times* noted, "Mr. and Mrs. White came here [Lenox] in June from their home in Washington, DC, in order to spend the summer in a higher altitude, which had been ordered for Mrs. White's health."[21]

Muriel kept a small keepsake envelope on which she wrote, "Darling Mother's hair cut off Sep. 3rd, 1916."[22] In 1906, Daisy had written to her husband on their twenty-seventh anniversary, "My darling Harry, This is our wedding day and I must send a few lines althou' it is late to say that I wish we were together. You have been a most wonderful husband to me and I pray that our happy life together may continue for many long years."[23]

Muriel was able to remain with their father longer than Jack, and she accompanied him back to Washington. She wrote to her brother,

> It was very sad coming back to this beautiful house which Mother's taste created & where one hoped that a long & happy old age might be in store for her at Papa's side. It is terribly sad to think of him here all alone & as he said to me when we were sitting yesterday evening out on the terrace his greatest consolation wld. be for you to marry.[24]

Henry White was very supportive of the establishment of a national Episcopal cathedral in the nation's capital. Chartered by Congress in 1893, the location atop Mount Saint Alban was chosen in 1898, and construction began in 1907. Muriel wrote to Jack about the visit she and their father made to the site: "We discovered a place in the crypt for Mother's last resting place. It is a sort of niche with a medium sized window. In the wall of the niche Mother's ashes could be placed with a marble medallion of her profile by French[25] & a window to her memory. . . . Darling Papa is very pathetic as he is so patient & unselfish in his

The French Commission meeting at Henry White's house in Washington, DC, 1917.
CREDIT: BAIN COLLECTION, LIBRARY OF CONGRESS

sorrow just as he is always about everything." After an appropriate interval helping their father, Muriel returned to Germany, taking her two older children with her.

To mark one year since Daisy's death, Henry wrote to Muriel. "This is the anniversary of your mother's death. How well I remember that day and her last words, 'Peace, peace, peace,' which is what she was at last attaining after so much suffering. I also remember what a great comfort your presence was that last week and afterwards, to me."[26]

Muriel returned home to family obligations that foretold her role as a diplomatic "fixer." Manni had a friend and family relation,[27] Count Hyazinth von Strachwitz. He had been training for the 1916 Olympics when war broke out in 1914, and he was appointed a lieutenant in the Hussars. He volunteered to lead a deep reconnaissance squad into France, where his unit freed some German prisoners before he, too, was captured along with several of his men. He managed to escape, but one of the men, Oberleutnant [upper lieutenant] Count von Schierstaedt, was seri-

Daisy in older age. COURTESY OF THE WILLIAM TAPLEY BENNETT, JR. PAPERS, RICHARD B. RUSSELL LIBRARY FOR POLITICAL RESEARCH AND STUDIES, UNIVERSITY OF GEORGIA LIBRARIES, ATHENS, GEORGIA, 30602-1641

ously wounded in the escape when he took a bullet to his leg. Count von Strachwitz gave a local farmer gold coins in exchange for civilian clothes, which the two were wearing when they were again captured by French forces. Because of their clothing, the French regarded them as spies and saboteurs rather than soldiers, and thus they had no legal rights.

There was talk of a firing squad; then the plan changed to sending them to French Guiana in South America, where they would be imprisoned and sentenced to hard labor.[28] Instead, they were sent to a French camp where only the worst offenders were imprisoned, and Strachwitz was routinely starved and beaten.[29] It was clear that he would not survive his five-year sentence there.

Muriel Seherr-Thoss was a longtime friend of Sophie Verdier Pichon, the wife of the current French minister of foreign affairs. Muriel asked Stephan Pichon to intercede on behalf of Strachwitz, who was being treated so badly as a spy. Pichon spoke with Minister of War Alexandre Millerand (who would later become prime minister, and then president, of France). As a result, Strachwitz was moved to Avignon prison, and his sentence was converted from five years of hard labor to five years in a military prison, where he would be treated far less harshly among other soldiers. The written commutation stated that it was done "to please the Countess von Seherr-Thoss in memory of our old and excellent relationship."[30] Due to Muriel's intercession, Strachwitz would not only survive but eventually become known as the "Panzer Count" and was the most highly decorated German regimental commander of World War II.

It would certainly not be the last time she was called on for help, and she became very skilled at it. The next year, her father wrote to relay a conversation he had with Baron Amaury de La Grange, a French aviator who fought in the Battle of the Marne, then as captain of an observation aviation squadron. He was severely wounded late in the war and in later years would be arrested by the Gestapo and sent to a special camp to serve as a hostage for Adolf Hitler before being sent to Buchenwald and then to the Tyrol. In 1915, he had married an American woman, Emily Eleanor Sloane.[31]

Young Emily Sloane was not a typical society debutante of her day. She allied herself with Mrs. William Astor Chanler, and the two served as secretary and president of the Lafayette Fund. Through their efforts, more than fifty thousand "comfort kits" were sent to French soldiers after Miss Sloane, who was in Paris at the outbreak of war, personally saw the sufferings of soldiers in the trenches by disguising herself as a local girl and being taken to the front. When she accepted the marriage proposal of Baron Amaury de La Grange, he was serving on the front lines, so they postponed their wedding. She never stopped her efforts on behalf of French soldiers, and at the end of the war, she did her best to find homes for injured soldiers.

At one point she was working in Belgium, but because of administrative roadblocks, she found herself unable to cross the border back into France. On learning of the situation, Muriel "wrote to General von Bissing saying that Baroness de LaGrange [Amaury's mother] was a Miss Carroll of Maryland, the same state as Papa, and that it would probably create a great outcry in the United States if she and her daughter . . . were detained in Belgium. It had the desired effect."[32] Henry White wrote to his daughter that the baron "asked to be particularly remembered to you. He is very grateful to you for your help in getting his wife out of Belgium early in the year and asked me to send you his special remembrances."[33]

As early as 1919, there were references to Muriel's opposition to German policy. Her father had lunch in Paris with family friends, the Count and Countess Jean de Kergorlay and their daughters. The countess was born Mary Louise Carroll, daughter of a governor of Maryland and directly descended from a signer of the Declaration of Independence. Her sister, Anita, married Baron Louis de La Grange. The Whites and the Carrolls had been friends for several generations. The de Kergorlays had two sons, Bertrand and Albert, who both served in the aviation corps of the French army during World War I. Bertrand was made a chevalier of the Legion of Honor, and both he and his brother were decorated several times for their service.[34]

Henry White wrote to his son Jack after the luncheon, "They asked particularly after you and seem to have quite a touching affection for Muriel who found means to help their brother when a prisoner in different German camps. There are many who speak of her with real affection."[35]

Henry White with his grandchildren, Margaret, Boysie, and Cincie.
CREDIT: ELIZABETH SEHERR-THOSS

Obviously, Muriel's contacts were extensive. All those efforts, how-ever, took their toll on Muriel, who was operating independently. As her father continued in that same letter, "I hope your *joie* will return and your health too when you get to a place of rest in Holland and I must say that I shall not feel easy until you are there safely. I quite understand your nerves being upset by all that you have been through."[36]

But the requests for her assistance did not stop. Again in 1920, Muriel's father wrote to her of a luncheon given by Senator Henry Cabot Lodge's daughter-in-law Bessie.[37] Also at the luncheon was Julia Meyer

Brambilla, wife of the counsellor at the Italian embassy and daughter of the US secretary of the navy. It was given in honor of Baroness Sternberg, born Lillian Langham of Louisville, Kentucky, whose late husband, Baron Speck von Sternberg, had been the German ambassador to the United States. In 1919, she returned to the United States to regain her citizenship "and take legal matters to have her fortune restored."[38]

Henry White wrote of the luncheon as follows:

> The baroness told me how you gave her food frequently and probably saved her life from starvation adding a description of the wonderful way in which you looked ahead and provided for your family and friends. She wound up by saying, "In fact Muriel was the only one that had any food in B. [Berlin] during those terrible times." She was of course delighted to know that I had heard from you and sends you her love. She is to have an interview with the Alien Property Custodian tomorrow armed with several letters—one from me among others—and I hope she will get her property back.[39]

Although Henry White had written to Muriel that his "greatest consolation" as a widower would be to see his son married, the father actually preceded his son to the altar. Quite naturally, Muriel and her brother wanted to see their father happy. They discussed with him the subject of his possible remarriage. He would have been a very attractive match for a widow. He replied to Jack that he was

> touched I need not say, I would merely remark that the only reason which would ever cause me to think of forming another tie of that kind would be the possibility of thereby adding to the amount which I could leave to you & M [Muriel]. This wd. involve of course a widow with no descendants and the only person filling that bill & who would be sympathetic & companionable would be Mrs. Kane, whom I like & who is very lonely with no one to inherit her very considerable possessions to which those of her elder sister, also with no descendants, are likely at no distant day to be added.[40]

It is almost certain that he was writing about Annie Cottenet Schermerhorn, a first cousin of *the* Mrs. Astor, who married John Innes Kane, a great-grandson of John Jacob Astor. He left Ann a widow in 1913, with no children. Her sister, Sarah, never married, and they had two brothers who died as infants. When their father died in 1903, his family sold their large estate, Jones's Wood, for $700,000 (equivalent to $22 million today) to John D. Rockefeller, for what became Rockefeller University. Annie Cottenet Kane lived until 1926 and never remarried. She left $4 million to New York charities, including $1 million to Columbia University, where her father had been chairman of the Board of Trustees.

Financial considerations aside, White also noted of his possible remarriage,

> But when I think of anyone else having the name which always meant beauty, distinction, cleverness, high standards—a combination the like of which I have never seen and which has been often & most touchingly alluded to since I have been here—I must say that I rather shudder at the idea . . . and there is always I suppose the possibility of which Mother used often to warn me of my becoming "ga-ga" with age, as so many others have done and falling a victim to some designing female.[41]

When Henry White did remarry, it was to an old friend who not only was not childless (contrary to his earlier stipulation) but also had five children, four of whom survived to adulthood, as well as several grandchildren. Emily Thorn Vanderbilt Sloane (1852–1946) was a granddaughter of Commodore Vanderbilt. One of her brothers was the father of Consuelo, Duchess of Marlborough, while another, George, built Biltmore Estate, the largest privately owned home in the United States. Emily was a philanthropist, creating the Sloane Hospital for Women in 1888, with an endowment of more than $1 million. She and her husband and his brother also donated the funds to create the Sloane Physics Laboratory at Yale. She and her first husband built Elm Court, their massive shingle-style cottage in Lenox, Massachusetts, not far from the Whites' home, the Poplars, where Daisy died. Emily had been a widow since 1915, when her handsome husband, William Douglas Sloane, died of a kidney ailment at Aiken, South Carolina. He and his brother, Henry T. Sloane, founded the carpet firm W. & J. Sloane, of whom Mrs. Astor sniffed, "Just because we walk on their carpets doesn't mean we must dine at their tables."[42]

The older couple (he was seventy, she, sixty-eight) wanted a small, private marriage ceremony. Rumors of an engagement the week before the wedding were denied by both families even though Henry White was known to be her guest at Elm Court. On November 3, 1920, "a group of near relatives assembled at St. Bartholomew's chapel, and the simple ceremony was performed by Rev. Dr. Leighton Park. . . . It was said later at the residence of the bride, 2 West 52nd Street, that they had married for companionship and would remain at the house, as there would be no honeymoon."[43] The article was careful to point out that Emily was an heir to her grandfather, who died "leaving a fortune rated at considerably more than $200,000,000."[44] The bride's home was one of the famous twin brownstones at Fifth Avenue and 52nd Street, both having been built by their father next to her brother, Cornelius, and his wife, "Alice of the Breakers." Most of the bride's family attended the small ceremony, as did Jack White, who had recently returned from Poland. Muriel wrote to him from The Hague about their father's marriage: "I am thankful that his happiness should be assured as I feel certain it is, with a wife who has so sweet & charming a disposition as our stepmother. All people seem to agree as to the sweetness of her character & I must say that it is a great comfort & relief to me to feel that we need no longer fear any loneliness for Papa in the future."[45]

Fortunately, her father's new marriage kept him from suffering with his daughter the worst excesses of the Silesian Uprisings that occurred in the wake of World War I. Silesia is a region of central Europe that now lies mainly within Poland, with smaller parts in the Czech Republic and Germany. Traversed by the Oder River, Lower Silesia was in the west and Upper Silesia in the east. The greater part of Silesia had belonged to the Kingdom of Poland in the medieval period, and then to the kings of Bohemia and the Holy Roman Empire, before falling to the Austrian Habsburgs. Prussia's Frederick the Great seized it from Austria's Maria Theresa in 1742. It then became part of Prussia and, eventually, the German Empire in 1871. Despite Germany's policy of "Germanization" and

Henry White with his second wife, Emily, his daughter, and two grandchildren at Elm Court, Emily's home in Lenox, Massachusetts. CREDIT: HENRY WHITE PAPERS, BOX 102, LIBRARY OF CONGRESS

its genocide of native Poles, Upper Silesia, where the Seherr-Thoss castles of Dobrau and Rosnochau were located, was then still majority Polish.[46]

The reason Silesia was always a target was its mineral resources. Almost a quarter of Germany's annual output of coal was from Silesia, as well as 81 percent of its zinc and 34 percent of its lead.[47] When the Poles and Czechs regained their independence after the end of World War I, eastern Upper Silesia again became part of Poland while the Austrian western parts were divided between Czechoslovakia and Poland. Upper Silesia was placed under martial law in August 1914 and remained so throughout the war. The Germans assumed that the Poles' Slavic heritage would render them loyal to Russia and thus ruled them harshly. Poles hoped for a reborn independent Poland after the war.

The Paris Peace Conference of 1919 created a strategic tension between British Prime Minister David Lloyd George, who wanted Upper Silesia to remain within Germany, and French Premier Georges Clemenceau, who thought it should become Polish. The signing of the Treaty of Versailles in 1919 cut the baby in half by ordering a popular vote to determine whether Upper Silesia should be part of Germany or Poland. Until the actual vote, it remained under German control, including its harsh police force. Germany warned that those residents who voted for Poland would lose their jobs and pensions.[48]

In 1919, Manni wrote a letter to his father-in-law about the "Bolshevist riots in Berlin." As expected from a German officer, he found his country blameless in every way:

> Let us leave apart a judgement about German methods of war, about Germany [*sic*] fault or partly fault as to the outbreak of war. Even the most fantastic slander against the German people cannot obliterate the fact that Germany belongs to the chief pillars of the monument we call civilized mankind. Would not the whole monument be endangered if the German pillar was completely broken down?[49]

Almost as an afterthought, the young soldier assured the ambassador that he "dare not doubt a moment" that White was doing all he could to promote peace.

Three separate Polish Uprisings took place in 1919, 1920, and 1921 (the last and longest). The French, in their desire to weaken Germany, supported Polish claims, while the British and Italians supported the Germans. They wanted to ensure that they were paid substantial war reparations by Germany, which insisted those payments could not be made if it did not have the revenue from the Silesian mineral industries. Giving all the mineral-rich areas to Poland would weaken Germany. In the subsequent plebiscite, those in urban areas voted to remain German while rural voters chose to remain Polish. Insurgents took over a large part of Upper Silesia, and fighting broke out, with charges of rape and mutilation by both sides.[50]

Wojciech Korfanty, a Polish activist, organized the Polish Uprisings in Upper Silesia and was known for employing terrorism against its German civilians.[51] The town of Oberglogau (now Głogówek), near the Czech border, voted by 95.9 percent to remain with Germany. Caught in the middle of it all, Muriel Seherr-Thoss wrote to a friend that her village, seven miles away on the left side of the Oder, gave "300 votes for Germany in the plebiscite and only 20 for Poland."[52] As she explained in her long letter written in French, "the French and the Poles were very surprised by this result, because they did not expect that our Polish-speaking peasants would vote *en masse* for Germany. They therefore allowed Korfanty to organize this insurrection and to take by force what they had lost by the plebiscite."[53]

The result was "terrible days . . . and I cannot express to you enough admiration and gratitude that we (inhabitants of Upper Silesia) feel for the brave Italian officers and soldiers who defended us with their lives against the bands of Korfanty whom the French have allowed to devastate our province without lifting a finger to protect us."[54] Ten railway bridges near Muriel between Neustadt and Oppeln were blown up on the night of May 2 by, according to her, a local veterinarian in complicity with a French officer. "We first wondered why these people had destroyed our bridges. As the bands of Korfanty advanced without being stopped by French troops, we understood it was to prevent troops coming from Germany to meet and stop them. . . . I sent my three children back to friends in Germany and had all the items of value at home packed (linen, silverware, clothes, etc.) in order to put them in a safe place." French officers had earlier searched local houses for weapons and "severely punished all those who hid some."[55]

Muriel had decided to "stay at home and try to save our beautiful castle from being looted, because I did not believe that the Poles would be cruel to women." But the parish priest, the mayor, and others warned her that "as my father-in-law filled the office of Landrat [high government official] I should not think of staying." Hearing shots in the distance, Muriel led the women and children in "a caravan of 8 carts and 25 people and left my pretty home at midnight, thinking of finding it in ruins. I would not wish such an experience on my worst enemy."[56] After an all-night journey, they reached the town of Tülz, where they learned the Italians had repulsed Korfanty's men. The women quickly filled the local church for a Thanksgiving Mass.

As locals gathered, Muriel heard many horror stories about the French troops. A young Prince Ratibor told her that his aunt and uncle, the Duke and Duchess of Ratibor, were at their castle when French soldiers forced their way in and held guns to the heads of the older couple. They were saved only by the quick thinking of one servant who told the soldiers that the Duke and Duchess were friends of the king of Italy, and, as Muriel recalled,

> the Italian officer could take them to the town of Ratibor. In the meantime, the insurgents had completely robbed the little house near the castle, inhabited by the Duke's eldest son. His young wife, whom I know very well, had her jewels torn off, as well as her mother, Princess Oettingen, who was visiting her. She, her mother, her husband and her children are left with nothing but what they were carrying. Not a piece of linen or any piece of clothing escaped the looters.[57]

It was young Prince Ratibor who told Muriel about the local schoolmaster's terrible fate. "It is impossible for me to tell a lady of the horrors that this poor man was subjected to, but his mutilated body was in tatters."[58] Muriel also learned that

> the castle of my sister-in-law, Countess Hans Seherr-Thoss, in Kzarnowitz, near Cosel, was robbed and the cattle taken away, also the castle of her neighbor, Count Hasslinge. . . . What the insurgents could not take away, they burned then cut into pieces the family portraits. . . . In all these places the peasants who had voted for Germany had their homes looted. School teachers and state officials who were not saved in time had their eyes gouged out, their noses and ears cut off.[59]

Muriel must have given an interview to a reporter, as her ordeal was reported in the United States: "Countess Seherr-Thoss conducted women and children of forty families from her home village of Kosnochou [Rosnochou] to Neustadt, the journey being made in carts."[60] In closing her long letter to her friend in Italy, as an additional reason for her to be grateful to the Italians, Muriel referred to "the two happy years of my youth spent in Rome, when my father was Ambassador there."[61]

Muriel's experiences in the Silesian Uprising also had a profound effect on her father and, by extension, on public policy, thanks to the first-hand information she supplied to him. Because Henry White, a Republican, had strong ties to both Britain and Germany, he had remained neutral in his sympathies. That position was shared by the Democratic US president Woodrow Wilson, who said of the issue, "the only real interest of France in Poland is in weakening Germany by giving Poland territory to which she has no right."[62] White was very pleasantly surprised, after the declaration of armistice, when President Wilson asked him to serve as one of five American peace commissioners who would go to France to work on a peace treaty with Germany.

One American publication noted rather snidely that Henry White, as the sole Republican appointee, maintained

> amiability towards the present Administration, which still retains his son in the diplomatic service.... Of his qualifications nothing is known except that he has money, pleasing manners and a knowledge of the French language not possessed by any of his colleagues from top to bottom. He also speaks German after a fashion and, if occasion should arise, will be able to act as interpreter for the President in conversation with the former Kaiser, whose intimate hospitality he has enjoyed. Also as the father-in-law of Count Seherr-Thoss, he undoubtedly will be able to obtain the privileges of that distinguished Prussian officer's undamaged castle at Rosnochau if the President should accept the kind invitation of the present German government to pay a visit of condolence to the afflicted Fatherland.[63]

Of all the delegates, White was the only one who had spent any time in Silesia: "His visits to his daughter had given him a substantial knowledge of the region, and she took pains to send him information. The comparative ease with which Wilson was brought to support the plebiscite was due to the efforts White had been making. . . . He had seen Wilson repeatedly on the subject, explaining the injustice of the wholesale cession of Upper Silesia to Poland."[64]

Paris Peace Conference. Henry White is seated second from right next to President Woodrow Wilson in the center. CREDIT: FLICKR, U.S. SIGNAL CORPS, NO KNOWN RESTRICTIONS

In the beginning of their dialogue, President Wilson questioned White's opinions. He asked at one meeting, "I have heard from the French and the Poles that you have a son-in-law in Upper Silesia who belongs to the class of German landlords who have been grinding the faces of the Polish peasantry for centuries."[65]

White explained that the Polish peasantry had been independent proprietors since 1848 and had operated amicably with their former landowners. He also pointed out that many residents of the region spoke both German and Polish, and, at the very least, it was unfair "to place a whole province upon what might prove a lower level of culture without consulting its people."[66] Thus, the plebiscite moved forward. White's position was that "the proud and headstrong nation [Poland] which had been imprisoned for so many generations by a league of neighbors should be released, and should have her rightful possessions restored to her."[67] President Wilson wrote that there should be "an independent Poland, with secure access to the sea, embracing all territories inhabited by indisputably Polish populations."[68]

Several years later, President Wilson, who had been awarded the Nobel Peace Prize, was retired and in poor health. Shortly before his death, Henry and Muriel visited him in his home in Washington, DC.

As they were about to leave, "he remarked to Countess Seherr-Thoss, 'But for your father I should never have known the truth about Upper Silesia: the French and the Poles had entirely misled me.'"[69]

Even with the Seherr-Thosses' long relationship with the royal family, Muriel's husband did not enjoy the same success with his own efforts at affecting diplomacy. In a letter written after a German torpedo's 1916 sinking of the French ship *Sussex* without warning, killing fifty crew and passengers and wounding two Americans, Henry White wrote to Muriel that "if Germany continued destroying American ships and breaking her promises, the United States would inevitably be forced into the war and would make a German defeat certain."[70]

Naturally, Muriel showed the letter to Manni, who "at once translated and sent it in the form of a report to General Ludendorff, who returned it with some rudely skeptical remarks in the margin."[71] Not to be put off, however, Count Seherr-Thoss took the letter to military headquarters himself but "was refused an audience by the Kaiser's aide-de-camp, on the ground that, 'We know the kind of reports you send to General Ludendorff about America. We don't wish the Emperor to hear them.'"[72]

Adding insult to injury, after dinner at military headquarters, Count Seherr-Thoss personally "approached the Kaiser, saying that he had a very interesting and important letter from his father-in-law in Washington; but the Emperor, visibly embarrassed by the presence of his *entourage*, replied coldly, 'I would rather you told me about your father's pheasant-shooting in Silesia.'"[73]

If it seems odd that a relatively junior officer had the access and temerity to approach his emperor personally, the Seherr-Thoss family had long connections to him. As Kaiser Wilhelm recalled in his memoirs, they were close friends from his days as a student in Bonn: "I have a vivid recollection of my contemporaries in the Corps 'Borussia,' and as I write, their various personalities pass before me. There was Duke George of Oldenburg, the Grand Duke Frederick of Baden—who was my companion on a walking tour through the Black Forest; also Baron von Seherr-Thoss, later Governor-General of Liegnitz; Baron von Thiele-Winkler, whose fencing in a duel I witnessed for the first time in breathless excitement."[74]

The emperor had often hunted at various Seherr-Thoss properties with Manni's father. In 1911, the emperor arrived for a hunt at Moszna Castle that included the senior count. From birth, the emperor had a short, withered left arm and could use only his right. His hunting perch was placed slightly higher than the others so he could rest the gun almost at eye level and shoot only with his right hand. He had three 20-caliber shotguns, which were quickly reloaded and handed to him by his bodyguard. A special beater forced the game to run straight into the emperor's gun.

As Muriel's sister-in-law, Betty White, recalled from personal experience,

> A shoot is a marvelous performance. The landowners would have "beaters" come, who would beat the game into a circle. The "guns" would stand a certain distance from one another, each one with a "loader" behind. One would fire, then the next man, and the next.[75]

After Manni's father died and he inherited the family estates, Manni continued hunting on their properties. Muriel's great-grandson recalled, "At least a few times Manni formally invited [Hermann] Göring to hunts

A hunt at Moschen near Dobrau. Kaiser Wilhelm II is standing left of center holding a cane. Manni's father, Roger, Count Seherr-Thoss, is standing right of center behind the arm of the man holding a cigarette. CREDIT: REGIONAL MUSEUM MOJMIROVCE

at Dobrau," including an invitation "from Manni to Göring to come for a hunting weekend. It's handwritten on Dobrau letterhead."[76] While Manni's long relationships may have, for him, mitigated the atrocities his friends and associates later committed, Muriel had no corresponding affinity to reconcile their actions. As their great-grandson asked, "Has it entered your thoughts that the S-Ts [Seherr-Thosses] played more than one hand as a means of bluffing?"[77]

In 1922, Muriel wrote to her father to tell him that Manni's father no longer recognized anyone and would probably not last the week. The count died on January 19. While waiting for the end, Muriel wrote to her father with disturbing news:

> It was very wrong of my Father-in-law not to give Manni an insight into things sooner as now it is very hard for him. It seems quite clear that his father has been putting all the money he could into Walzen [another Seherr-Thoss property] for Dodel [Manni's mother] and that includes all the estates which Manni is to inherit [that] are in great disrepair. There is far less ready money than his Father told him at the Bank & from all he can see; during the last six months of his Father's illness, his employees have been cheating him as was to be expected. Amazing that he never once would let Manni help in any way although he repeatedly offered to do so.[78]

Walzen, located only eleven miles from Dobrau, had been owned by Manni's brother, Count Roger Seherr-Thoss.[79] He went heavily into debt, and the estate was taken by the state in December 1919, under the Reich Settlement Act of August 22, 1919.[80] Originally, much of the Seherr-Thoss land holdings near Zabrze and Katowice contained valuable coal deposits, but that mineral was not prevalent near Dobrau and Rosnochau. Once it was depleted, "it became harder to keep it all up. Manni struggled with and resented the burden."[81] Evidently, Muriel's father-in-law had been appropriating the money meant to be spent on the upkeep of Dobrau and Rosnochau and applying it to redeem Walzen, perhaps as a dowager castle for Manni's mother, who lived until 1925.

Muriel had been spending all the money she could solicit and borrow from her family, and she was now fully aware of impending financial doom:

Manni is very nervous and upset & I think it is just as well that till
things have shaken down a bit & he has found his way about I shall be
away as I am bound to be the scape-goat of his worry & bad temper.
Now he will visit what annoys him on his Mother, in which there will
be a certain amount of justice as she encouraged his Father to squeeze
everything out of the estates . . . for the younger children to keep Manni
out of things.[82]

As Muriel's sister-in-law, Betty White, recalled about the Seherr-
Thoss family's finances, "There was always a question of money because
he [the count] had to support his brothers."[83] Now there was a dowager
countess to support as well as four brothers and several uncles and all
their families. And to Muriel descended all the liabilities as chatelaine of
Dobrau Castle. As her father wrote to her, "In view of all that you have
written as to the heavy charges which M. [Manni] has to meet at once, I
agree with you in thinking that it will be better to go slowly in respect to
Dobrau and not to think of moving into it for several years."[84]

Schloss Dobrau, the principal Seherr-Thoss home. CREDIT: LANDESBIBLIOTHECK BERLIN,
WIKIMEDIA, PUBLIC DOMAIN

Chapter Four

I wish it were really possible to make our people at home understand how definitely this martial spirit is being developed in Germany. If this government remains in power for another year, and it carries on in the measure in this direction, it will go far toward making Germany a danger to world peace for years to come. With few exceptions, the men who are running the government are of a mentality that you and I cannot understand. Some of them are psychopathic cases and would ordinarily be receiving treatment somewhere.[1]
—US Foreign Service Officer George Messersmith

DESPITE BEING SEPARATED BY AN OCEAN, MURIEL'S FATHER KEPT her informed of family events, including those of his new wife's family. Although Henry White had remarried, to his father's dismay, Jack was still single. Muriel, who was almost four years older than he, had always been close to Jack. When they were children and often traveling, she wrote him letters beginning "Most Precious piece of masculine humanity"[2] or "my treasure boy, Jack."[3] In another from onboard the R.M.S. *Teutonic*, she called him "my darling precious Jack" and told him, "Mr. and Mrs. Ogden Mills are on board. They have 2 twins of 11 who are *very* shy and a nice little boy. Franklin Roosevelt is onboard & wishes you were here. He has very much grown & is very pleasant & intelligent."[4]

Muriel remained intensely interested in her brother's development. She wrote to her mother when she was twelve,

> I am rather glad that he is going [to school], as I think it will amuse him to be with other boys, and nicer for him to do his lessons in company....

He has a nice little parcel of his books and he is going to take some bread and an apple for his lunch and it remains to be seen what accounts he will give when he returns at 10:00 . . . [writing hours later]. We have just come back from leaving Jack at school, there was only one boy there who judging from his copy books was uncommonly stupid so that I expect that Jack will gain an easy victory.[5]

Later, in 1895, Muriel wrote to her brother, calling him "my treasure boy Jack," from the Priory, Reigate, a house that had been taken by the American-born former Mary Leiter, who only six months earlier married fellow Soul George Curzon and became Baroness Curzon of Kedleston. Muriel, when she was thirteen, wrote her mother from Washington only six weeks before the Curzon wedding: "It went very well with Daisy Leiter. She is very nice only I would give her a credit for twenty in looks at any rate."[6] She also mentioned that they went "with the Roosevelts for a long walk."

Muriel was delighted to hear that Jack had finally become engaged and was especially pleased to learn that his betrothed came from a family of distinguished diplomats. Elizabeth "Betty" Barclay Moffat (1898–1993) was a daughter of Reuben Burnham Moffat, a New York City attorney, and Ellen Low Pierrepont Moffat.[7] She was descended from the first chief justice of the United States, John Jay, and his wife, Sarah Livingston Jay. Betty Moffat graduated from Miss Chapin's School in New York City. When she was twenty-two, in 1920, she accompanied her mother to Warsaw to visit her brother Pierrepont, a career diplomat, and saw firsthand the life and experience of foreign service, so she was well prepared for her life with Jack.

Learning of the engagement, Muriel wrote to Betty, whom she had not met, "to tell you with what joy I welcome you as a sister and how much I am longing to know you." She assured Betty, "Jack has always been such a kind good brother & such a model son that I am sure he will make you the best of husbands and deserve his good fortune in having won a wife as charming as I have heard you to be."[8] Muriel asked Betty to send her a photograph of herself.

On April 9, 1921, Jack White married Betty Moffat at St. James Church in New York City. Afterward, her widowed mother held a reception at her home at 660 Park Avenue. Eleven months later, on March 4, Betty White gave birth in New York City to their only child, Margaret Rutherfurd White, also named for her grandmother and always referred to in the family as "Lolly" to differentiate from her grandmother, her aunt, and her first cousin. The baby's parents were at that time stationed in Venezuela, but Betty went home to New York City for the birth. When Lolly was only two, her parents sent her from Paris, where her father was at the US embassy, to Czechoslovakia, in the charge of her nurse. Her parents would join her there at her father's new assignment.

In 1925, Manni and his mother were being driven by their chauffeur from Ohlau to Breslau when a steering failure caused the car to crash into a cherry tree. Manni and the driver were thrown from the car, but the dowager countess suffered internal injuries and broken legs and died as a result of her injuries.[9]

Only two years later, in 1927, Muriel and Manni were with Henry and his wife at Elm Court, his wife's summer home in Lenox, Massachusetts, not far from the Whites' home, the Poplars, where Daisy died. The evening before he was scheduled for an operation, Henry had been engaged in a conversation with Muriel about an English book, *Where Freedom Fails*. She was surprised to hear him say about the author, "I agree with him that we ought to remit the European debt"; he thought it would be in the interest of the United States, as it would lead to "the increased well-being of Europe and her greater good will toward us."[10]

Tragically, Henry White failed to rally from the shock of an operation on July 14, 1927. His long support for a national cathedral in Washington had been partially realized, as only the crypt and part of the choir had been completed; thus, "In the Bethlehem Chapel of its crypt, after a memorial service held on November 10, 1927, his ashes were laid to rest, not many feet from the grave of the great war President [Wilson] whom he had so loyally served." His memorial proclaims, "Blessed are the peacemakers."[11]

Margaret, Boysie, and Cincie as children. CREDIT: PAUL CHURCH

Elm Court, where Henry White died. It was the home of his second wife, Emily
Vanderbilt Sloane. CREDIT: NATIONAL PARK SERVICE, FREDERICK LAW OLMSTED NATIONAL
HISTORIC SITE

In the year after his father's death, Jack White was named counselor
of the US embassy in Buenos Aires, where he served until he was transferred to Berlin in 1933, for two years, placing him in close proximity to
Muriel at another very difficult time when she was extremely fortunate
to have his support and counsel; indeed, events might have turned out
much better had he not been transferred away from Berlin after such
a short time.

Jack White served under an academic scholar, liberal Democrat
William E. Dodd, who was appointed ambassador to Germany in 1933
by Franklin D. Roosevelt and instructed to do "unofficially" whatever
he could to protest Nazi treatment of Jews in Germany while still
maintaining "cordial official diplomatic relations."[12] Before Ambassador
Dodd's departure for Berlin, he was instructed by his friend, the poet

Carl Sandburg, "to find out what this man Hitler is made of, what makes his brain go round, what his blood and bones are made of . . . and be brave and truthful, keep your poetry and integrity."[13]

Ambassador Dodd was suspicious of career diplomats. He wrote in his diary on November 5, 1933,

> John White, son of the famous Henry White, Republican member of Wilson's mission to the Paris Conference, 1918–1919, and Orme Wilson, a relative of Pierrepont Moffat, State Department official, arrived to take up their work. The one will be Counsellor of the Embassy here, the other Second Secretary. Both seemed to be good men—White a little too English in bearing and with a distinct Harvard-Oxford accent.[14]

Dodd was correct about the family relationships. M. Orme Wilson Jr., a grandson of *the* Mrs. Astor and nephew of Cornelius Vanderbilt III, was a career diplomat who, in 1944, followed Jack White as US ambassador to Haiti when White was named ambassador to Peru. Jay Pierrepont Moffat's family connection was as a cousin to Moffat as well as Jack White's brother-in-law. He was a career foreign service officer and eventually US ambassador to Canada.[15]

It was a large and convoluted family web that directly affected US foreign policy for decades.[16] It was also the kind of aristocratic diplomacy that Ambassador Dodd at first distrusted. He believed "to a degree larger than generally recognized, I think they are responsible for the reduction in our Foreign Service appropriations . . . [and march with] the ranks of privileged capitalists."[17] Fortunately, Moffat wrote to his brother-in-law, Jack White, that Ambassador Dodd "approves of your work, but there is no doubt that he feels . . . you are living on too elaborate a scale and is preaching this doctrine not only in relation to you but to a great many others."[18]

Reliant on her husband's family's limited wealth and without access to her own funds, Muriel was often dependent on her father and his new wife for financial support. She wrote to "Mother Emily," as she called her, from her recently leased apartment in Rome: "I am so grateful to Papa for being willing to lend me the money so that I am able to arrange this nice apartment which is brand new with every modern convenience,

Muriel's brother, Ambassador John C. "Jack" White. CREDIT: DUMBARTON OAKS
ARCHIVES, WASHINGTON, DC

streaming sunshine & a lovely view of St. Peter's dome over the Villa
Borghese."[19] But in the same letter, she wrote of a visit to

> Miss Kemp . . . [who] asked Margaret & me to tea the other day after
> I had called on her & the first thing she said to us was, "I suppose you
> realize that no Germans are invited anywhere here in Rome." I replied
> that this being the case I wondered that she had invited Margaret and

me to tea with her but I thought she was mistaken as far as the Italians were concerned as Margaret and I had met with nothing but kindness & amiability. She replied rather tartly that no one regarded me as a German & that she was referring to the German diplomats. It was certainly one of those remarks which would better have been left unsaid. The good lady gave a *thé dansant* [tea dance] soon afterwards to which she did not invite us.[20]

While most American diplomats in the region were doubtful that Hitler would come to full power, one man, George S. Messersmith, held the opposite view. Messersmith was a career foreign service officer who was appointed head of the US consulate in Germany, where he served from 1930 to 1934. While there, his most controversial act was his decision to issue a visa to allow Albert Einstein to travel to the United States. He personally called Einstein to tell him the visa was approved. Messersmith was strongly criticized by conservative groups and American media for his action. Messersmith was both early and vociferous in his warnings to the US State Department. He wrote from Berlin in an official memo to William Phillips, undersecretary of state, in 1933, the excerpt at the beginning of this chapter.

In 1933, Jack was posted to the US embassy in Berlin, and his wife, Betty, and daughter, Margaret, joined him at the end of that year. The American ambassador was away, so Betty's husband was chargé d'affaires. Within days of her arrival, she recalled,

> there was a tremendous gathering at the Sportspalast to raise money for the Winterhilfe [Winter Relief, the principal Nazi charity]. They were going to play the fanfares written by Frederick the Great. We were given special places. The huge floor was absolutely crammed with people. Then all these enormous klieg lights were playing all around. Music started, a group came forward, and then as the music ended, the lights full on him, Hitler came forward and everyone raised their arm in salute HEIL HITLER! All very dramatic.[21]

Not long afterward, the Whites attended a party given by the German foreign minister and met many members of the nobility who hadn't been to Berlin since the Republic came in. They were oh so glad to see each other. . . . And then it seems that they were looking forward—they all thought that Hitler was going to bring in the Crown Prince as Kaiser . . . after World War I, when the republican regime came in, the nobility never set foot in Berlin again until Hitler came. They thought Hitler was going to restore the monarchy. . . . Maybe they thought he was going to bring in the nobility.[22]

They were greatly surprised when, the night after the Sportpalast event, "Hitler raided the Stahlhelm,[23] which was the upper-class group that believed they were going to restore the Kaiser. He came into their building on the Tiergartenstrasse, where they were having dinner. The stories were that the raiders tore the women's dresses; it was very rough. That ended the Stahlhelm organization."

As chancellor, Hitler invited Betty and Jack White to a dinner party, where he "kissed my hand and then pushed it out of the way like a political handshake." At the end of the evening, "when I said, in English, 'Good night,' I was aware of a look of fury." They met Hitler again at a dinner party given by Joseph Goebbels. With the ills of World War II far off on the horizon, Betty found Goebbels "charming, as was his wife. Hitler was there, and again he kissed my hand—kissed his thumb holding my hand."[24]

The Whites' daughter, Margaret "Lolly," who was twelve, was enrolled in a small private girls' school. She recalled, "I asked my father. We were supposed to say, 'Heil Hitler' and do the salute and all that. I said, 'What do I do?' He said, 'Do as they do, but don't go out of your way'. . . . And periodically Hitler would make a speech and we'd all have to listen to it on the radio. Boring!"[25] She was required to go to a couple of Hitler rallies and remembered, "He wasn't that impressive, but my goodness, there was something magnetic about his voice. And then of course this orchestration of great shouts and all that."[26]

She had one classmate who was a member of the Bund Deutscher Mädel (Band of German Maidens), the female section of the Hitler Youth movement.

She apparently had been told that she must do something about the Jewish girl in our class. And she had one very good friend who was quite a nice girl who was her special sidekick, but the good friend wasn't in the BDM. . . . But apparently in the recess yard, the BDM girl chose that moment to go up to the von Spiegelberg girl and call her a couple of nasty names, "You something Jewess", something like that. And, interestingly enough, the Jewish girl burst into tears, but the whole school rallied around her and sent this girl, the BDM girl, to Coventry.[27] And when I got back to class, my American pal said "We're not talking to her anymore." And the whole class has agreed— will you pass the pencil, please, yes, but I mean nothing other than that. So only her good friend stood by her, and for the rest of that year, we did not talk to her.[28]

President Franklin D. Roosevelt, in 1934, appointed George Messersmith as minister to Austria, where one of his unofficial duties was to spy on the Duke of Windsor, formerly King Edward VIII, and his American wife. Messersmith actually became friends with the duke but continued keeping his superiors informed of his actions. He was the first to discover that Nazi Germany and Fascist Italy held secret negotiations and that the Windsors had serious Nazi connections.

In 1934, Messersmith wrote from Vienna to diplomat Jay Pierrepont Moffat, then at the US State Department, that Moffat's sister, Betty (Mrs. Jack White),

> was down here for a few days with Countess Seherr-Thoss' daughter [Margaret], who is a very charming girl, but unfortunately it was during the very first days of our stay here, when I was making calls on a half-hour schedule. We were able, however, to take a drive to Semmering, and we hope later that both she and Jack may be able to come down and see us after we get settled in the house.[29]

At the beginning of 1936, the Whites were reassigned to Calcutta, and their daughter, Lolly, was sent home to her maternal grandmother in the United States after finishing her school year. In July of that same year, George Messersmith sent a seventeen-page, single-spaced letter to US Secretary of State Cordell Hull. He related personal instances of growing violence in light of the recently completed "Juliabkommen"

[July Agreement] between Austria and Nazi Germany, brought about by negotiations with the support of Fascist Italy. It would last less than two years until Germany annexed Austria.

As part of his letter, Messersmith reported on a visit to

Countess Seherr-Thoss at her home near Klagenfurt in Carinthia over the weekend. She is, as you know, the daughter of Henry White and the sister of Jack White, our Consul General in Calcutta. Her husband belongs to a well known family in Germany and she lives most of the year in their castle in Silesia. She is of course German, and spends the summer here in Austria in Carinthia. On the day that amnesty was pro-claimed, I was with her in her car which has a German license, in front of the post office in Klagenfurt. Two young men, probably about twenty, looked at the German license on the car and after talking with each other one of them came and opened the door of the car and said to me, "Where is your Hackenkreuz [swastika]?" I could hardly believe that I heard properly so I asked him what he said. He replied very energetically and in a nasty way with the same question. I again, hardly believing my ears, said to the young man, "We are strangers here and I think you will wish to mind your own business." To which he replied, "But this is a German car, and where is your Hackenkreuz?" He was so offensive that in spite of my desire to do nothing, I felt that I could not permit him to annoy Countess Seherr-Thoss in this manner so got out of the car and a young man, who was in my car behind, took one of the boys who had done the talking (the other ran away) to the nearest policeman to whom I related what had happened and said that the political aspect of it didn't concern me, but that I thought he would want to know that a young man was disturbing strangers and as he seemed like a very foolish young man, his parents and the authorities should know what he was doing. I said, however, that I did not wish to make any complaint against him and that if the policeman arrested him it was not to be at my request.[30]

Following the end of World War I, in March 1919, Henry White let Jack know that he had taken a villa for the summer for Muriel and her family at The Hague, but

I am still uneasy about the children, however, whom she left in the apartment at Berlin with Manni's brother and two Swedish diplomatists in charge, in view of the threatened revolution there again; the more so, as M [Muriel] herself was to return there this week to get them but thought of paying Delie a visit between times & returning from Switzerland via B. [Berlin] to Holland picking up the children en route.[31]

The ambassador had very good reason to be uneasy about his grandchildren's safety. The November Revolution in Germany, lasting from November 1918 until August 1919, had brought about the replacement of the federal constitutional monarchy with a democratic parliamentary government known as the Weimar Republic. The revolution was driven by the growing disparity between the common man and the aristocracy. Families such as the Seherr-Thosses owned at least six major residences while many Germans could barely afford rent and food.

Knowledge of the abdication of Tsar Nicholas II in Russia, in 1917, fueled the unrest in Germany (even though very few people were aware of the royal family's brutal assassination). Kaiser Wilhelm II abdicated as emperor of Germany and king of Prussia on November 9, 1918, and signed on November 28 the official document in exile in the Netherlands. His family's House of Hohenzollern ended a five-hundred-year reign over Prussia. The German nobility, until then protected as a legally defined class, was abolished, and on August 11, 1919, all Germans were declared legally equal. Twenty-two princely heads of constituent states of Germany were toppled (including kings of Bavaria, Saxony, and Württemberg). The world as the Seherr-Thoss family knew it was over.

Muriel wrote a lengthy letter from Holland to her brother describing recent events. She was more aware of their new position than was her husband.

> You are quite right in thinking that it is a mercy the children are so young & Manni & I mean to bring them up in order to cope with the world they will have to live in. He & I personally feel that we can be contented with far less than his expectations entitled him to. If only we have a nice little home somewhere we can live peacefully & happily with our children. It seems terribly sad that by fighting this war *"a outrance"* [to the death] against German militarism, that Bolshevism & extreme socialism (which are so much worse) should have been let loose on the world.[32]

Muriel's husband, "Manni," Count Seherr-Thoss. COURTESY
OF THE WILLIAM TAPLEY BENNETT, JR. PAPERS, RICHARD B. RUSSELL
LIBRARY FOR POLITICAL RESEARCH AND STUDIES, UNIVERSITY OF
GEORGIA LIBRARIES, ATHENS, GEORGIA, 30602-1641

Muriel's father had a much more practical impression about how
his son-in-law would react to their changed circumstances. He wrote
to Muriel from Paris, "I quite understand, as I have written you, and
deeply sympathize with Manni's feelings and disappointment at such an
eventuality in view of his traditions and of what he had been brought up
to expect. Still, I cannot doubt that there is a useful life ahead for him

in helping to restore his country, even if it be not as agreeable or of the nature which he expected."[33]

Muriel tried to sympathize with her husband, writing about Manni to her brother, "When the Revolution came, the Emperor gone & all his traditions & all his expectations had fallen around him like a pack of cards, he was like a person stunned. His resignation was very touching & he seemed to be much more upset abt. losing his Emperor than abt. his & his children's very material losses."[34] Although Manni thought about remaining at home, Muriel had family members impress on him that "he would be more useful to his country in Holland than elsewhere & that he might mitigate the fate of someone else by going there. . . . As the son & heir of a Silesian magnate & as an officer in the G.S. [General Staff] he was the first person the Bolshevists would have imprisoned or shot had they come into power (which they were always on the verge of doing)."[35]

Muriel and the children had arrived in Berlin from Rosnochau just two days before scattered shooting began in the streets. Sailors in uniform tried to remove the epaulettes from Manni's uniform, but he was able to calm them. "The next day the order came that all officers in B. [Berlin] were to wear civilian clothes. They all decided to remain at their posts & to support any government which cld [could] maintain order. Had they & the government officials & the people in the Foreign Office not done this, I suppose we should have reached the stage of Russia very shortly."[36]

The next day, Muriel took little Margaret to Mass but found afterward all the streets were blocked, and they could not return home without a pass proving who they were. "You can imagine how alarming it was to be in the midst of shooting with a child & not be able to get home. Heaven sent me assistance in the person of a young Jew in the Foreign Office who had a pass & who got us through as his wife & daughter!"[37]

It was only a brief escape. As Muriel tried to move all her family,

One felt as helpless as a rat in a trap about getting away & even the foreign office people seemed powerless to help one. Barbed wire was drawn across the streets, the shooting went on all night & a good part of the day. Two officers were killed on the bridge behind our house & the Bolshevists took possession of one of the suburbs of Berlin called

Lichtenberg & there murdered lots of police & officers including some of their wives & children. I had hitherto not believed the Germans capable of murdering women & children and this made me realize how great the danger was.[38]

Muriel's father telegraphed her that he had taken a house for them in Switzerland, and they should leave immediately. However, they could not secure permission from the Swiss government, which rightly feared a major influx of refugees who would bring Bolshevism with them. Ambassador White used all his resources to secure permission for Muriel, her children, and their nurse to enter Switzerland for three weeks. Because the exception did not include Manni, Muriel wrote, "Of course I could not have heard of leaving him & I therefore turned my attention to the possibility of getting to Holland."

Muriel ventured out to the train station to learn whether they might be able to travel to Holland and learned that the train was still running.

When I came out of the station shooting had begun in the Friedrichstrasse. From the roofs, from the windows, from everywhere you can think of. Two women were killed quite near me & a soldier told me I should go home at once as it was no place for women. I remember wondering if I should ever see Manni or the children again & praying as hard as I have ever done in my life. I ran like a hare to Unter den Linden. Here, however, they were again shooting with machine guns. I dashed across Unter den Linden & finally got into a quiet street. Before I got home I had to pass some more shooting at one point & I don't suppose my life was ever in such danger as that morning except during my terrible illness the winter before last.[39]

With the intervention of the Dutch diplomat, Baron Willem Gevers, son of the Dutch envoy to Germany, permission was granted for all of them, including Manni, to enter Holland.[40] In light of Muriel's friendship with Gevers, it should be noted that he was given responsibility for "looking after the interests of the British prisoners of war"[41] while there was no British representation in Berlin due to World War I. In 1919 and 1920, there was only a British chief of the military mission to the Weimar

Republic in Berlin. A British ambassador was not appointed until the twenty-first Earl of Erroll was named counselor in November 1921.

It was also in 1919 when Muriel wrote to her brother from the seaside resort in Scheveningen, The Hague, where her father had secured a villa for them. "That you are going to Poland is too delightful for words as you will be so near us & be able to visit us often at Rosnochau."[42] As a retreat, Muriel's father purchased for her a private apartment at The Hague in Holland. Eventually it would become the only property she owned in her name. As her niece explained,

> Right after WW1 Muriel was able to live in a house in The Hague that HW [Henry White] had given her; she and Manni would make trips back to Germany. There was a heavy duty on tea, as well as cigars and other luxuries. Ever anxious to circumvent the authorities, she would pack the other luxuries well hidden in other things, and declare 1 pound of tea. (Worked like a charm!)[43]

The family also had a large apartment in Berlin that they used when necessary.

Additionally, Muriel wished to have someplace she could escape the frequent arguments with her husband, usually concerning money or conflicts about their children. As she wrote of their younger son, "Whatever pleasure I manage to give the children has to be given them in secret as Manni raises Cain! Cincie's very nice Austrian tutor says he has never seen a father who begrudged his children the most harmless pleasures. For instance, he got into a fearful rage because I had a tiny theatre party here for Boysie and Cincie at Xmas time."[44]

She found and purchased, in 1931, Krastowitz Castle in Austria, located near the summer resort of Wörthersee on Carinthia's largest lake. She wrote to her brother,

> Imagine that I have bought a small place in Southern Austria. There was a mortgage on it which is so arranged that it will be paid off in 45 years by paying the yearly interest of about 600 dollars a year.... I didn't buy it in my name, or the Austrians would demand income tax from me. Cincie is the owner. One can arrange 2 separate residences in it so

that later on if he marries, Manni & I won't clash with him. . . . I shall be glad to live in a house which is my own & where the furniture is not so precious that Manni can't bear to have it used! Also where I can ask young people which is impossible here.[45]

For his part, Manni "decided that he must close up Dobrau and has bought a villa near Klagenfurt in Southern Austria with some money he received from the German Govt. [government] for land which they forced him to sell for making an electric cable through the Dobrau forest."[46] The two new residences, Krastowitz Castle and Villa Herzoghof, were very close to one another. As Muriel explained, "The Fürstenbergs (who are the richest landowners in Germany) had to close up Donaueschingen and have moved to a villa near Vienna. One can only live in Germany now when one owns nothing but debts, thanks to their idiotic system of taxation."[47]

Boysie, seeking to placate the Nazis while keeping them at arm's length, greeted attendees at an annual harvest festival event at Rosnochau. Note the family servants gathered in the doorway. CREDIT: JOHANNES PREISNER

Manni and Muriel could then both live their own lives separately without the daily stress of arguments. Their great-grandson thought their solution worked because "Muriel was essentially through with Manni and Dobrau before the war started. Herzoghof is a lovely villa, a quarter mile from Krastowitz which was rather compact. Herzoghof offered separation in the failing marriage and room for guests in the high season."[48] Despite their new purchases, Dobrau would remain their principal residence and the one to which they always returned.

In April 1937, Muriel faced a domestic nightmare when her oldest son, Boysie, heir to his father's title and estates, became engaged to Constance "Mutzi" Masirevitch. She was the beautiful daughter of a Serbian diplomat, Dr. Szilárd Masirevitch (1879–1944), who was then the Hungarian minister to the Court of St. James[49] (although he often referred to the fact that he had no Hungarian ancestry). The wedding was announced for April 22, in London, and the *New York Times* noted the half-American heritage of the groom, who was an officer in the Royal Prussian Cuirassiers.[50] The bridesmaids had been chosen, including the groom's beautiful cousin, Countess Geraldine Apponyi,[51] who would become queen of Albania.

This was not the marriage Muriel envisioned for her first-born son. Not long after the announcement, she wrote to her brother that Manni was on his way to join her in Krastowitz, having

given his consent very grudgingly & most unwillingly to Boysie's engagement to Mutzi Masirevitch subject to proofs being produced as to the reality of the property she is to inherit from her father & a childless Uncle & Aunt. This consists of a street of houses in Budapest which brings a revenue of 75,000 pengoes[52] a year. Manni also wants her yearly allowance from these relatives put on a legal basis & proofs of her pure Aryan descent. Subject to these documents being produced he has given his consent & they will be married in London on April 22nd at the Westminster Catholic Cathedral.[53]

Evidently the bride's income was crucial to the union. Muriel wrote to her brother,

The young couple will live in the little old house on a farm adjoining this estate [Krastowitz] which Boysie bought with the money left him in trust by Mother which he is going to run. I bless her memory every day for having left him these 10,000 which have now rolled up to 24,000. . . . But for Mother's having done that poor Boysie cld. [could] never have married unless he found an heiress, as Manni would never have agreed otherwise.[54]

With Muriel's excellent sources within the diplomatic community, however, she was able to learn shocking details that caused the engagement to be broken. Her prospective daughter-in-law, the supposed successor to the title Muriel proudly held, was illegitimate. The engagement was broken. She explained in a letter to her sister-in-law, Betty White,

There was nearly a duel between Manni & Herr von Masirevitch[55] over this broken engagement and a challenge also came for Boysie by

Manni and Boysie Seherr-Thoss with hunting trophies at Dobrau.
CREDIT: ELIZABETH SEHERR-THOSS

registered mail. As he was *fortunately* in bed with high fever when the registered letter came I signed for it and opened it. I wrote the seconds (Count Teleki & Baron Pronay in Budapest[56]) that my son was very ill & that the doctors had forbidden me to give him any disagreeable letters or worrying news till he is completely restored to health, which won't be for at least a month.[57]

She was determined to clear her son's name even if that would necessitate making public what she had learned.

Meanwhile, I have taken steps to inform the Hungarian foreign office (through one of my oldest friends, Prince Festetics[58]) that if Herr von Masirevitch doesn't realize that *he* is the person who should apologize to my son for keeping him in the dark as to his daughter's being illegitimate, I shall write the following facts to my old friend Lady Helen Graham, Queen Elizabeth of England's lady in waiting:

1stly: Why my son's engagement was broken off.
2ndly: That the Hungarian Govt. has sent as Minister Plenipotentiary to the Court of St. James a man who married his mistress with that person as Chéfesse du Mission.
3rdly: That his former mistress & present wife was a cocotte in Munich who came from the provincial town of Rosenhain in Bavaria & that he married her 2 years after their daughter was born. I imagine this will bring Masirevitch to his senses!

Evidently no duels took place, so perhaps Muriel did make use of the information she had gleaned. Under the name "Constance de Masirevitch," the would-be bride undertook a literary career including the translation of Hungarian and other foreign plays into English. She would eventually write about the "Four Quartets" of the poet T. S. Eliot.

Muriel did, however, commit to paper, after discussing the issue with her husband, the requisites for Boysie's eventual marriage:

I finally wrote him [Manni] from Vienna that as Boysie would not marry a German because he thinks them dull & uninteresting (any more than Manni himself had been willing to marry one) & as the newly imposed *death penalty* on German residents who do not give up all their foreign money they own to the German govt. would preclude any girl with money in a free country like America & England from marrying him.[59]

Not surprisingly, the experience only added to the stress and anxiety Muriel was enduring in addition to her marital and financial challenges. She continued writing to her sister-in-law:

> You are sometimes surprised that my nerves are so bad; but I have had more than the usual share of *most* American women of experience which are a strain on one's nervous system.
>
> > 1stly: Four years of war in a country I detest with constant terror about Manni & a fight to have enough food for my family. The right kind of food was unobtainable.
> >
> > 2ndly: Rescuing myself & my property from the German financial authorities & Manni from the clutches of 2 harpies in succession who wanted to marry him; at the most critical moment in a woman's life! [*menopause*]
> >
> > 3rdly: This charming idyll with these bandits of Serbian extraction who nearly hooked poor Boysie.

Political tensions were continuing to worsen as well. Muriel's daughter, Margaret, had a close friend and exact contemporary, Gertrude Schley (1910–2008),[60] whom she had known since their days at Miss Nightingale's Finishing School in Manhattan. In the summer of 1937, Gertrude enjoyed a lengthy visit with her mother to Krastowitz, where they were treated as members of the family. Years later, Gertrude was very kind to Margaret's oldest grandson, Paul Church, who never knew his great-grandmother Muriel. She invited Paul and his wife, Linda, for tea and told them about her visit.

> While staying at Krastowitz in the Summer of 1937, your great-grandparents and I were enjoying a lovely dinner, whereupon there was loud banging on the entrance doors. Two SS Officers marched into the house followed by a dismayed butler. Muriel barely glanced at them, not

wanting to acknowledge them intentionally. Hermann remained seated at the opposite end of the table. Muriel continued cutting the food on her plate, rather loudly saying, "Who do you think you are to burst into this house, frightening our guests, and disrupting the evening?"[61]

The officer responded to her, "There are no party flags hanging at the front of this house!" To which Muriel replied, "Why would a family hang a flag for a party they don't support?" Gertrude clearly remembered,

> The officers erupted in anger. Hermann stood up and said, "Gentlemen, what do we need to do?" The officer with the flags over his arm thrust them forward and said, "Hang the flags!" Hermann nodded to the footman who stepped forward to receive the flags. As the officers turned to leave, Muriel waited until their boots entered the hall, yet close enough for them to hear her say, "Very well, hang the flags upside down in the hall bathroom, and make sure they trail on the floor!"

Even their young guest knew that Muriel was courting danger. Gertrude told Paul Church, "Early the next morning Hermann woke us, telling us that telegrams had been sent reserving our immediate return sail to the U.S, and to our families in New York City. Your great grandfather [Manni] said, 'It is not safe here for either of you, there are soldiers in the woods and on the streets. Gertrude, you are our dear friend and guest, both of you must be protected.'" Within days, on July 29, 1937, she and her mother sailed on the S.S. *Deutschland* from Hamburg, arriving in New York City on August 6.[62]

For Muriel herself, returning to the safety of the United States was not an option. Muriel had already suffered financially for years. Her substantial fortune, used to improve and restore at least two Seherr-Thoss family castles—Dobrau and Rosnochau—was steadily declining even before she was denied access to her funds.

Soon after their marriage, Muriel had surrendered control of part of her fortune.

> With excellent intentions but very much against my better judgement, Manni over persuaded me to get Papa to send the money he had put

aside to ensure me an income when I married over to Germany to invest in German papers. I felt at the time it was an act of folly but Manni was afraid that if the break came with America Papa couldn't have sent me anything more. I wanted it sent to Holland but Manni said that war with Holland was also on the cards. With infinite trouble I managed to get these papers to a Dutch bank where they are now. . . . It has been a lesson to me not to give way to Manni's wishes when my instincts tell me a thing is foolish.[63]

Realizing that a reduced principal would produce a substantially smaller income for her, Muriel hoped, "In Rosnochau we shall be able to live on what we have with the income of what I have inherited from Mother in dollars."[64]

Once she was mistress of Dobrau, however, expenditures became even more costly. She made expensive changes, adding "cupboard rooms, bread ovens, ice coolers, and ironing rooms built in the basement of the palace, and meals were delivered to the banquet hall via a crank elevator."[65] As she wrote to her father,

Alterations in Dobrau cost more than what Mother Emily so kindly gave me because the walls are so thick that making the necessary windows in the basements cost far more in masons' work than we expected. It had to be done as one cannot let servants work in dark damp holes as my parents-in-law did. . . . There was no water supply for washing up in the kitchen and the pantry. Water was fetched from the pump by bare-footed kitchen maids.[66]

Early in her marriage, Muriel adopted and supported the policies of her husband's nation. With time and personal experience, however, her loyalty diminished until she eventually wrote of never wanting to return to Silesia or Germany. Her opinion of her husband underwent the same shift. Having just read Emil Ludwig's biography of Kaiser Wilhelm II released in 1927, she wrote to her brother,

It is a marvelous description of a nature unbalanced by being neurotic. In many ways Manni is very like him only a love of money and old furniture take the place of the Emperor's of publicity and a big fleet. Even down to the detail mentioned by Ludwig of the Emperor's upsetting the flower vases before guests arrive which is just what Manni does! Both have the characteristics of excitable unbalanced women rather than men and require intimidation for keeping them in order.[67]

In the same letter to her brother, Muriel wrote of her scheduled visit to attorneys to pursue what legal options she might have, including the possibility of divorce. She referred to her husband as "'the weaker half.' I have alas long ceased to regard his as a 'better half.'"[68] Manni had directed her to give to him the annual salary Muriel was paying for a tutor for their younger son Cincie, as well as her annual expenditure for their children's clothes. She wrote, "Of course I refused to do [so] as he would keep the money and they would have nothing to wear but his old clothes, which is all he gives them. As long as I was gentle about declining he went on bullying. He only let me alone when I screamed at him. You will admit that such things do not make home life pleasant."[69] Going forward, she made a promise not to continue paying for Manni's holidays with the family, particularly since "Manni has put aside more in the last two years (after all taxes and expenses were paid) than I shall have a year to live on!"[70]

Similarly, her opinion of the "Jewish question" changed as well. She initially shared the antisemitism prevalent in her social milieu, although not as stridently as many others. After her subsequent meeting with the attorney, she wrote to her sister-in-law Betty White, "The lawyer is a very nice man and not a Jew but a gentleman and a former officer . . . [who told her] Manni's abnormality in money matters is not at all uncommon in men of his class, i.e., the Prussian landed proprietor whether he be prince or peasant."[71] When she went for an interview in New York City in 1928 to try to regain her US citizenship, she wrote that "all the judges were Jews and most of the candidates for citizenship."[72] By 1933, Muriel's views seem to have hardened against her German compatriots. Though her letters still had echoes of antisemitism, she wrote in one,

> I am glad to get anyone I love out of Germany because I feel anything may happen there, at any moment owing to Hitler's policy having incurred the concentrated hatred of the chosen race all over the world.

To have provoked such rich, powerful, and unscrupulous enemies as the Jews is to court certain trouble in my opinion. Also to bottle up public opinion inside the country by imprisoning everyone who differs from the government in concentration camps is to my mind like sitting on a powder-barrel. My Anglo-Saxon common sense tells me that however good it may be to eliminate Jewish influence from the government and to incapacitate the Communists, it isn't good to tread deliberately on very poisonous snakes or to sit on explosives. I am terribly afraid of a war's coming in time to kill my darling boys! . . . Not only has Hitler managed to rouse all the Jews of the world against Germany but is at daggers drawn with Austria![73]

In the same letter, she told her brother that she had written to his wife Betty "asking her to help me save Boysie's life in case of war. Germany is in for serious trouble before long I feel certain."[74]

Later that summer, Muriel received happy news. She learned that the will of her recently deceased Aunt Sophie, wife of Henry White's brother, Julian LeRoy White, would bring her and her brother a bequest of $300,000 each. Her euphoria was diminished when she learned that the funds would not be distributed to them until the death of Sophie's sister, who would enjoy the income for her life. Muriel wrote to Jack about her long-standing resentment concerning her constant financial concerns.

She revealed that she had asked their father years earlier to

advise her [Aunt Sophie] about making a will so that you and I should be sure not to loose [sic] Uncle Julian's capital to the Beylard family or to poor Russians. He demurred at first until I began to cry and told him that as he had allowed Mother to prevent my marrying a very rich man in my youth and as I had been worried about money during most of my married life, the least he could do for me now was to try and save this for you and me or at least for our children and to use his diplomatic talents for our benefit. Papa admitted then that I had had "a rough deal in life" (those were his very words) and promised to do what he could.[75]

She wrote to her brother that their aunt's sister "may live till she is 95. I doubt whether you or I will profit greatly by this inheritance but I trust our children may."[76] Sophie's unmarried sister, Mary, died at Rabodanges, her home in France, in 1947, four years after Muriel's death, so Muriel was correct that she would never benefit from the bequest.

Just as Muriel's allegiance to her husband and her adopted country evolved, so did her earlier antisemitism. By the summer of 1937, she was openly courting danger at a dinner at Berlin's Adlon Hotel for the chairman of IBM, Tom Watson, who was visiting his company's German subsidiaries. Along with Manni, another guest at the table was Norman Ebbut, the Berlin correspondent of the *Times* of London, who made note of the conversation. As the dinner was ending, Muriel said to a Nazi party official sitting at her table,

> "Is it true the Party sometimes rewards deserving Jews by making them honorary Aryans?", she asked. When the gauleiter [district leader] conceded that this happened on occasion, the countess followed up with a line that she must have been mulling over for quite some time. "Can you tell me then how I could become an honorary Jew?" That kind of bold behavior was hardly typical by then, either for Germans or their American spouses.[77]

There were quite a few American-born women—most of them heiresses—who were married to German husbands. The *Chicago Tribune's* Sigrid Schultz, a rarity as a female war correspondent, recalled of Berlin society at the time, "Foreign women married to Germans often became fervent Nazis. One American-born countess refused to be introduced to me because I 'maligned Nazi Germany!'"[78] Schultz, the first female foreign bureau chief of a major US newspaper, sent a prescient telegram to her editor declaring, "Year two of Hitler's Fuehrer Germany finds Germany comparable to a mass of cooling lava after a volcano eruption with some people getting burned and nobody certain where the lava will finally settle."[79]

By 1939, Muriel was actively working to help Jews escape from persecution and death. Arthur Lederer was a highly skilled Jewish tailor who in 1921 joined the well-known atelier of Franz Schlaf in Vienna, tailors by appointment to the emperor since 1908. He had designed and produced livery uniforms for Muriel's senior house servants.[80] Lederer frequently worked for the royal court, where he created regalia uniforms and formal dress for "Hungarian counts, the Knights of Malta, the Prince

Arthur Lederer modeling an ambassador's uniform he created. CREDIT: FLICKR, AUSTRALIAN NATIONAL MARITIME MUSEUM, NO KNOWN COPYRIGHT RESTRICTIONS

of Japan, the Maharajah of Jaipur in India, King Farouk of Egypt, the Vatican, [and] the Vanderbilts in America."[81] "The night after Hitler marched into Vienna, Arthur was working on King [Archduke] Otto's robes, thinking the monarchy was returning,"[82] according to Jean Lederer, his eventual daughter-in-law.

Trying desperately to escape, "Arthur wrote to his exalted customers from around the world, asking them to invite him into their country because the bureaucracy made it impossible to get exit papers. They all wrote back, 'Sorry, but good luck.'"[83] Although several, including the emperor's aide-de-camp,[84] wrote letters of recommendation for him, they were obviously afraid of being persecuted for helping Jews. In fact,

> a postcard from family in Prague contains a request that the Lederers cease contact out of fears for their safety. With all of these doors closing, one finally opened. Help came in the form of Countess Seher[r]-Thoss, a wealthy former client who placed Arthur in contact with English aristocrat Lady Max Muller. Through the Quaker relief organisation Germany Emergency Committee, Lady Muller arranged to pay the family's fare to Australia as well as the £300 arrival money required by the Australian Government. In June 1939, the family began their journey to their new home, Australia.[85]

Muriel's funds were sequestered and out of reach, so she asked for financial support from her friend Wanda, "a Norwegian-born woman with the German-sounding maiden name of Heiberg."[86] Wanda was in fact Lady Max Muller, wife of the former British minister to Poland, Sir William Grenfell Max Muller. She and Muriel had almost certainly known one another since Wanda's husband was appointed to Poland in 1920, but, as usual, there was also a family connection. Sir William Max Muller was a first cousin of Muriel's aunt, Georgina Grenfell Walrond, wife of Henry White's half-brother, Willie Buckler.

In November 1938, the Lederers attempted to flee escalating Jewish persecution in Nazi-occupied Austria. They took a taxi from Vienna to the Austria–Czechoslovakia border but were arrested there by the Gestapo and imprisoned. After three days they were released and returned to Vienna.[87] One month later, they purchased tickets and took an Austrian Airlines flight to Prague. There they were given by the League of Nations (forerunner of the United Nations) Nansen passports issued to stateless refugees.

On February 14, 1939, Arthur Lederer wrote from Prague to Lady Max Muller thanking her for her generosity. His letter began, "H.E. Countess Seherr-Thoss has written to me to tell me what you are doing for me."[88] On March 3, 1939, he, his wife Valerie, and their son Walter received visa approvals to emigrate to England. It is highly likely that Muriel used her extensive contacts in London, where her father had been posted as first secretary for years, to obtain the visa approvals. The three Lederers had only ten shillings each and took a train and ferry for their journey. They traveled through Germany and then through Holland to Rotterdam, where they boarded a ferry to Harwich. On June 17, 1939, they boarded as class B passengers on the Orient Lines' S.S. *Orama* at Tilbury on the Thames, bound for Australia.

Their journey took them to Toulon, France; Naples, Italy; Port Said, Egypt; and Aden, Yemen. On July 8, 1939, they arrived at Colombo, Ceylon (now Sri Lanka). "On the ship to Australia, Arthur Lederer sent a Marconigram (telegram) from ship to shore to the Maharajah of Jaipur, to advise they were passing through Colombo in Ceylon . . . the Maharajah welcomed them and took them to lunch. They were seated at a long table and behind each guest there was a male servant in livery. Luxury sublime!"[89] The last leg of their journey took them to Fremantle, Western Australia, and finally to Sydney, Australia, on July 26, 1939. Arthur Lederer was able to establish his family in Australia and died only one year later, secure in the knowledge that they had escaped and were successfully resettled. His son Walter "became a bespoke tailor following in his father's footsteps."[90] He recalled that the £300 Muriel had requested of Lady Max Muller "actually gave us the very first start to begin life in Australia."[91]

When Arthur Lederer escaped the Nazis with his family, he took with him as proof of his professional success a paper copy of a completed order from Franz Joseph, emperor of the Hungarian-Austrian Empire, "for a field marshal's uniform as a gift to King Edward VII of England."[92] Forced to leave behind all their belongings, Valerie Lederer took with her the front door key to their home in Vienna as a reminder of their former lives.[93]

Arthur Lederer, his wife, Valerie, and son Walter on their journey to Australia.
CREDIT: FLICKR, AUSTRALIAN NATIONAL MARITIME MUSEUM, NO KNOWN COPYRIGHT RESTRICTIONS

On December 27, 1939, Muriel wrote a postcard to Arthur Lederer in Australia, which included a photo of her with her pet spaniels. She asked whether the Lederers had arrived at their new home and "have been able to settle in and begin anew?" She acknowledged his appreciation, writing, "I'm happy that my efforts were successful (with the kind help of Lady Max Muller). She wrote me about your visit and we both are impressed by your courage." She asked that he write to let her know about their new homeland and assured him that she and her husband "send our heartfelt best wishes for this new beginning."[94] She signed the card "Muriel Gfn. [Countess] S.T. geboren [born] White."

The picture postcard Muriel sent to the Lederers after their resettlement. CREDIT:
AUSTRALIAN NATIONAL MARITIME MUSEUM

Chapter Five

Zog had every reason to be pleased with his Queen. For one thing, she became pregnant within three months. For another, her natural informality promised to westernize the monarchy's image.[1]
— Jason Tomes, *King Zog: Self-Made Monarch of Albania*

GERALDINE OF ALBANIA WAS AN UNUSUAL QUEEN AND MURIEL Seherr-Thoss the appropriate mentor to guide her onto the world stage. Widely referred to in the days leading up to her wedding as "the white rose of Hungary," Geraldine was born in Budapest on August 6, 1915. Her grandfather, Count Lajos Apponyi de Nagy-Apponyi, was grand marshal of the Hungarian Court and a member of an ancient and noble family in the Kingdom of Hungary since the thirteenth century. Her father, Count Gyula, served as a soldier before entering law school at the University of Budapest. He was elected a member of parliament from the Bazin district from 1901–1905 and then "launched a bank undertaking in Paris, which ended in complete failure due to World War I."[2] Geraldine's American-born mother, Gladys Virginia Steuart (variously spelled "Stewart," 1891–1947), was a daughter of US diplomat John Henry Steuart and his wife, Mary Virginia Ramsay Harding, a member of a wealthy family from Virginia and North Carolina.

John Henry Steuart, Geraldine's grandfather, was a native of Baltimore, served as the US consul in Antwerp, Belgium, and was well acquainted with Henry White from their shared Baltimore heritage and diplomatic careers. As a child, Gladys grew up "educated in the different capitals of the Continent."[3] In 1912, the year Gladys reached her majority, she met, at a dinner at the Austro-Hungarian embassy in Paris, a man who was to change her destiny: Count Gyula/Julius Apponyi. He met Gladys when he was asked to escort her in to a dinner party.

> Even their first talk was not a conventional conversation, and it was evident that the young people felt a deep interest in each other—a much deeper one than a first meeting would ordinarily warrant. It was perhaps a quality which his descendants inherited: the young officer fell in love "at first sight" with the beautiful American girl, his feelings were reciprocated, and a month later Count Julius Apponyi and Virginia Gladys Stewart became engaged in Switzerland.[4]

Gladys Virginia Steuart accepted the marriage proposal from Count Gyula Apponyi, but war intervened in their plans. She registered as required with the US consul office in Geneva on July 17, 1914, giving her local address as the Hotel Bellevue and reporting the purpose of her visit as "being married."[5] They were scheduled to marry in Geneva on August 5, 1914, but the groom received a telegram ordering him to join his regiment at the front immediately. After a quick discussion with her mother, the couple met the mayor of Geneva and a priest at the town hall at 3:00 a.m., and they were married by a special license on July 30. The small group then immediately retreated to St. Joseph's Roman Catholic Church, where they had planned to marry, and a quick religious ceremony was performed as the sun rose. At her husband's request, Gladys converted to Catholicism, and her first-born daughter, Geraldine, would remain a devout Catholic all her life.

Count Gyula took a train to the war front while the bride announced her plans to join the Austro-Hungarian Red Cross as a nurse.[6] The groom's widowed mother was notified of the wedding after her son left for the front. Born Countess Margarete Seherr-Thoss (1848–1931) and referred to by friends and family as "Mutti," she would bring Muriel and the White family deeply into this extended family circle. "Mutti" was the sister of Muriel's father-in-law—thus Manni's aunt.

Despite her husband's military duties, Gladys's daughters would arrive early in the marriage—Geraldine on August 6, 1915, and Virginia on December 26, 1916. The two would remain inseparable and even died only two weeks apart.[7] The young family lived in the home of Gyula's mother in Budapest,

> or rather the two women, mother and daughter-in-law, lived in Budapest. . . . In his absence the young wife worked as a voluntary nurse in a Budapest military hospital. . . . The children spent the first years of their life in the house of their grandmother, and it was she who educated them. Their mother did not want to neglect her duties as nurse beside her duties as mother—it was probably some sort of pledge—while their father came but seldom home, and, as it was discovered during his last visit, suffered from a dangerous illness he had contracted at the front.[8]

It is not surprising that the two women found it difficult to live with one another. "With her husband absent on military service, Gladys felt isolated and unhappy. By the time the United States declared war on Austro-Hungary in December 1917, she was staying with her mother and stepfather in Switzerland."[9]

On November 11, 1918, World War I ended for Austro-Hungary with a complete military defeat for the former empire. The Apponyi family fled to Switzerland and could not return to Hungary until 1921. The 1920 Trianon Treaty reached at the Paris Peace Conference divided much of Hungary. Their family castle, formerly in Hungary, renamed from Appony to Oponice, was now located in the newly created Czechoslovakia, which denied the count a visa. Gladys and Gyula, in 1921, visited the Seherr-Thosses at Dobrau, where Muriel and Gladys, both Americans, got along well.[10] The Apponyis finally found renewed hope for the future on December 28, 1923, when they were joined by a son, Gyula/Julius, called "John." Only five months later, tragedy struck when Gyula, the husband and father, died of lung disease at the relatively young age of fifty. Geraldine never fully recovered from the loss of her father, which occurred when she was only eight.

There were also pressing financial challenges. As Geraldine would later write,

> My mother was an heiress but her money was held in trust in America until the day of her marriage when she gave over everything to my

Geraldine, future queen of Albania, with her sister,
Virginia, and their parents. CREDIT: JOSÉPHINE DEDET

father to manage. He being a patriot put it all in bonds in Austria and
Hungary from which he recovered nothing after the sinking of the two
monarchies and the inflation that followed. My parents managed to
exist through my grandmother's help. It was fortunate that my father
went into exile as when the Bolsheviks pillaged the family house they
also hung up an effigy of him as he was on the list of prominent aris-
tocrats who were to be killed.[11]

Before his death, Geraldine's father "could live in Budapest in reasonable comfort" with financial assistance from his mother, "but he brooded on his misfortunes."[12]

She and her sister and brother were sent to France to visit their American grandmother, who "loved her grandchildren deeply and did everything to surround them with every comfort."[13] Her grandmother would steadfastly provide Geraldine with emotional support well into her old age. Meanwhile, in France, Geraldine's mother met a French officer. Barely a year into her widowhood, Gladys introduced her children to him as their new father. Geraldine was devastated. The "remarriage struck Geraldine as an appalling betrayal, and several years of family discord ensued."[14]

The newly remarried Gladys wished to maintain good relations with her late husband's family. She brought her husband and children to meet the Apponyi family, at which time he "was received with great kindness and accepted in the aristocratic circle."[15] However, the family strongly believed that the Apponyi children should be brought up and educated by their birth father's family. "The Girault family lived under rather modest circumstances. . . . Julius Apponyi's estate left a comparatively small residue for his widow and children, hardly sufficient to keep up the standard of life for the children."[16] There would be even less when the Giraults started having children of their own, and, indeed, Geraldine's mother lost no time in creating her second family, with two daughters and a son born between 1927 and 1932.

Even for a family of diplomats as experienced as the Apponyis, this situation called for someone uniquely suited to the task of retrieving the children and bringing them back to Hungary to be educated and guided by their father's family. Muriel recalled how she became an integral part of the future queen's life. As she was organizing a charity event,

> My husband's aunt, Countess Margaret Apponyi, née Countess Seherr-Thoss, widow of Count Louis Apponyi, the last Marshall of the Hungarian Court, asked me to visit her on my way to the Riviera. This dear old lady, then begged me to persuade her daughter-in-law, the

widow of Count Julius Apponyi . . . to allow me to educate her eldest daughter Geraldine among her mother's people. Countess Apponyi's younger granddaughter Virginia was already under her charge and had urged that her elder sister be educated with her.[17]

Countess Margarete, or "Mutti," was a devout Catholic and suspected Gladys's new husband of "anti-clericalism. She sent Muriel, as her nephew's American-born wife, to negotiate the future of the Apponyi children, and by 1930 they were back in Hungary.[18] Thus began a long association between the future queen Geraldine and Muriel Seherr-Thoss.

"Mutti," Countess Margarete Seherr-Thoss, Geraldine's grandmother who enlisted Muriel's help to mentor the future queen. CREDIT: PUBLIC DOMAIN

As Muriel herself later wrote, "The negotiations entrusted to me by my husband's relations were not easy; but finally I succeeded in persuading Madame Girault to sacrifice her own feelings, in the interests of her daughter's future and she agreed that I should undertake Geraldine's education."[19] Muriel was entrusted with physically bringing her back from France to her father's family, and Geraldine "was once more shuttled across Europe to Hungary."[20] As Virginia's son recalled,

> Mother and Geraldine were taken away by close family from the Girault household when very young, brought up by Madeleine Károlyi their aunt. The Károlyi family was very rich and famous and one of the oldest nobility in Hungary. The family council estimated it was not proper for the daughters Apponyi to be brought up in France by Gontran Girault, an officer in the French army who on his military income was not wealthy enough to care for them. So Countess Károlyi repatriated the girls and Gyula to Hungary where they were brought up.[21]

After the two girls had been immersed in the German language, Geraldine and Virginia were enrolled as boarders in a Sacred Heart convent school at Pressbaum in lower Austria. Evidently the two sisters needed a higher level of discipline than what was offered there. Muriel wrote to her husband's Aunt Mutti,

> Has Adèle done anything about finding another school for Geraldine and Virginia? . . . I don't see how we can leave them at Pressbaum. . . . Countess Rumerskirch and several other ladies told Adèle and me that they took their daughters away because they learn so little at Pressbaum. . . . Neither of those two children [Geraldine and Virginia] have any idea of discipline and they must learn it besides learning lessons. They are also fearfully untidy so they need a really strict school.[22]

"During the next few years, I mostly saw the child whom I had come to regard as an adopted daughter, clad in the dark blue uniform worn by the scholars of the Sacred Heart Convent."[23] Muriel advised wisely (perhaps because her own daughter, Margaret, was five years older and had experienced some of the same issues), and the Apponyi family was grateful for her expertise. As Muriel wrote, "The Apponyi sisters look back to this time in their lives, as a most happy one. The atmosphere of that abode of religion, refinement, learning and peace was everything that the most exacting parents could wish for their daughters' upbringing."[24] Geraldine, "though outwardly glamorous . . . never aimed at witty sophistication. There was also her unusual height (6 ft.) and her known shortage of capital. The Czechoslovak authorities expropriated part of the Apponyi estate at a nominal compensation price."[25]

Muriel Seherr-Thoss had developed a reputation for presenting "tableaux vivants" for various charity organizations. They featured scenes containing one or more people, usually in stationary and silent poses, and normally in costume. In 1928, she was lauded for a program she organized and directed in New York City for the benefit of the Franciscan Foundation in America. It followed one she organized in Washington the year before under the patronage of the women of the diplomatic corps.[26]

Early in 1930, Muriel was asked to repeat scenes representing the lives of the saints for the benefit of the Queen Victoria Memorial Hospital in Nice and for the Hospital for Tubercular Children at Monaco. It was the first time she asked young Geraldine to be part of the program.

> This lovely blue-eyed child of fourteen, appeared for the first time before the public eye, at the afternoon performance of my Tableaux entitled "Les Belles Existences," on Monday, March 10th, 1930, in the Casino of Monte Carlo. Her part was that of Sofie of Thuringia, the eldest daughter of St. Elizabeth of Hungary, from whom nearly all Europe's crowned Heads are descended. Among the distinguished audience were Their Royal Highnesses Princess Louise, Duchess of Argyll and the Duke of Connaught; who subsequently expressed his surprise and satisfaction, that my cast of over one hundred ladies and children included so many beauties![27]

Princess Louise, a sculptor, was the most artistic of her siblings. If any royal could—and often did—appreciate a pretty face, it was her brother, the Duke of Connaught, favorite son of Queen Victoria. As Muriel wrote of Geraldine then, "her good looks were even exceeded by the great

Geraldine, future queen of Albania (second from right), with cousins and friends at Dobrau. CREDIT: ELIZABETH SEHERR-THOSS

sweetness of her disposition; coupled with the charm of distinction of a budding woman of the world."[28]

After Geraldine and Virginia finished at their boarding school, "the girls prepared themselves with great pleasure for their new lives as young ladies of society. . . . They were grown-up girls now and had to be introduced to society. Their aunts gave many a large, gay party for them, other invitations followed, and after a series of dances came the great Opera Ball with its exciting preparations."[29] The Apponyis "subsidized her lifestyle in order to help her make a good match, but her ideas on matrimony appeared to owe too much to the sentimental novels which were her favourite reading."[30] Geraldine and Virginia's beloved paternal grandmother, "Mutti," died in 1931, while the girls were teenagers, and their Aunt Muriel tried to ease that loss by offering her continuing guidance.

Geraldine went home with Muriel to Dobrau, Silesia, where she spent "a few weeks pleasantly . . . at the castle of an Austrian aunt."[31] It was there Geraldine had an emotional experience she related to her eventual lady-in-waiting:

In the library of my aunt [Muriel] I found a family album and in it a picture of my parents; Father in uniform, Mother in a nice summer frock; probably a photograph taken at the time of her engagement. At the bottom of the picture I saw Father's handwriting, only two words: "For ever." So theirs was a love match which was destined to last for ever. . . . No, I did not fall in love with anyone in Dobrau—but with the idea of eternal love.[32]

Family photo albums show a radiant Geraldine driving, playing tennis, and enjoying the company of other young people at Dobrau. If any of the young men were seen as possible suitors, it appears that no one there captured her heart. It is interesting to speculate whether Muriel may have entertained thoughts of Geraldine's interest in "Boysie," her own son, who was three years older than Geraldine and destined to inherit the castle and title. Their degree of blood kinship—her grandmother and his grandfather were siblings, making Geraldine and Boysie second cousins—would not have prevented it, although perhaps Geraldine's lack of money might have.

An often-told tale about Queen Geraldine concerned a Magyar fortune teller who prophesied, "A crown I see in your hand. A golden crown. Much joy and pride around the crown but also there will be suffering and anxiety." It was Muriel Seherr-Thoss who took her adopted niece to the fair that day and heard the comments that Geraldine committed to her diary that night.[33] "Many months later, when Geraldine had become Queen of Albania, the diligent Countess Seherr-Thoss returned to the fair to look for the gypsy and so was able to recompense her."[34]

Geraldine was also developing a strong sense of independence. "She was invited by Aunt Muriel, Countess Seherr-Thoss, to the winter Olympic Games at Garmisch-Partenkirchen [1936]. During a walk in the town Geraldine found a ravishing ski suit which she simply had to buy." She entered the shop and asked the saleswoman the price of the suit. Although she first said "Guten Tag" to the clerk, the saleswoman's sharp reply was that she should have first said, "Heil Hitler!" "Thereupon Geraldine promptly told her that she was not a German and would not do so."[35] She left the shop without the ski suit.

Boysie Seherr-Thoss with his cousin, Geraldine, future queen of Albania, at Dobrau.

The 1936 Olympics, often called "the Nazi Olympics," allowed Germany to showcase its efficiency:

> No one could ignore that order reigned in Garmisch. An impressive order considering the crowds—more than a million visitors—and the modest size of the city. At no time were there traffic jams on the roads or jostling on the platforms of the small rail stations of the region.
>
> Throughout the duration of the Games, the Bavarian Alps were the smiling and affable showcase of the new Germany. At the time of the festivities, the merchants took care to remove the signs prohibiting Jews from entering the shops, but the routine returned quickly.[36]

Geraldine greatly enjoyed the Olympics. She later recalled, "We slept no more than five hours a night because in addition to the competitions we attended, we took advantage of our stay to ski and, in the evening, to go dancing—all of this without ever feeling the slightest fatigue as the climate was healthy."[37] She also had an opportunity to observe Hitler firsthand.

> Geraldine found it hard to understand why he was the object of such adulation, not only from Germans, but also foreigners, especially women. "When he got out of his car or entered a room, they became hysterical, throwing kisses and favors at him." She studied him carefully but had to confess that, if he hadn't been surrounded by such deference, she wouldn't even have noticed him.[38]

She particularly noticed his "glaucous eyes, color indefinite, blue it was said when they came to life."[39] During the opening ceremony, "all the spectators stood up to listen to the national anthems. The last to be played was that of the National Socialist Party. What surprise, then, for this young Hungarian [Geraldine] when her neighbor forcibly lifted her arm, shouting, 'If you don't salute you can't stay seated with us!'"[40]

During the Olympics, Muriel and Manni were seated in the VIP viewing box of Hermann Göring, whom Manni knew from their military service. Göring, a veteran World War I fighter pilot, was second-in-command to Adolf Hitler and was invited to Dobrau for several hunt-

Geraldine, future queen of Albania, at Schloss Dobrau. CREDIT: ELIZABETH SEHERR-THOSS

ing parties. Hitler also was seated in the viewing box that day. The Seherr-Thosses' daughter, Margaret, had with her Gertrude Schley, her close friend whom she had known since they were fellow students at Miss Nightingale's finishing school in Manhattan, founded in 1920.[41] Gertrude personally relayed to Margaret's grandsons that the group's conversation that day "turned to politics, Muriel making the inquiries. She turned to A. Hitler and H. Göring and boldly said, 'I know who you are and what your aim is, and I shall work against you.' A. H. [Hitler] tossed his head back and laughed, saying, 'Oh, Madame, don't be so serious.'"[42]

Years later, Margaret's two great-grandsons

were viewing the marvelous photo albums of the Seherr-Thoss family's lives. In the year 1936 there were several pictures of the Summer Olympics held in Berlin. One in particular was of Jesse Owens sprinting along the Track course. The most compelling photos were of our Great Grandparents, Hermann and Muriel Seherr-Thoss, in a viewing box with Adolf Hitler, Eva Braun, and Hermann Göring. My brother and I were stunned to identify the Fuhrer, etc. Our grandmother stood behind us on the sofa, hands supporting her. My brother exclaimed, "Oma, your parents are with the Fuhrer?" "Yes," Oma replied. "But, why?" I asked. "Because they knew each other." The way in which she replied, suggested an end to the discussion.[43]

Before going to the Olympics, the Seherr-Thosses and Geraldine stayed at the family's Grüben Palace (Schloss Grabin, which burned down in the 1950s), in Opole Voivodeship, where Manni's father and Geraldine's grandmother had been born. Baby Geraldine had been cared for by a nurse, Elisabeth Boebel, who was brought from her post at Grüben Palace, so the family had close associations with the property. While there, Geraldine noticed

strange comings and goings. . . . Officially, Uncle Manni and his wife Muriel received "old friends" to talk about "the good old days" or hunting. These friends arrived at the castle one by one and also left separately, very late in the evening. The men shut themselves up in the large smoking room and the young people of the house were asked to keep watch at the door after giving the servants leave. From cross-checking and hearing snatches of conversations, Geraldine quickly understood that the "old friends" were in fact senior officers of the Wehrmacht and, like Manni and Muriel Seherr-Thoss, they did not approve of Germany's political direction.[44]

During the Olympics, a famous World War I pilot, Ernst Udet, who in 1933 had joined the Nazi Party and would become a Luftwaffe officer during World War II, performed flight loops for the crowd. Manni noted, "As a pilot he is an artist, but as a politician he is not."[45]

That Olympics year of 1936 was pivotal in other ways. The large family estate in Hungary, Appony Castle, was the one Geraldine most associated with her childhood. Begun in the sixteenth century, it remained "in the Apponyi family in an unbroken line until 1936 when it was taken over by a Slovak for debts incurred."[46] Now that her mother lived in another country with her second family, this would have been the time Geraldine could have relied most on a father. But, even if he were still alive, they would have faced a bleak existence. When Gyula had finally been able to reach Hungary after the war, "he returned penniless so my paternal grandmother sold her court jewels and made three dowries for my sister, Virginia, our cousin who was the daughter of Uncle Anthony Apponyi, and myself. . . . My dowry enabled my parents to buy a lovely villa with a large garden in the suburbs of Budapest."[47] After her mother was widowed, she sold the villa, but "the notary who sold the house in Budapest vanished and by the time he was found and charged he had gone through all the money."[48]

Then, on January 6, 1937, Geraldine's younger sister, Virginia, married a Hungarian count, Andras de Baghy Szecsenyi. Evidently there was no impediment due to Virginia's lack of a dowry, since his family was prosperous. Virginia's husband, never healthy, "struggled with cancer from a young age. His father did everything he could to treat him. He called famous doctors to his son even from abroad and set up a contemporary hospital in a separate building to ensure the patient's undisturbed peace of mind."[49] They had a daughter, Julia Geraldine, born April 4, 1939, and a son, André Peter, born October 13, 1941. Unfortunately, the young father died at the age of thirty-one, less than two weeks after his son's birth.[50] Muriel wrote to her brother, Jack, "Geraldine's younger sister Virginia has just lost her very charming young husband (owing to an operation) when their baby-boy was only 10 days old. Really terribly sad! My news from Geraldine is quite recent & good."[51]

Geraldine had no dowry and yet insisted that "only people in love must marry; if she were to do so one day, she would choose only someone whom she loved and would demand the same feelings on his part."[52] As Muriel recalled,

> The two lovely sisters aroused great admiration in Budapest, and suitors were not lacking. Virginia married very happily, almost as soon as she made her appearance in society. In spite of much good advice, proffered by the older ladies of her family, Geraldine firmly declared that she refused to make a marriage of convenience, and that she would only give her hand to him who could win her whole heart.[53]

Geraldine took a job out of financial necessity, selling souvenirs at the Hungarian Historical Museum (now the Budapest National Museum), which she obtained through the intervention of her kinsman, Count István Zichy, the general director. Fortunately, she greatly enjoyed her work. "This was immense joy for her! The first decisive step towards an independent life was made. She threw herself into her work with heart and soul."[54] Muriel wrote that Geraldine

> was working in a library in Budapest, when she was suddenly caught up in a modern edition of the fairy-tales which used to charm our childhood. A country neighbor in Hungary, of her Aunt Countess Karolyi, was greatly attached to Geraldine, like most people who came in contact with her. This lady was invited by friends in Albania to visit them during the festivities which took place there in the autumn of 1937. She then showed King Zog a photograph of the chief belle of Budapest.[55]

Geraldine had given the photograph of herself to the sisters of King Zog of Albania, whom she first met at a diplomatic reception and then again when visiting her grandmother on the Riviera. They exchanged letters, but Geraldine had forgotten about the photograph "by the time the letter of the princesses arrived, saying how happy they would be if they could see Geraldine again."[56] A different source said the photograph was sent to the king, at his request, by his economic representative, Miklós Ghycy, who had been tasked with finding an appropriate consort.[57]

King Zog began life as Ahmed Muhtar bey Zogoli (1895–1961). Born to one of the four landowning tribes of Mati in Ottoman Albania, he fought on the side of Austro-Hungary in the First World War. Although exiled in 1924, he returned that same year with backing from Yugoslav and White Russian support. Zog was elected prime minister of Albania from 1922 to 1925 and then was president until 1928; on September 1, 1928, President Zogu became Zog I, king of the Albanians. He proclaimed a constitutional monarchy and took the oath of office by swearing on a Bible and the Koran. The next year he abolished Islamic law in Albania. Zog did away with requirements for women to wear veils, and, in 1938, he opened the borders to Jewish refugees fleeing Nazi Germany. Although a constitutional monarch, Zog retained powers that created what many claimed

Geraldine, future queen of Albania, playing tennis at Schloss Dobrau.

to be nothing less than a military dictatorship. Other European monarchs effectively ignored Zog as a self-proclaimed king, even though some royal families in the Arab world maintained contacts with him. There was no possibility of his marrying a European royal.

It is no wonder that there was speculation Zog might marry an American heiress. "It was rumored in America that King Zog would settle on an American heiress if she brought a dowry of $5,000,000."[58] Other sources insisted that "he would marry any presentable American heiress who could bring him a dowry of $1,000,000 cash. Zog had read glowing accounts in the European magazines about the impoverished princes who had re-couped their lost fortunes by marrying rich American girls."[59]

The letter that came from Zog's sisters invited Geraldine to visit their court for an official function. "It ended by saying that a friend of the princesses would visit Geraldine and her family in Budapest to repeat the invitation by word of mouth. Naturally the letter caused a tremendous sensation in the family; somehow it was felt that this was not a simple invitation for a visit."[60] "King Zog fell in love with a photograph. It was as simple as that."[61]

> As one historian noted of the different stories of the origin of the photograph, they had only one thing in common, namely that the protagonists, Zogu and Geraldine, fell in love with each other at first sight. ...Romantic novels were published one after the other about the prince of a small state who lived in exile but did not give up the fight for the liberation of his country but then met the daughter of a millionaire, fell in love with her and finally could return to the prince's motherland.[62]

Geraldine did not immediately jump at the chance to visit Albania's capital, Tirana. She would have heard rumors that the king was looking for a wife and was astute enough to know she was to be "on display." "The Apponyi family decided that if the visit was arranged discreetly and Geraldine did not wish to become engaged, then she could return to Budapest and her work at the museum and the Press would never have to hear about it."[63] For his part, the king knew Geraldine was not an heiress and would not bring a dowry to her marriage. But she was beautiful, came from one of Hungary's most influential families, and fluently spoke five languages—English, French, German, Hungarian, and Italian.[64] With his excellent sources, he would also have known she was a virgin. Marrying an Apponyi bride would, in his mind, secure his position within Hungarian aristocracy. However, Geraldine's nephew recalled that

> her marriage to Zog was not popular among certain nobility in Hungary. They considered, "Why is our Apponyi countess going to marry this peasant revolutionary leader and self-proclaimed King of Albania?" There was a council meeting of Apponyi, Karolyi, and other families about letting Geraldine go to the invitation of Zog. But then she did fall in love with him, so it was a very consensual marriage.[65]

One of Geraldine's close friends since their days at Sacred Heart in Pressbaum, Countess Katalin Teleki, was sent ahead to Tirana as a "scout" to give her opinion of what she saw. She wrote back with encouraging news of the country and its ruler. On her return, "The two girls spent several days together in intimate conversation and Geraldine was tactfully spared any family pressure . . . [and] listened intently before telephoning Aunt Fanny [Karolyi] 'I've decided. I'm going to Tirana. . . . I'm coming back straight away if I don't like him.'"[66]

The proud but newly poor Apponyi family "accepted the funds sent by the King to meet all the expenses during the journey. He also offered to pay for a small travelling trousseau but this the proud Hungarians refused. The whole family got together to provide a modest wardrobe so that Geraldine would not feel obliged to anyone, and certainly not to her host."[67]

Geraldine finally met King Zog face to face and found him "a handsome, tall man impeccable in the white uniform of Colonel-in-Chief of the Army. It was his eyes that I noticed mostly—blue piercing eyes."[68] They spoke in German, a third language for each of them. Their conversation continued for several hours until they heard the clock strike midnight, and he ordered champagne.

> He never looked away from me as he offered me a glass. Our fingers touched and at that moment the lights dimmed. Because I was anxious, I dropped the glass, which shattered into thousands of tiny crystals. "Splinters bring good luck," he said in a friendly tone and stroked

my hand with a spontaneous movement to reassure me. . . . Is there a greater luck and happiness than to find a man who loves me and whom I love? Because I love him, and I am going to marry him![69]

After much conversation, King Zog asked her, "'Do you think you could love me for eternity no matter what happens in our lives?' 'Oh, but I already love you,' came the reply without hesitation."[70] Her cousin's governess, Baroness Rüling, acted as Geraldine's lady-in-waiting on the trip and later recounted, "It was so touching to see our little friend was more and more attracted to the King's personality . . . two people had really found each other."[71]

When the engagement was announced, some of the American press portrayed Geraldine as a sacrificial lamb.

What so many other women had spurned as too foolhardy a venture, the young countess calmly accepted. Those who know her best say she is a high-spirited girl and that she was fascinated rather than terrified by the adventurous idea of becoming Queen of wild and woolly Albania. She is something of a daredevil herself, having won her spurs in bravery as a bareback rider in the Hungarian cowboy country.[72]

Not surprisingly, the fanciful last sentence bears no truth. The same article seemed to offer at least a hint of optimism:

In the last decade or so, Zog's grip on his enemies has become much firmer and he has made amazing strides in curbing blood feuds, disarming the mountaineers, and otherwise making his little kingdom a safer place to live in. Aware of the lingering antagonism in the hinterland against his marrying a "foreigner," the King cautiously had his rubber-stamp Parliament proclaim its approval of the match beforehand.[73]

Jealousy may have entered into the observation that Geraldine, a beautiful twenty-two-year-old who was earning a pound a week at the National Museum, was marrying a wealthy man twenty years her senior. "The imputation was unfair. Though she may have been carried away by the adventure of marrying a king, Geraldine was never a gold-digger. As a museum porter declared, 'She was a nice sweet little countess.'"[74]

Some within the aristocracy were outraged at the surrender of this young virgin:

> A poor fatherless Hungarian girl is taken to Tirana and simply sold to a Balkan chieftain. What life will that poor girl have in Albania! Zog himself, though said to be an elegant and nice-looking man . . . has hardly any culture apart from some language facility . . . and the story goes that she is all day long with the king's sisters who do nothing else but teach her Albanian and anoint her with smelly oil, fattening her according to the good old Turkish tradition, as it is known that bodily charm means bodily lard to Balkan taste.[75]

Muriel was pleased at the news of the successful visit, but she did have one concern about "what I had heard, before arriving in Tirana, as to difficulties with the Vatican. These I was assured by my radiantly happy young hostess, had been most satisfactorily arranged as there would be a private Catholic marriage besides the public ceremony."[76] Muriel, who was physically with Geraldine as preparations were made, was much better informed than the mother of the bride, who was quoted from Nice:

> First the idea of becoming a Mohammedan made her daughter, Countess Geraldine Apponyi, hesitate, but on becoming better acquainted with Albania's sovereign the thought had not troubled her. It is not yet known whether the future queen will be obliged to become a practicing Mohammedan, according to her mother.[77]

In fact, the king offered not only that she would retain her religion but also that he would build for her a Catholic chapel at the palace. "Zog, being a Moslem, and the Countess, a Catholic, there were religious complications but it was agreed that neither would switch faiths and Zog made the additional concession of pledging that any children they have would be raised as Catholics."[78] But the question of religion caused more problems than were made public.

> Zog persuaded her to agree to Islamic education for their children on the understanding that he would obtain a dispensation from the Pope. When the Vatican refused he resolved to carry on regardless. Geraldine

137

was deeply upset. Her Jesuit confessor told her that she would be no more than a concubine. Then he left for Rome—obviously a spy! . . . Furious with the Pope, Zog ordered every Catholic church in Albania to celebrate the royal wedding with a Te Deum.[79]

Rather than Geraldine returning home before their wedding, the king insisted that she remain in Tirana, where she would begin to be taught Albania's history and its difficult language. Muriel, who had played an integral role in rearing Geraldine and imparting the social skills necessary for her success, was "invited by the future Queen of Albania to stay with her at Tirana in the charming villa which King Zog had placed at her disposal until their wedding."[80]

Muriel wasn't quite sure what to expect, but,

> as soon as I met the monarch of that most endearing little country, I was not surprised that he had won my Geraldine's heart. King Zog's charm, good looks and intelligence, as well as his record as a national hero for daring courage and his chivalrous devotion to his beautiful fiancée, entitled him in every way to be the most perfect hero of romance.[81]

Muriel told someone else, "He was not mysterious but only reserved and had a great deal of self-control and was always polite."[82]

The king wrote to Geraldine's legal guardian, Count Charles Apponyi, to ask for official permission to marry. The prospective bride also wrote to her uncle assuring him of her happy acceptance. "Next day King Zog presented to the Hungarian Countess Geraldine Apponyi the document which raised her to the rank of 'Princess of Albania'; the following day the Albanian parliament met and in a full-dress assembly took enthusiastic notice of the fact that King Zog the First had chosen Princess Geraldine for his consort."[83]

An engagement celebration was announced for January 26, 1938, and the wedding was set for April 28. After the announcement, three of Zog's sisters traveled to New York City, where they "received the sort of reception more often accorded to film stars. . . . A high point of their tour was tea at the White House with President Roosevelt—the first time members of the House of Zogu had been officially received by a Head of

State."[84] Obviously Geraldine's and Muriel's American credentials were already opening doors that had been heretofore closed.

In the absence of Geraldine's mother to deal with these matters, Muriel remained with her to help with the bridal preparations. On the night before the formal wedding, a gala dinner was held at the palace for family members, including those who had come from Budapest and Vienna.

Since Muriel's husband, Manni, Count Seherr-Thoss, is not mentioned, one must assume he did not attend, although their oldest son Boysie, who was a contemporary of Geraldine as well as her cousin, "was present at the recent royal wedding in Tirana."[85] One highly visible attendee at the wedding was Dr. Imre Hunyor, Geraldine's friend and personal attorney, who "brought as his wedding gift a gypsy band"[86] that had been her favorite.

The American newspapers covered the wedding in great detail, reporting that the bride "was followed by her mother, Mme. Gladys Stewart Girault and her grandmother, Mme. Virginia Harding d'Ekna, both formerly of New York. One of her closest friends, Countess Muriel

Geraldine's marriage to King Zog, 1938. Standing on the left as best man is Count Galeazzo Ciano, foreign minister for his father-in-law, Benito Mussolini. He was already planning the invasion of Albania. CREDIT: SÁNDOR BOJÁR, FORTEPAN, PUBLIC DOMAIN

White Seherr-Thoss, American-born, was in the group surrounding the bride."[87] Among Geraldine's eight bridesmaids, one was her cousin, Marianne Szápáry de Muraszombath, Countess Széchysziget et Szapár, who would become the mother of Princess Michael of Kent.[88] At the marriage, Geraldine became "the second youngest queen in the world; only King Farouk of Egypt's consort, Queen Farida, was younger."[89]

The morning after the wedding, Geraldine found that "her nightgown had vanished. Zog bashfully explained that proof of virginity was required by the President of the Parliament."[90] Nevertheless, it didn't matter that it was the first day of their honeymoon when Count Galeazzo Ciano, the foreign minister in the administration of his father-in-law, Benito Mussolini, arrived for lunch and stayed for four hours. "Zog suggested that Mussolini should avoid too closely tying himself to Hitler. Ciano replied that it was onerous having Germans as friends, but having them as enemies would be terrible. The outlook was uncertain, he agreed, but Albania could count on Italian friendship. He wished the couple a long and happy reign."[91] Ciano noted in his diary, "I leave Albania more firmly convinced than ever of the need for a radical solution."[92]

After the wedding celebrations Muriel was able to return to her own home, Dobrau, in Silesia, secure in the knowledge that she had performed her duty to her husband's family and to Geraldine. She later wrote, "As the wedding guests sailed away from Durazzo looking up at the palace crowning a hill, where the Royal couple were spending their honeymoon, we all felt that the stage in this most modern of fairy stories had been reached, where 'they lived happily ever afterwards.'"[93]

It would be natural to assume she was correct, but nothing could be further from the truth. After their wedding, the couple drove away in a present from Adolf Hitler, "a long scarlet super-charged Mercedes, with three large chromium exhaust pipes, a removable roof and lined throughout with white leather. It was a replica of his own and this was the only other one in existence."[94] Given Geraldine's anti-Nazi bias, this gift may have been a jarring surprise on such a happy day. Not to be outdone in celebrating a Hungarian bride, Admiral Horthy, the regent of Hungary, sent a "phaeton drawn by four prancing white Lipizzaner horses which was to be used to carry the bride to the palace on her wedding day,"[95] as well as a full set of Herend porcelain china. The Turkish government sent twenty-four Oriental rugs, while President Lebrun of France (one of the few European leaders to recognize the event) gave the couple a Sévres porcelain table-piece; Great Britain's King George VI sent a telegram of congratulations.

During the following year, Italy continued to press Albania for more control over its government, infrastructure, and finances. It was no accident that Count Ciano had attended the royal wedding as best man and stood prominently in many of the photos. The king originally asked him to be the chief witness to make up for the fact that the bride was not Italian, but Count Ciano "seemed set on turning the event into a triumphal progress for himself."[96]

> The world's press were quick to comment on Ciano's presence but in his courting of Albania over the past years, Mussolini had been adroit to advance considerable loans for public works, money that Albania desperately needed to build up the country's resources. A modern port at Durazzo, new roads, bridges, air services, electric power installations had all been provided since 1926 when the Treaty of Tirana was signed under which Albania became, in essence, a dependency on Italy.[97]

Ciano thought the king's sisters snubbed him at the wedding, confiding to his diary, "The royal princesses are peasants."[98]

Whatever the genesis of their unusual alliance, Geraldine and Zog were happy. "Zog had every reason to be pleased with his Queen. For one thing, she became pregnant within three months. For another, her natural informality promised to westernize the monarchy's image."[99] The marriage

> was manifestly a relationship that worked on some level. The Queen liked to be liked, seemed eager to please, and tried always to look on the bright side. A husband resembling her father had been her explicit desire. The King had sought a loyal, attractive, and pliable wife. His face softened when he was with Geraldine, to whom he showed kindness, courtesy, and consideration.[100]

Having been so instrumental in ensuring the happy wedding of her young ward, it must have been doubly painful for Muriel to return to her home and her own very troubled marriage. Her experiences writing and producing *tableaux vivants*, her skill in tactfully retrieving Geraldine from her mother's family, and her diplomatic expertise would be of little use to her back at Dobrau. While her father was still alive, she wrote to him, "The tragedy of my life is that I ever came to this country where all my natural gifts have been wasted and where the mental atmosphere has been like a prison."[101] That opinion only deepened with time.

She had earlier drafted a long letter to Manni for her father and brother's signatures, listing the injustices Muriel had faced in her marriage. "The letter was succinctly to the point, acknowledging their awareness of Manni's habits relating to anger and control issues with Muriel and the children, and taking advantage of Muriel's finances. That they would step in if necessary and for Manni to see a Doctor for his mental incapacities."[102] The letter explained,

> She cannot face living at Dobrau any more under present conditions, as she does nothing but cry or fight against crying when she is there. . . . Apparently the loneliness of the place isn't only responsible for this but also the fact of her being perpetually worried about money. . . . Unless you can enable her to run your Silesian household comfortably and to invite a few visitors without constantly making her feel that the expense is too great and that they are therefore unwelcome to you, she must give up any further attempts to live there.

It was Muriel who was paying for most of their needs. The draft letter continued,

> I understand that the arrangement between you is that she gives you a fixed sum (outside of Germany at your own wish) as *her* contribution to the household expenses and that your estate office runs expenses there . . . the husband is bound under German law to defray all household expenses as well as his wife's expenses and those of his children. Muriel has hitherto never claimed this from you, having done so without your financial cooperation, nor can she feed 15 servants on air.[103]

It would not be a happy homecoming.

Chapter Six

I hope I may live long enough to see her [Margaret] happily married and that God may then take me to a better world as the thought of living to an old age in Upper Silesia gives me such a fit of the horrors but that for my religion I would take poison to avoid it.[1]
— Muriel Seherr-Thoss to Henry White

Having escaped "those bandits of Serbian extraction who nearly hooked poor Boysie,"[2] Muriel's first-born son was still unmarried. A handsome young man six feet in height with blonde hair and blue eyes, Boysie was a boarding student at the picturesque Benediktiner Gymnasium Ettal, a secondary school in Ettal, Germany, operated by the Benedictine Brothers (OSB), from May 1922 until Easter 1926, although he did not graduate.[3] He recalled his time there as "romanticized. A beautiful church in that valley in Bavaria. That sort of thing doesn't exist here [the United States]. Imagine singing a mass there by Mozart or Hayden in that church. In retrospect it was so beautiful."[4]

Although Muriel had been pressing both her sons to leave Germany and move to the United States to join her extended family there, Boysie wasn't certain that was his wish. As he recalled, "I had an immigration visa to the US but I let it lapse twice because I didn't want to go and I was perfectly happy. I had a new girl whom I liked." But, he said of his family, "they saw the writing on the wall because they had lived through this once before." Asked about deserting his friends in Germany, he responded, "You leave your friends when your house is burning."[5]

Not surprisingly, Boysie was an excellent skier and was in Interlaken in the Swiss Alps when he met his future wife in 1937. Marian

Cannon Kingsland, born in Lenox, Massachusetts, on July 20, 1916, was also skiing in Interlaken when she was invited to a debutante ball there. Marian's mother, born Marian DeForest Cannon (1894–1935), had died in Paris two years earlier while married to her third husband, Sir Charles Duncan, third baronet.[6] Marian made her debut at the 1935 Autumn Ball in Tuxedo Park.

Marian's father, George Lovett Kingsland Jr. (1884–1952), was a member of an old and distinguished family and was a great-nephew of *the* Mrs. Astor.[7] His grandfather, Ambrose Kingsland, was the mayor of New York City who originated the creation of Central Park.[8] The Kingslands, while still socially prominent, had been very wealthy, but after several generations, their funds were rapidly being depleted.

Marian, also an attractive blonde, was four years younger than Boysie[9] and was introduced to him at the debutante ball. The pair promptly fell in love, and he decided to pursue her to the United States when she returned home. Boysie sailed from Boulogne on the SS *Statendam*, arriving in New York City on December 16, 1937.

His quest was successful, as their engagement was announced in May 1938.[10] The marriage took place on June 28, 1938, at Manette Hill Farm, the estate of Marian's mother's sister, Mrs. Edgar W. Leonard, at Hicksville on Long Island, New York. The bride's father walked her down the aisle while Boysie's sister, Margaret, served as one of two maids of honor. Boysie's parents arrived in New York City two days before the marriage on the SS *Statendam* from Rotterdam, although they were not mentioned in news reports of the wedding. The *New York Times* proclaimed the event to be "of international interest," including the fact that the groom was a cousin of the queen of Albania.[11] Boysie's brother, Cincie, served as best man. After a honeymoon in Europe, where they lived for an extended period of time with Muriel and Manni at Dobrau, the couple returned on the SS *Normandie* from Le Havre to New York City, arriving on November 19, 1938. On the ship manifest, under the heading of "Occupation," his was—perhaps presciently—listed as "none" while hers was "housewife."

One would assume that the golden couple could expect flower-bedecked roads ahead of them, but that wasn't the case. First, the bride's father was a staunch Protestant and had no desire to acquire a Catholic son-in-law, even though he did what was expected by giving her away at the wedding. Marian's mother was not alive to mediate, although her mother's sister, Adelaide, who hosted the wedding, served as a surrogate mother. Second, what was to be Boysie's profession? He had helped his father to a small degree in running their various farms in Silesia but had no other professional training. He was reared to be master of all the family properties and to assume his father's seat in the Prussian House of Lords (even though it no longer existed). He served for a time in the German army as a young man, though "somehow Muriel had been able to shorten"[12] the length of his service. Because he was very familiar with horses, he was assigned "cleaning out the hooves of horses with a toothpick."[13] Finally, there was the increasing public sentiment against Germany with Hitler on the rise, and Marian's family members were not eager to have a blonde, blue-eyed German in their midst. Boysie said, "When I left I knew that if Germany won the war I would never be able to go back. If they lost the war that was a different thing."[14]

On March 13, 1938, only two months before their wedding, Hitler had annexed Austria into the German Reich in what became known as the Anschluss, even though that action was forbidden by the Treaty of Versailles. In September, only three months after the wedding, Nazi Germany negotiated the cession of the Czechoslovak Republic's Sudetenland in order to gain control of key military defenses in the area. It was obvious World War II was about to begin, and it would have been difficult for anyone to miss an Aryan German with a double family name speaking English with a "slightly British"[15] accent, no matter how handsome and charming. Boysie was a realist, however, and said of his options at the time,

> You were German. You were going to have to fight for Hitler whether you wanted to or not. If you go and fight and if you survive and Germany wins the war you are going to be expropriated because Germany will have the British empire and half of Russia. There would be no need for large estates anymore. They are all going to be expropriated. And if Germany loses the war and Russia wins you're also going to be expropriated and maybe you'll be dead too in Stalingrad to boot.[16]

His mother had earlier expressed the same opinion: "If there is any danger of Germany's fighting the civilized world again I shall have done with them forever & neither Manni nor my three children will keep me amongst them!"[17] She wanted Boysie safely in the United States. Even if that made him an enemy alien, at least he would be alive. She advised him, "You are the eldest son and you have been brought up to inherit the property and continue the family tradition. I hope you never inherit it because you will have a millstone around your neck for the rest of your life." He remembered she said to him at the time, "It was a matter of avoiding the war—survival."[18]

Marian's family was not alone in their prejudice. Nica de Rothschild recalled, "This was a Germany where the impact of the financial crash was fuelling the rise of support for Adolf Hitler and his National Socialist Party. 'It was during Hitler's rise, but we weren't aware of what was going on, until it finally occurred to us that the people who were behaving boorishly were those who knew we were Jewish.'"[19]

Through a German friend who worked for Lever Brothers in Canada, Boysie was interviewed for a job at a top Madison Avenue advertising agency. When asked what he was good at doing, he replied, "The only thing I do really well is shoot pheasants. And he gave me a job—in the depression!"[20]

He painted a much rosier picture in a letter to his Uncle Jack, who was then the US ambassador to Haiti: "The work here at Young & Rubicam is extremely interesting and I just love the whole 'outfit.' In short, I am very happy here. It is a very good firm with 650 employees alone in the N.Y.C. office." He subsequently asked for advice about possible positions in South America but added, "Please don't bother to answer this part of my letter if it means any trouble at all."[21]

With Boysie married, Muriel turned her attention to her only daughter. Margaret was born on April 4, 1910, and when she turned eighteen, it was time for her to make her debut. In 1928, she and her mother sailed to New York for that purpose. Muriel's stepsister, Mrs. John Henry Hammond (née Emily Vanderbilt Sloane), generously allowed Margaret to use her residence at 9 East 91st Street for "*Thé Dansant* from 4 until 7 o'clock."[22]

If any marital prospects arose because of Margaret's presentation reception, they never came to fruition. In the intervening eleven years before she married, it was a subject that was very much on her mother's mind in light of her own unhappy marriage. Muriel wrote a family member, "I hope I may live long enough to see her [Margaret] happily married and that God may then take me to a better world as the thought of living to an old age in Upper Silesia gives me such a fit of the horrors but that for my religion I would take poison to avoid it."[23]

She wrote to her brother, Jack, from New York City, that Margaret had been successfully "launched as a debutante and has been asked everywhere." While there were no suitable marriage prospects in line for her hand,

> we cannot keep clear of Spanish beaux. There is another Don Whis-kerandos here who has proposed to her and is deeply in love and fearfully jealous without a *gleam* of a sense of humor. He is full of the finest sentiments and is I believe a very decent young fellow though I should be bored to tears with a son-in-law who is so solemn. That quality of his may save me, but I fear the worst as he is good-looking and has curly hair. . . . I think she would be bored to death with him before the honeymoon was over. If a Spaniard in Spain had fallen in love with her one might have expected it but it really is bad luck that her only serious "beau" in New York should be one. She is evidently the type which they admire.[24]

Margaret did receive at least one proposal of marriage, but perhaps his lack of American citizenship was his undoing. Margaret

> refused young Count Deym, the grandson of the former Ambassador to London. Funnily enough Uncle Stuyve [Stuyvesant] and my father-in-law were both in love with his grandmother, old Countess Deym, before she married, so there seems to be a sort of inherited attraction! . . . I am sorry about it as the boy is nice, has a place near here in Tchecho-Slovakia [Czechoslovakia] and enough to live on without being rich. He was also really very much in love with her and came to New York last winter just to propose to her. I am rather sorry about it. Manni however is not keen about it unless she finds someone really

very rich. She told him (though not me) that that would be the only inducement for her to take the responsibilities of marriage. As very rich men are hard to find nowadays, I think she will probably remain an old maid . . . when she gets to be about 30 she may regret the nice men whom she turned down in her youth![25]

One particular candidate for Margaret had aroused great hope: Count Claes, the oldest son of a Swede, Marquess Lagergren, who served as papal chamberlain to Pope Leo XIII. Muriel sought information from her father about him and his family because, she wrote, "they asked Margaret and me to a big dinner and the eldest son has been making up to Margaret."[26] Claes Leo was born in 1892, making him eighteen years older than Margaret, and he had two younger brothers who had also been created counts. He attended agricultural school in Bonn and trade school in Ghent and then studied in France before practicing import and export banking in New York with his mother's family firm, Howland & Aspinwall, from 1915 to 1923.

Muriel wrote to her father that the Lagergrens had taken Princess Brancaccio's apartment in Rome and were entertaining a great deal.[27]

They are very rich and have a fine castle in Sweden. They must be well off to entertain the way they do. The parents are apparently anxious for the son to marry a Roman Catholic of which there are few in Sweden. Also as Lagergren is of no particular family they want a girl of good family.[28]

Obviously Muriel thought of her own family as superior. Of course, there were other considerations. Another informant "told me the son had been fast but of course he is rich and mothers with daughters are bound to tell one things like that. I should be so grateful if you can find out something about the family from the Swedish minister in Washington," she wrote to her father.[29] Fortunately, "Margaret likes the young man and he is well-mannered and nice-looking, very dark. Of course she couldn't marry him before she is 17."[30]

Muriel wrote again to her father months later on the same subject, saying she still had not received sufficient information about the Lagergren family and their fortune. Muriel had asked the young man

A 1931 family photo at Schloss Dobrau. Margaret is between her brother, Boysie, and their father, with brother Cincie standing behind. On the ends are cousins "Baby" and "Didi" Hunyadi. CREDIT: ELIZABETH SEHERR-THOSS

to come and stay with them during the summer. "He asked Margaret if she would prefer to marry a German or a foreigner. Margaret replied that she would only marry an American and he said to her that in that case he would remain a bachelor. His mother's fortune is what I would like to find out about. She was an American from New York and Lagergren's first wife."[31] Alas, nothing came of Muriel's hopes. Claes Lagergren did inherit his father's marquessate in 1930 and married twice—both times to Swedish wives.[32] Neither he nor his two brothers had sons, and the male line is now extinct.[33]

Not until September 8, 1939, when Margaret was twenty-nine, did she cross alone on the SS *Rex* from Genoa to New York City. Her engagement was announced, and in only a few weeks, she was married on October 21, 1939. Her husband was Edgar Moore "Ted" Church Jr., an alumnus of St. George's School in Newport (class of 1929), Yale (class of 1933), and Yale Law School (class of 1937). His parents, natives of Philadelphia, were deceased. His father, an investment broker who had captained three football teams at the University of Pennsylvania, served as the head football coach at Union College in Schenectady, New York, for one season in 1895.[34] He outlived Church's mother, Alice Kennedy Sands. The groom's grandfather, William Augustus Church, was treasurer of the Reading Railroad, while his aunt, Elizabeth Inskeep Church,

Margaret in her wedding dress. CREDIT: PAUL CHURCH

married cotton merchant William Morris Longstreth from an old Philadelphia Quaker family. The couple reportedly met when they crossed the
Atlantic on a 1938 sailing of the SS *Bremen* from Cherbourg. Margaret
had obviously abandoned her vow to marry only a rich husband.

Margaret's "aunt" (actually the mother-in-law of Muriel's brother,
John), Mrs. R. Burnham Moffat, hosted the wedding ceremony and
reception at her home at 660 Park Avenue.[35] Muriel and Manni did not
attend the wedding, perhaps because of financial constraints or due to
the continuing illness that exempted him from the battlefield. Margaret
was given away by a White cousin, George Francklyn Lawrence Jr.,[36] so
evidently her two brothers also did not attend. There is some question
whether Muriel ever met her son-in-law. If so, it could only have taken
place the previous year when Muriel and Manni went to New York City
for Boysie's first marriage. Muriel did write on the day before Margaret's wedding, "As you say, it is the greatest blessing that she is marrying
such a really nice American in every way as Teddy Church especially in
times like these."[37]

Cincie was three years younger than Boysie and had always dreamed
of becoming a rancher. As the second son, he knew that primogeniture
would dictate that he did not inherit the family properties, so he would
have to make his own way. He went to the United States in 1937, arriving
on the Dutch liner SS *Veendam* on February 8, when he was twenty-one.

Two inches shorter than Boysie, Cincie's eyes were gray instead of
blue. He, too, was handsome and available and quickly joined a young
social set whose amusements were reported in newspapers at such well-
known resorts as Palm Beach. Cincie was reported as a roommate of Prince
Mikhail Alexandrovitch Goundoroff, whose mother was the German-born
Princess Elizabeta Stolberg-Rossla. As one newspaper reported:

> Anybody worrying about the sudden disappearance from Manhattan
> society of handsome young Count Herman [Cincie] Seherr-Thoss will
> be reassured and amused to learn that the extremely decorative youth
> has just arrived in Wyoming to take up a new career. He'll find it easy to
> squander his wages. Of all things, for his new job as a ranch hand Her-
> man will receive for his services the magnificent sum of $20 a month.

Margaret and Edgar Church at their wedding. CREDIT: PAUL CHURCH

Fortunately for the Count, he won't have to depend on his salary alone. He gets about $300 a month from his mother, Countess Herman Seherr-Thoss. Cincey [*sic*], as he's known to his friends, since his return from Palm Beach, had been sharing an apartment on E. 68th St. with Prince Mikhail Goundoroff. . . . When he flew off for the western cow country, Cincey had a fine send-off from his best girl, Beatrice Procter, soap heiress and daughter of Mr. and Mrs. Rodney Procter.[38]

Cincie's wife, whom no one in the family had met when Boysie received a telegram from his brother informing him of their marriage, was Virginia Madeline DeLoney (1914–1999), called "Virgie" in a family that always used nicknames. Cincie could not have met a wife more perfectly suited to his stated plans. They were wed on January 5, 1943, in Des Moines, Iowa, but the marriage wasn't announced until March 3 in the *New York Times*. Although Cincie's family connections were all recounted in the article, only Virgie's parents' names, Mr. and Mrs. Charles DeLoney, were included, as well as her hometown of Jackson, Wyoming.[39] Virgie came from solid pioneer stock, her grandfather, Charles "Pap" DeLoney, having opened the first general store in Jackson before serving as one of Wyoming's state senators. Her grandmother, Clara Burton DeLoney, was from an early Mormon family who had walked more than five hundred miles over the plains from New York to Utah and eventually settled in Jackson, Wyoming.

Muriel's grandson recalled that his mother, Margaret, "voiced tempered objections to the union as supposedly Virginia was a Mormon." But since Cincie's son by a later marriage spoke to the grandson "favorably about Virginia, he must have known her."[40]

The letter Boysie wrote to his uncle Jack mentioning prospects in South America had also included the surprising family news about his only brother:

Cincie, who as you know was in Des Moines at X-mas time sent me the following telegram on Jan. 11th: "Just got married, on way to Miami." That was all. We still do not know who the young lady is or what her name is, what she looks like and where she comes from. The only thing I know about her from a letter I received from Cincie last night is that

she is a WAAC[41] and a lieutenant at that. Cincie says he is very happy
and that they are saving to buy a ranch as soon as they can. Apparently
he met her out West on a ranch and he also stated that she grew up on
a ranch herself. He said also that she is a very fine rider and very fond of
horses . . . the girl must be quite a girl to be a lieutenant in the WAAC.
Furthermore, if she likes the kind of life that he likes and has the kind
of background he says she has, the marriage is perhaps a very good idea
in this day and age, where in my opinion lack of great wealth is an asset
and happiness and harmony with the people around you is all.[42]

His last sentence would soon be tested. Boysie added correctly, "It is
probably impossible to inform my parents of this event until after the war."

Muriel had for some time been urging their family attorney and
trustee, her cousin Lewis Spencer Morris, to give Cincie the funds to
purchase his ranch even before he married. She came back to the same
subject in a subsequent letter, reminding him that Cincie and Margaret
were the beneficiaries of a substantial trust, adding, "I have written you
by two different routes as to Cincie's great desire that the family trustees should enable him to invest in a ranch."[43] Cincie had written to his
mother earlier from Wyoming, "I am very happy here. I wish I could have
a little ranch which I could make into a lovely place. If I had a little capital, then I could marry a nice wife." He wrote again to her two months
later to say he was working for "an old lady" who owned a ranch and paid
him for his work.

He added, "I am so glad I can save my allowance," although he was
worried that he "had to register for the Army here and they put me in *first*
class. That means they can call me at any time. It is certainly not pleasant
for me to have to fight in a war against my own country. Other aliens
are put in Class Three."[44] While Muriel had gotten her sons safely out of
Germany, in the United States, they were legally enemy aliens, and she
feared they could be arrested and detained.

Boysie recalled of his own draft experience:

Here I was, an enemy alien. The war started. There was the draft. My
draft number came up and I had to go before the draft board and they
said to me, you can refuse to serve and we will intern you and send you

back to Germany after the war, or you can serve. I said, look, gentlemen, I came here of my own free will and I cannot live with myself if everybody else, regardless of whether German, American, English, or French are bearing their share of the burden of this disaster that has befallen the world. But you've got to make me a citizen. Right now I am not allowed to own a gun, I can't own a camera, I'm just a third-rate nobody. You can't just expect me to carry a gun for Uncle Sam so long as I am not a citizen. The whole draft board applauded.[45]

Boysie officially applied for citizenship on March 7, 1938. He took the oath of renunciation and allegiance and was sworn in as a citizen on October 22, 1943, while serving as a private in basic training at Camp Wheeler in Macon, Georgia.[46] He would very quickly have the opportunity to fight for his new country.

Naturally also concerned about Cincie's possible military draft, Muriel instructed Lewis Morris, "C. [Cincie] always has been quite helpless regarding legal or official matters! Please get in touch with the authorities concerned in Wyoming and have the matter straightened out if you can do so; *even if it is expensive.*"

Having discussed the matter with her older son, Muriel said that Boysie wrote to her, "Quite aside from other conditions of a political nature which might result in his (C's) being locked up when and if this country goes to war, what would happen then to his ranch and cattle?" Muriel explained to Morris, "I am not unnaturally worried at Boysie's writing as to this possibility; which would of course apply to Boysie as well as Cincie."[47]

At the same time she was worried about her sons' possible military service, Muriel wrote in the same letter, "Manni had an order to hold himself ready for some military post. Only his doctor's declaration as to the condition of his kidneys made them rescind it a day or two ago. Apparently they are letting agriculture go hang; for they are taking people like Manni whose presence is imperative for running big estates. His [farm] director has been away since the war began."

Muriel remained in her "protective mother" mode, suggesting to Lewis Morris another possible avenue of appeal. Aware that, in war time, her letters were probably read by censors, she often wrote in a code understood only by her correspondents. She told Morris, "I was so afraid of this possibility [conscription or arrest of her sons] that I wrote to my former playmate (who is now so exalted) congratulating him on his renewed raise to power."[48] Her subsequent letters made it clear she was speaking of the recently reelected president Franklin D. Roosevelt, with whom she had played on the RMS *Teutonic* when she was only fourteen. She continued, "In this letter I asked him 'please to hold a protecting hand over my sons in case of certain eventualities.'"

She received a gracious reply, but it was not what she hoped for. As she related to Lewis Morris, "I received a very nice answer dated Jan. 31st 1941 in which the great man replied: 'As regards your two sons as to whom you have expressed anxiety, I have no doubt that, sensible as they must be of the distinguished and good name of their family they are making themselves welcome visitors. I shall hope for further news of them.'" She had hoped that his reply "would *avert* the danger of a concentration camp. The sentence which I have quoted from Boysie's letter looks as if that danger were still acute. If Cincie is in class 1 and can be drafted at any moment for the U.S. Army, I don't see how he also can be put in a concentration camp in case of war. But of course it is imperative that that matter be put straight as soon as possible."[49]

Muriel was known to be resourceful and had already used her connections and access to wealth to help many who needed her assistance. As long as she achieved her result, she had no fear of approaching anyone. In the same letter, she wrote, "Another person who would be very helpful in that direction (if she could be induced to intervene) would be my aunt Lucy Rutherfurd (Winty's wife)."[50] This was an instance in which she may have been skating on thin ice.

Her mother's brother, Winthrop Chanler Rutherfurd (known to all as "Winty"), was "celebrated for really breath-taking good looks."[51] He had been secretly engaged to Consuelo Vanderbilt before Consuelo's mother cut off all contact with him and forced her to marry the ninth Duke of Marlborough. Winty married, in 1902, Alice Morton, whose father had been US vice president and was so helpful to Henry White in obtaining his first diplomatic posting. After Alice's death in 1917, leaving Winty with six children to rear, he hired as a governess the very attractive Lucy

Page Mercer, who in 1914 became social secretary to Eleanor Roosevelt and promptly fell in love and began a relationship with FDR. Although Eleanor became aware of the affair in 1918 when she discovered Lucy's letters to her husband and threatened to end the marriage, Lucy married Winty in 1920, and the affair continued. Eleanor's mother-in-law intervened, knowing that her son's political career would be ended by a divorce scandal. He promised to end the relationship but did not. As late as 1932, FDR secured for Lucy a front-row seat to his presidential inauguration. After Winty's death in 1944, she resumed the relationship and was with FDR when he died in Warm Springs, Georgia, in 1945. Lucy had to be quickly removed from the cottage before the first lady arrived. Artist Elizabeth Shoumatoff, who was painting her famous "unfinished portrait" of FDR when he slumped over in his chair, packed up their things and hurried Lucy into a car. The two were not certain that the president had died until they reached Macon, Georgia, and saw telephone operators in tears at the Dempsey Hotel.[52] Although that event was still in the future when she wrote to Lewis Morris in 1941, Muriel was obviously aware that her aunt was still seeing FDR while Winty was very much alive. There is no indication whether Muriel approached Lucy with a request to intervene with the president, but she certainly would have done anything to protect her sons.

With a German war almost certain, soon to include the United States, Marian's father-in-law made his opposition to a German son-in-law plain by cutting off his daughter's family funds. George Kingsland had never remarried after his 1922 divorce from Marian's mother and spent much of his time in Palm Beach. He lived until 1952, and although he was said to be planning to restore his daughter in his will, he died before doing so.[53]

Of course, Boysie had no direct contact with his parents except by messages that may have been transferred through friends in the diplomatic service. He recalled, "I was very unhappy at the beginning in the US. The whole world was different."[54] With income cut off and lacking any job skills, he took a job selling vacuum cleaners. The couple had just enough money to buy a car and drove to the Berkshires in western Massachusetts. They came across an idyllic property called Blueberry Hill at

West Stockbridge near Lenox, the town where both Daisy and Henry White had died. "Marian and I bought a little place in Massachusetts. We were very lucky. A nice house—ugly at the time but it had the most wonderful views. We dug into that place and fixed it up and from that moment I was happy in America."[55] The family of Henry White's second wife, Emily Vanderbilt Sloane, lived in the area along with extended family, and "that's why it was so nice to come and live in this part of the world. Because there were some people in that part of your family. That made an enormous difference." Marian and Boysie traded in the car as the down payment and bought Blueberry Hill in 1938 for $5,000. It remained the family home for four generations until it was sold in 2024.

Muriel was pleased that Boysie seemed happy despite his in-laws' rejection, but her concern for him was unabated. She wrote to her new daughter-in-law, Marian, "We are the two people who love Boysie best in the world and both our hearts are wrung with anxiety for him."[56]

Muriel was astounded by the negative reaction of Marian's "near relations" to having Boysie in their family. She wrote to Marian after Margaret's recent marriage, "I am amazed and *shocked* at the attitude of your family as Margaret writes that she has met with nothing but kindness on *all sides* since her return. A few American relatives and acquaintances were rather horrid to me after the last war, but my beloved father and my stepmother never were anything but kindness and affection itself to me and your father-in-law, also Jack, my dear brother."[57]

Muriel's grandson recalled a conversation with "Aunt Marian" when she said that Manni was "complacent about the entire Nazi business and the beginning of war" because he thought "if war began, it wouldn't last long and all soldiers would be home by New Year 1940."[58]

Boysie had mentioned interest in relocating to South America in the letter to his uncle, so perhaps he had also discussed that possibility with his mother. Muriel wrote to Marian of her friend, Bertie Lansbery, who had extensive properties in Brazil: "No one can detest the Nazi regime more than he does and he has countless friends among the nicest people in England. He looks upon you and Boysie as victims of those wicked gangsters who are governing Germany as indeed you are, together with the German nation and the Poles and all the other people whose homes, lives, property, trade, etc., are being ruined by them."[59]

Obviously, the young couple's financial precariousness, linked with the family's antagonism toward Boysie, were doubly worrying for Muriel, who wrote to Marian, "It is only a most ignoble fear of what other people think which has made your family adopt that outrageous attitude. I fear it is a case of 'their hearts not being in the right place' or perhaps they haven't got any hearts! Never mind, my pet! You are now in a family who have very warm hearts and who love you dearly and who cling together as a family should."[60]

Amid all the machinations and celebrations of her children's marriages, it was obvious to Muriel that hers was irretrievably broken. She had endured a great deal, including Manni's mistresses, his temper, and his refusal to give financial support to his family. As early in the marriage as 1925, she wrote to her aunt, "Manni has happily now realized that I cannot stand this lonely place without some company (he being away all day) and the children at their lessons. So he has at last been willing to let me have some visitors and to go around the neighbourhood about which he has hitherto invariably made scenes."[61] Not long afterward, she wrote that "a wife in this country must either be a shrew or a martyr. I notice that the moment I become too gentle or affectionate I get trampled upon."

Two years later, she had sought the advice of a priest, who was very helpful. As she wrote to her brother,

> It was my duty to write to my husband and tell him in the plainest possible language that unless he could make me happy at home there was no obligation for me to stay in his house for another day. I have done this (more plainly than I have ever done before) and one cannot be *too* plain with a German! I have also told him that I did it on the advice of a priest. Of course it is a nervous trouble (coupled with his hereditary avarice) which makes him so unkind in Silesia (because he cannot bear to spend money), then the only solution will be for me *only* to see him abroad. The Catholic Church includes avarice among the seven deadly sins. After being at close quarters with it for 18 years

I feel more disposed to include it among the different forms of hereditary insanity . . . the talk I had with the priest cleared my brain.[62]

However, the marital problems not only persisted but also increased.
Manni even tried to bring an "undesirable" young woman along with
Muriel and their family on a crossing to the United States.[63] It was left
to Muriel to untangle the situation. He once threatened her with divorce
when she was ill in bed and a package containing bed clothes for Boysie
arrived with 250 marks due on delivery.

Manni did not enjoy the same popularity with staff and servants as
his wife. "The count was rough, he didn't let the children play loudly, and
he didn't like it when his wife played the piano. His malice was known to
the servants and local residents. My aunt said that he would deliberately
make litter and order the servants to clean it up, even though they had
just done so. . . . [Manni was] more interested in playing golf and hunting
than in [his and Muriel's] children."[64] "The count was not supposed to
be an affectionate father. Children were not allowed to play too loudly in
their home and their friends were also unwelcome."

His oldest son, Boysie, recalled one incident:

When we came back from America we brought some gramophone
records with us and we played them. These were very nice early jazz
records. They were thrown around and he said, "I won't have any of
this stuff," with a loud voice roaring at us. "Stop this noise! I don't like
this in my house. This is barbaric American stuff!" He would shout at
people on the estate, this was par for the course in or out of the house.[65]

Boysie confirmed that his parents' marriage was unhappy: "I saw her cry
very often."

Their frequent issue was finances: "There were always scenes, usually
about money. When my mother bought me a bicycle, a tremendous
scene. When I bought a house in Austria, a scene. When I bought my
car, a tremendous scene. There were always scenes." Most people outside
the family were spared these bitter disputes. "There were often rows about
everything, starting at breakfast about anything that passed through
my father's mind. He was the most deceiving character, because he was

An older Manni Seherr-Thoss, Muriel's husband.
CREDIT: ELIZABETH SEHERR-THOSS

absolutely charming to everyone to meet but at home he was an absolute devil."[66] In fact, of the three children, Boysie claimed, "I got along with him least well. My brother's rather perceptive tutor said, 'He doesn't like you because of your intelligence.'"[67]

Manni seemed to oppose Muriel on every domestic issue. "He brought a stable boy from Dobrau here with lice in his head. . . . I have finally told him that as long as I am mistress of his house I will not keep and feed servants with lice and that if he had wanted a wife who tolerated them like his Mother he should not have married an American. Since then he has stopped worrying me on that subject but as long as one is gentle he thinks he can trample on one."[68]

Manni had certainly done very little to make Dobrau profitable. His grandson recalled a conversation with Manni's son, Boysie, who said that

> he didn't think that Pappi, as he called his father, had done a very good job of *managing* the entire Dobrau estate. Boysie then went on to tell me what *he* would have done with the resources on that large tract, especially in the forestry sector, which was of special interest to Boysie. As I recall, Boysie related that if his father had applied himself differently to the resources of Dobrau that would have brought in much more *income*, which was needed at that time . . . later on, when I was a teenager, my recollection of my grandfather was that he was more interested in hunting on the place and pursuing other gentlemanly activities relating to entertaining visitors and family. . . . I can say that Manni was complacent about most important matters![69]

As a Catholic convert, Muriel's faith was strong. At some point prior to October 1939, she traveled to Breslau, the seat of their diocese, to seek spiritual guidance once again. At the Cathedral of Saint John, she met at length with the parish monsignor and told him of her many travails and asked how to prevail in a difficult marriage. "To her utter surprise, the Monsignor succinctly tells her that he knows her husband and there is no need for counsel; he will grant her a divorce immediately."[70] Obviously Manni's reputation was well known.

Church records were destroyed and lost during the subsequent war, so there is no document certifying her divorce. However, later official German and US government records list her as "divorced." Muriel wrote to her daughter-in-law, Marian, "Everyone in Germany *screamed* when I got that extremely useful divorce from your father-in-law (which counts as a mere scrap of paper for a Catholic Christian) and now the *loudest* screamers all tell me what a clever woman I was to do it and what a good and useful wife and mother that step has enabled me to be to him and the children."[71] Perhaps she took her cue from another of her cousins, of whom she wrote, "Newy Morris's sudden death was very sad and sudden but I don't believe his wife minds. There was another ill-sorted couple such as the world is full of, but they got along quite nicely by being very little together."[72] Margaret White Bennett wrote to Paul Church, "I remember that when we were in Buenos Aires—after Deidu [Margaret] (your grandmother), had visited, hearing that Muriel and Manni were getting a divorce—for financial reasons. It was all very hush-hush, and I don't know if it actually happened."[73]

If Muriel thought her divorce was "a mere scrap of paper," her husband did not agree. He almost certainly had already begun a relationship with the woman who would become his second wife. His cousin, Count André de Baghy, confirmed that he had several affairs. As Muriel's great-grandson recalled, "After the divorce, Muriel left for Holland. My understanding is that Hermann and Ursula von Hirschfeld had been in a relationship for some time." Ursula's husband, Caspar, Baron von Berlepsch, was away at war while Manni remained at home on medical leave. Baron von Berlepsch would be killed in action in Austria in 1941.

After the divorce, for her trip to Holland,

> Muriel disguised herself frequently, and in this case took a train to her home in Holland not knowing when or if she would ever see Silesia again. Upon arriving in Holland and going to a bank in which she had accounts, the Manager told her regretfully that her accounts had been frozen. He felt badly and sent telegrams on her behalf to Hermann [Manni], who gave her permission to return to Dobrau as Head of Household.[74]

Her son recalled, "Later on in her life when currency regulations were imposed on anybody living in Germany she was told by the government that she should deliver her assets in America to the German government. She then got a divorce from my father. She was a very strong fighter." After she spent six months living at the Westbury Hotel in New York City, she was able to regain her citizenship so "when the currency regulations started to get tough, it was relatively easy for her not to give anything to the German government because it was in trust."[75]

Now openly divorced with some of her funds cut off (she couldn't touch the capital in her trust), Muriel had to plan more carefully for her future. She wrote to her brother,

All interest from my Canadian and U.S.A. certificates is frozen, as well as from my securities in the Dutch colonies. . . . I certainly couldn't afford Switzerland. I *could* live very cheaply with my children's relations in Hungary or in Italy with friends as a P.G. [paying guest], but I am not allowed to go there. Margaret has written me a touching letter, offering me hospitality in a little "dependence" of the country home which she and Teddy have acquired. . . . I would be dependent for every cent on Margaret and my son-in-law, until the war is over. Devoted as you are to your dear child Margaret [Lolly], I don't think you and Betty would enjoy having to ask her (and particularly her future husband) for every cent of money you require.[76]

It seemed her options were limited. Manni had said she could return to Dobrau as an unpaid head of household, and that became the most viable solution. As she explained to Jack,

I was always a blameless and faithful wife to him, until we were divorced, but he was a most unfaithful husband (not once but several times). So I see no reason why I should feel shy about letting *him* provide me with food and a roof over my head! Besides, I earn my keep, for running his household under present conditions is the job of a well-paid housekeeper. Manni doesn't have to give *me* any salary.[77]

Chapter Seven

No Austrian lady . . . , let alone an American one, would put up with the dull, lonely life I lead here coupled with such unreasonable stinginess, undeserved reproofs, ingratitude, and bad-temper. I have certainly done my best to be a faithful and loving wife to him and to stick to him for better or worse (and there has been a good deal of for worse lately) but do what I will I can't please him.[1]
— MURIEL SEHERR-THOSS

LESS THAN A YEAR AFTER QUEEN GERALDINE'S MARRIAGE TO KING Zog, Muriel was summoned to Tirana again in 1939 "to await the arrival of what everyone hoped would be an heir to the Albanian throne."[2] Geraldine's sister, Virginia, could not be present because she was expecting her own child. In fact, their babies would be delivered only hours apart. Muriel was pleased by what she saw when she arrived on March 12:

> I found my dear little Queen quite blissfully happy; so there could be no doubt that King Zog was proving to be the best and most devoted of husbands. I spent many happy hours with her, during which she told me of the plans which she was making for the welfare of the Albanian people. I also admired the beautiful christening robe, all trimmed with lace, which the young Queen's clever fingers had fashioned; as well as many other dainty garments for the tiny stranger.[3]

Muriel had experienced diplomacy and state affairs as few others had. Her father and brother were both ambassadors, and she had been presented at several courts. Her first-person account of Italy's invasion of Albania in 1939 and the exile of the king and queen is particularly valuable, as it was both contemporaneous and insightful.

> My first intimation that all was not well with this apparently peaceful little country, was on Friday evening March 31st. His Excellency the Turkish Minister, whom I met at dinner, then told me that the Italian fleet was off the port of Valona and that an ultimatum would shortly be presented to King Zog by the Italian government, making extensive demands on Albanian independence.[4]

Trusting her instincts, Muriel made her way to the American legation at Tirana headed by Ambassador Hugh G. Grant. Her first priority was her very pregnant ward, Geraldine. She asked the ambassador whether, should the palace be attacked, the queen could be guaranteed safety at the legation. "Mr. Grant and his kind and charming wife gladly answered in the affirmative and she showed me an attractive suite of rooms, which they placed at once at Her Majesty's disposal."[5] The ambassador also told Muriel that he had just received a coded telegram informing him that Italian troops were massing at Bari and were headed to Albania. Diplomats from other countries were alarmed, and several had been trying, without success, to arrange a meeting with King Zog to discuss the situation. Muriel knew that she could gain access to the king, and "I thereupon wrote His Majesty a letter, in which I repeated what the Turkish and American ministers told me, and also informed him of Mr. and Mrs. Grant's kind offer of hospitality to the Queen, in case of danger."[6] Muriel reported to her diplomatic friends that the king already knew "the Italians decoded his ciphers, tapped his telephone, and opened Foreign Ministry correspondence."[7]

It was almost midnight when Muriel personally handed her letter to the officer on duty, who promised to deliver it immediately even though the king was then meeting with his minister of foreign affairs, Ekrem Libohova. Within ten minutes, the minister came down himself "and smilingly asked me how I could possibly believe such alarming rumours. He assured me that it was quite untrue that the Italian fleet lay off Valona, or that the Italian government had any aggressive designs on Albanian independence. He said the Italians merely wanted some arrangement, whereby they could close the Adriatic in case of war."[8]

While Queen Geraldine, in her last stages of pregnancy, was shielded from what was happening outside the palace, others began to fear the worst. King Zog was not aware that his enemies—including his own foreign affairs minister—were so close at hand. Only minutes after Muriel's conversation with Libohova, the king's nephew came down to see her at his uncle's instruction, "to reassure me. The young officer in question looked very pale and upset, and admitted that the Italians were making extensive demands on Albanian independence which must be refused. He said there was no fear of hostilities or any danger to the Queen. I retired to rest somewhat reassured, though I still had my doubts!"[9]

On April 2 and 3, there were peaceful demonstrations in front of the palace and at several legations, urging Albania to refuse to concede to any of the Italian demands. On April 4, Muriel again took the initiative to visit the German minister, Eberhard von Pannwitz,[10] who was an old friend. He had just returned from a week in Italy, and she knew he would have the latest information. "Herr von Pannwitz was just as cheerful as the Minister of Foreign Affairs and confirmed the assurances made by Monsieur Libohova on the previous Friday, as to the peacefulness of Italy's intentions. This I suppose it was the German Minister's duty to assert being the representative of their Ally!"[11]

With perfect timing, amid a tightening noose around Albania's fragile neck, there was momentary elation.

On Wednesday morning, April 5th, at 3:30 a.m., a fair-haired, blue-eyed prince was born. The delirious joy of the Albanians knew no bounds when they were informed of the happy event at sunrise, by the discharge of 101 cannon shots. Soon after his birth, the King's youngest sister placed her nephew's tiny hand on a loaded revolver. She explained that this was an Albanian custom to ensure that a boy should be brave and strong.[12]

It was certainly a portent of the life of that newborn boy. He was named Alexander/Iskander but called the Albanian derivative, "Leka."

The queen's sister had safely delivered a daughter, named Julia Geraldine, before midnight on April 4, thus giving the first cousins different birth dates. As her brother remembered, the two babies "were considered as twins and they remained friends till the end."[13]

Despite the happy birth, events were moving at a rapid pace. As Muriel recalled, "That very morning the Italian government sent an ultimatum to King Zog, demanding an answer in 24 hours. On Wednesday evening, at about 6:30, Herr von Pannwitz came to see me and advised me to leave Albania as soon as possible, as he had now reason to believe that the situation was pretty serious."[14]

The queen's grandmother, Madame Strale d'Ekna, had also been summoned for the impending birth, and Muriel heard from her just hours later. She reported

> that the best hotel in Tirana, the Continental, which was owned and run by Italians and where she was staying, had been closed; so that she had to move to the American legation. The Italian aviators, who lived at the Continental Hotel, had then carried off all the remaining Italians in their aeroplanes. The flying field, planes, etc., in Tirana were in Italian hands.[15]

The closure of the Hotel Continental finally convinced Tirana's upper-crust clientele that the situation was serious. "They had lived through many an invasion scare, but never before had they lost their favorite bar."[16] The US minister, Hugh Grant, who had been so accommodating to Geraldine's family, finally obtained an audience with the king and recorded his recollection:

> The King's general demeanor was calm but during the course of the conversation which lasted for nearly an hour he manifested his strong emotion. . . . He referred with a touch of bitterness in his voice to the fact that the Italians launched their offensive at the very moment when the Queen was giving birth to a child. At this particular moment he gazed out of the window and I could see plainly tears welling up in his eyes. He gave the impression of a man who felt bitter disappointment and that he had been grossly betrayed.[17]

King Zog had to tell Geraldine that she and their newborn son must be ready to leave at a moment's notice. "Geraldine was thunderstruck. Gladys Girault nearly fainted, and some Hungarian ladies-in-waiting wept as Mrs. Strale d'Ekna tried to get them to pack."[18] The next morning at 9:00 a.m., the queen sent for Muriel,

> and she presented a lovely and pathetic picture, with her baby boy lying beside her and the King's miniature under her pillow. With admirable calm and courage, this poor young mother told me that she must leave that afternoon for Greece, over a very rough mountain road, in an ambulance; which involved a trip of about thirteen hours. Queen Geraldine was fully aware that her enforced flight might cost her her life in her condition; but her only real dread was lest anything should happen to her beloved husband who was remaining in Tirana.[19]

Muriel immediately insisted on accompanying the queen and baby Leka. Geraldine replied that she and the king had already decided she should not do so, as Muriel had her own family to consider. The king generously provided a car and driver to take Muriel into Yugoslavia, "as the harbours were already under blockade and no sea-trip was possible."[20] As a special mark of appreciation, King Zog officially granted Muriel Albanian citizenship, a gift on which she would eventually try to rely. "Their Majesties both expressed their thanks that I had been willing to stay for as long as they could keep me, and I was thus obliged to bid my dear one and her baby a very anxious farewell."[21] Muriel was asked by the American ambassador's wife to take with her three American guests who were visiting: William Danforth, the founder of the Ralston Purina Company in St. Louis; his wife; and their grandson. Muriel was happy to accommodate them.

The *New York Times* announced the birth of baby Leka ("Prince Is Born to King Zog and Part-American Queen"); on the same page, two adjoining articles were titled "Albania Is Sought by Rival Powers" and "Italians Pressing Albania in Talks."[22] The issues were irretrievably linked. The Italians insisted that "the tension results from a systematic boycott of Italian interests on the part of King Zog, who has sought to hinder Italian economic penetration of Albania. . . . It is reported that the King took steps unfriendly to Italy and . . . it is not known what form Italy's action might take."[23] Perhaps readers did not know what action Italy would take, but it was evident to anyone there that Albania's "economic penetration" had already begun.

Geraldine's mother fled to Dubrovnik eighteen hours earlier, although the grandmother, Mrs. Strale d'Ekna, refused to leave and stayed with her and the baby.[24] Muriel's small group left at 3:00 p.m. on Thursday, April 6, for Scutari and its proximity to the Adriatic. On their arrival, they found it "all bedecked with pictures of the King and Queen, green garlands and Albanian flags, in honor of the Prince's birth. I reflected sadly on the ironical fate, which would probably deprive this baby of the fair heritage, where his arrival was so joyously acclaimed, almost as soon as he had entered it."[25] As the *New York Times* reported years later, "Salutes fired in honor of the birth of the Crown Prince almost blended with the sound of the guns covering the Italian advance."[26]

Muriel's little traveling party left the next morning, having enjoyed celebratory bells at their arrival and now the artillery from the sea at their departure.

> As we left Albania at about 6:00 a.m. on Good Friday morning, April 7th, we, and the excited parents, could hear the sound of heavy artillery booming from the sea. We therefore correctly assumed that this brave little country was attempting to preserve its independence and was being bombarded in consequence. Fortunately, my cruel anxiety was soon relieved by the welcome news that the young Queen's terrible ordeal had not injured her health and that King Zog had joined her in Greece. As Queen Geraldine's whole happiness is centred in her husband and her son, those who love her can only thank a merciful Providence that her fate is no worse.[27]

Muriel later learned that the back seat of a limousine had been removed so that Geraldine and her three-day-old son could lie on a mattress as the car traversed dangerous rocky roads taken to avoid detection. The doctor who had delivered her son had made the necessary incision to allow a Caesarean birth, and, with good reason, there was fear that the difficult escape might prove fatal for her. As the car was about to leave, the king, who tried to stay as long as possible, "bent and kissed the baby on the head. His last words to the Queen were, 'Oh, God . . . It was so short.' The Queen replied, 'God bless you.'"[28] "So hasty was the departure that Geraldine left Tirana in only the nightgown she wore—the maid had packed her furs but overlooked the need for dresses and underwear."[29] When the king finally escaped, despite years of intrigue and machinations, he would never again set foot in Albania, although his wife and son would.

The same Count Ciano, son-in-law of Benito Mussolini, who figured so prominently in the wedding photographs of the king and queen, had been making plans for the Italian takeover of Albania. He knew that Geraldine was very near her due date and confided to his journal on March 25, 1939,

> It is not possible to foresee what will be the development of events but it seems probable to me that Zog will yield. I am counting on the birth of his child. Zog loves his wife and in general all his family. I think that he will prefer to ensure a quiet future for his dear ones. And, frankly, I cannot imagine Geraldine running around fighting through the mountains of Unthi or of Mirdizu in her ninth month of pregnancy.[30]

Count Ciano was furious, then, when Geraldine, Zog, their newborn son, and the entire royal family escaped just before his arrival at the palace. He went immediately to the queen's suite, where he found the birthing room and "saw linen that indicated a birth, and a hasty departure. Kicking the linen across the room, Ciano exclaimed, 'The cub has escaped!'"[31]

Despite protestations that annexation was not their goal, the Italians militarily occupied Albania in 1939. Italy coveted the port of Vlora and the island of Sazan at the entrance to the Bay of Vlora, as these positions would guarantee Italy control of the Adriatic Sea, thus affording a base for Italian military operations in the Balkans.[32] Mussolini's invading forces faced very little resistance. King Victor Emmanuel III proclaimed himself king of the Albanians on September 16, 1939, having already, in 1936, claimed the throne of Ethiopia. In 1940, Mussolini used Albania as a staging ground for his unsuccessful invasion of Greece.

In 1943, King Victor Emmanuel III deposed Mussolini and signed an armistice with the Allies. Facing a German invasion, the king and his government then fled to Brindisi. With few options left, Victor Emmanuel switched strategies and declared war on Germany. In a last-ditch effort to save his throne, in 1946, he abdicated in favor of his son (who became King Umberto II) and escaped into exile in Egypt, where he died that same year.[33] After the end of World War II, Albania became a Communist satellite state of the Soviet Union, with Enver Hoxha as its new leader.[34] Viscount Harcourt, who was stationed at Tirana, thought Hoxha "a fat, pudgy, self-indulgent fellow with pink and white face. He speaks good French but has a nasty way about him." He told US reporter Cyrus Sulzberger that "it was decided in the end to back Hoxha because his outfit appeared to be the best of a very bad lot."[35]

Unable to reclaim the throne, King Zog, Queen Geraldine, and Prince Leka lived a peripatetic life, traveling from country to country. In 1939, Geraldine received a serious offer from an American film company to act in Hollywood. It received so much attention that her family attorney, Count Imre Hunyor, issued a public statement that Queen Geraldine would not be accepting the movie offer, nor would King Zog be embarking on an American speaking tour as reported.[36] Zog indeed had far greater concerns on his mind. He was heavily burdened by the large court he was forced to support, including his six sisters who felt entitled to his largesse as their birthright. Hotel reservations required at least twenty-five rooms, and "full court etiquette was observed."[37] The sisters also insisted on their superiority to Queen Geraldine. When Leka was small, he developed pneumonia and bronchitis and was seriously ill. The sisters "were convinced that he had caught tuberculosis from Gyula [Geraldine's brother]."[38] They blamed her for endangering the health of the heir by allowing the two to play together. Her brother, never healthy, would die of tuberculosis in 1946, in Aix-en-Provence, at the age of twenty-two.

Guy Girault, Queen Geraldine's half-brother, recalls that he and his family "fled from Tirana [Albania] to Dubrovnik then Klagenfurt [Austria] where Muriel and Manni had a castle." When they arrived there, "Muriel begged them to flee again because the Gestapo was threatening her and she was afraid the Gestapo could catch them and send them to concentration camps."[39]

Queen Geraldine's sister, Virginia de Baghy, widowed at twenty-four, reportedly worked actively in World War II "alongside Raoul Wallenberg . . . and on March 19, 1944, the Gestapo dragged her from her house in Buda Castle. As punishment for her activity in rescuing Jews, Virginia was then deported to Mauthausen, from where she could escape only after the intervention of a relative, Prince Karl Anton de Rohan."[40] However, her son, Count André de Baghy, disputes that account, saying she was never sent to a prison camp.[41] The truth is probably somewhere in the middle, as a declassified CIA document from 1949 reveals that she "worked with G-2 [the US government's military intelligence unit] in Hungary during the war. She is in very poor physical and mental shape as a result of her wartime experiences with the Nazis in Hungary."[42]

Queen Geraldine was present at St. Joseph's Catholic Church in Cairo on February 10, 1947, when Virginia married Joseph B. Blackburn (1921–1963), district manager of TWA Airline's Egypt office.[43] Blackburn had served in the US military and supported the family for several years while they lived in Tunisia. At the suggestion of the Countess of Darnley, Virginia's son, André, was sent to boarding school at Broadstairs and then to the elite Gordonstoun, where Prince Philip, Duke of Edinburgh, and his three sons and two grandchildren were all educated. André's time at Gordonstoun overlapped with that of Alexander, Crown Prince of Yugoslavia.

Virginia and her second husband had a daughter, Eleanor Virginia, and a son, Joseph Apponyi, both born in 1948, eleven months apart. In 1949, the family moved to Colorado, where she filed a petition for naturalization as a US citizen, listing her occupation as "housewife."[44] Then, in 1953, Virginia, her husband, and her two de Baghy children by her first marriage (who were listed as "stateless") arrived in New York from Cherbourg on the RMS *Queen Mary*. Joseph Blackburn died on March 19, 1963, and was buried in Pittsburgh.

Widowed again, Virginia married a final time in Munich, Germany, on January 15, 1971, Joseph Markus Máriássy de Márkus et Batizfalva (1914–1989). It was a marriage her son termed "a mistake," as she had known him when he was much younger. "At the time, she didn't really have a balanced life and she thought it would be a good thing to marry him. . . . Even though he seemed like a very nice guy they didn't stay together very long and she then moved to live with Geraldine."[45] Virginia remained very close to her sister and died only two weeks after Geraldine on November 5, 2002, in Budapest. As her son recalled, "They were inseparable. . . . It is amazing that when the two sisters were separated they couldn't continue to live."[46] Virginia's body was returned to Baghymajor in Hungary, where she first married and became a mother.

Geraldine and Virginia's devoted and loyal American-born grandmother, Mrs. Strale d'Ekna, became an author, writing crime fiction and screenplays. Muriel's son-in-law, Ted Church, wrote uncharitably of her in 1949, "She has a vivid imagination and has just written a book on Zog she wants to sell to the movies." In another memo, he called her "just an old lady with a vivid imagination" and reported that King Zog sent her a monthly check of $115.[47] She died in New York City on January 30, 1950.

And what of King Zog's plans for a dynasty? They came to naught. "He's dreaming of a white uniform. . . . He came from nowhere. Now he has nowhere to go. Morose, sullen and bored he wanders along English country lanes with his bodyguard dreaming of pageantry and power. Because once this strange, pathetic individual was a king," reported the *Sunday Pictorial*.[48]

Fortunately for King Zog, in his flight he had not only taken what funds were left from the sale of his family's lands (about £50,000) but also carried off substantial amounts of the Albanian treasury's gold from the National Bank of Tirana and Durrës.[49] His nephew, André de Baghy, recalled playing in his sandbox as a little boy. He uncovered something very shiny, and his mother came over to see what he had found. It was gold coins, obviously hidden there by someone in Zog's entourage. "That saved us for a while . . . since we didn't have very much," he said.[50] "When we left Hungary she [Geraldine] was very helpful to us. . . . We ended up going to Egypt where Zog was stranded."[51]

Queen Geraldine and Muriel Seherr-Thoss tried to remain in touch, but World War II made communication difficult long before Muriel's death behind enemy lines in 1943. Muriel sent coded letters through her brother, who, as a diplomat, had access to private mail pouches. She referred to Geraldine as "G" or "My Dearest." In 1940, she wrote to him, "If you have any news of G.'s whereabouts please let me know. Over a month ago, I applied for a visa to visit her sister in Hungary."[52] The next year she wrote to him, evidently after receiving funds from King Zog, "I wonder if you have heard any more as to G.'s whereabouts? But for her husband's gift I should have been nicely in the soup and all I ever did for her has been amply repaid to me."[53] Muriel further let her brother know, in July, that she had "found another & nearer means of communication with G" but didn't elaborate.[54] Later that same year she wrote, still wary of identifying locations,

> I was very happy to receive a letter from "Dearest" recently, sent on by my Margaret. Fortunately she & all her large family have moved to a nice little country home. Her little boy is the one bright spot in his parents' lives. I am more than thankful that they decided to move that dear child to the country for I feel sure that the climate there will be far more healthy for them all than in the city where you first saw the light.[55]

Muriel's family would later reenter Albania's political sphere at the behest of the US government in an important way through her son-in-law. Margaret's husband, Ted Church, was an attorney, and CIA documents from 1949, declassified in 2007, attest that he represented King Zog in the United States. He kept the CIA fully briefed through Lyman B. Kirkpatrick (1916–1995), inspector general and executive director of the agency. As Church wrote at the time, "My influence with Zog is through [Queen] Geraldine and his [Zog's] gratitude to my late mother-in-law."[56] The description of Ted in the agency's internal file included these observations:

> Is judged to be a hard worker, cooperative, willing and conscientious, easy to get along with. Is neat and presentable in appearance. No sign of nervousness. Seems to be a very good man but not classed in "creative-imaginative" bracket. Claims to know Switzerland well. Has travelled for pleasure in Italy, North Spain, England, Corsica. Claims

to know French Riviera well. Speaks French good although not perfect. Also speaks fair German.[57]

After Zog's exile and the Italian takeover of Albania, the Office of Strategic Services (OSS), forerunner of the CIA,[58] had made a policy decision:

> Because resistance groups spent most of their time and effort fighting each other, OSS policy was to limit the supply of weapons and ammunition provided to any one faction. By November 1943, the Communist National Liberation Front (FNC) controlled most of the country and was the only effective force known to the Allies.[59]

As conditions worsened in various countries where they had fled as refugees, Zog's large group would be forced, once again, to pack up and try to find favorable countries whose governments would grant them safe passage. They fled to France but had to escape when Hitler's forces invaded in 1940. They were helped to England by Ian Fleming, author of the James Bond books, who was then a young naval officer. As a contemporary of Fleming recalled,

> From time to time German bombers came, but nothing stopped the evacuation, and by dusk nearly all refugees were away. Then came a coup de théâtre. The last boat was nearly filled when motor-horns were heard in the distance; and over the cobblestones rolled a cavalcade of enormous motor cars carrying King Zog of Albania, his family, and mountains of luggage, including the crown jewels of Albania. Somehow, Fleming managed to get the royal party safely off.[60]

After the Italian invasion of Albania on April 7, 1939, the British government accepted the annexation while "the United States . . . following the Wilsonian principles of respect for democracy, sovereignty, liberty, and self-determination, considered Albania a victim of Axis aggression and withdrew its mission to Tirana."[61] At the beginning of World War II, "the U.S. and its British allies encouraged and supported the resistance of the Albanian people against Fascist and Nazi forces of occupation."[62]

Many viewed Albania, after the Italian takeover and the advent of Communist rule, as having been abandoned by both the United States and Great Britain. One critic found it "a totally unnecessary sacrifice to Soviet Imperialism. It was British initiative, British arms and money that nurtured Albanian resistance in 1943, just as it was British policy in 1944 that surrendered to a hostile power our influence, our honour and our friends."[63]

It was not until after the war that, finally, the two great powers decided to collaborate.

> Operation BGFIEND began as a British enterprise. Sanctioned by Whitehall in February 1949, it was aimed at displacing Hoxha with the exiled Albanian King Zog, thereby enhancing Britain's position as a political force in the eastern Mediterranean. What stood between London and the fulfilment of these aims was money, or more accurately the lack of it. It was with these considerations in mind that MI6 and the British Foreign Office lobbied CIA and State Department officials to secure American financial backing for the project.[64]

That joint program called BGFIEND (later known as OBOPUS) was the framework for enlisting the assistance of Muriel's son-in-law, Ted Church. The stated goal was "a country project for the purpose of selecting, training, and infiltrating indigenous agents into Albania to effect and support resistance activities for the purpose of overthrowing the Communist controlled government in Tirana."[65] There were many problems with its implementation, which began in 1949. For example, a declassified document boasted about having dropped from aircraft three million leaflets in Albania,[66] but "80 percent of the Albanian populace was illiterate . . . [and the] launch of the short-lived Radio Free Albania proved equally futile, given that the country had little in the way of electricity and very few radio sets or batteries."

A long and acerbic memorandum declassified by the CIA in 2007 detailed a week-long trip Ted Church made to Egypt to visit King Zog and Queen Geraldine at the home they were building (and eventually had to abandon) at 16 Rue Ekbal, Ramleh, Alexandria. The queen personally showed him the site as well as the accommodations then being provided to them by King Farouk. Despite his in-laws' relationship with the royal family, Church cast aspersions on virtually everyone connected with the Albanian royal couple, including accusations of incest within the court. His comments were misogynist and bordered on racist. One of the few who received faint praise was a palace courtier of whom Church wrote, "He is a clean-cut (as Albanians go), good-looking military individual and relatively honest." Of another, Church wrote that "he is a slick individual and entirely crooked. In former years he used to smuggle dope to France in the diplomatic pouch."[67]

Even Margaret, as his wife and conduit to Zog and Geraldine, did not escape his criticism. Ted wrote of her, "My wife is a fine girl but can not help talking about anything she know [*sic*], so do not say anything to her which you do not wish repeated. Her brothers, both US citizens, are even more indiscreet."[68] He insisted that

> Zog can be handled . . . he should be separated from the female influence [his sisters] and made to think that he is heading up some military project towards the liberation of Albania. Then he can be handled easily. He is "chafing at the bit" to go back and fight for Albania and told me that he would return in any capacity in which his people wanted him. He further has said he would submit to a plebiscite and would bow out if defeated.

Because of Zog's continuing lack of funds, Church reported that the king's "black market operator" was trying "to get the remaining $750,000 of Zog's gold out of Egypt."[69] Yet he reported that Queen Geraldine asked him to order a "seven-passenger Cadillac limousine" and gave him the name of the court official who would arrange for payment. He also claimed that the king entrusted him "with closing $120,000 in the bank on behalf of his wife and son."[70]

On Monday, May 2, 1949, Ted Church visited the CIA offices in Washington to report on his trip to Egypt.[71] He was taken to meet with Frank G. Wisner. It seems probable that Church would have known Wisner, who had served in the OSS and was one of the founding officers of the CIA. The men were exact contemporaries, both born in 1909, and both attorneys. Directly out of law school at the University of Virginia,

Wisner worked for the Wall Street law firm Carter, Ledyard & Milburn, while Church worked for Simpson, Thacher & Bartlett, another old and established New York law firm founded in 1884. Church later moved to Shearman, Sterling & Wright, a different firm known for its transatlantic regulatory expertise.

In setting up the meeting, a declassified document that redacted the name of the sender and the recipient noted of Ted Church:

> He has not sought employment from the CIA or any other state agency, but has expressed his readiness [for] as many opportunities as are presented to him. He was brought to meet me by Mr. Prescott Childs, after hearing Mr. Church's story he let him know that the OPC [Office of Policy Coordination] and OSO [Office of Special Operations] would like to connect and speak with him directly. At the moment I do not believe that OSO has contacted him, but I have referred his name to (deleted) and (deleted) as well as the information in question, should OSO be interested.

Although Church wasn't asking to be hired by the CIA, the memo does not deny that he might formerly have worked with the OSS. Other documents make it clear that Frank Wisner was the principal in the meeting, and he may have known Church from their OSS days. If Ted Church worked for the OSS, it seems likely that Wisner would have been his handler. Wisner's first station assignment was Cairo, and he later was head of the OSS office in Bucharest. Wisner eventually became head of OSS operations in southeastern Europe and played a major role in CIA operations throughout the 1950s. Wisner is remembered as having organized "the first state-sponsored propaganda network in the United States . . . designed to create a positive picture of capitalism versus the deprivation and want caused by communism in eastern Europe."[72] But Wisner's work as a covert intelligence officer took a serious toll. He suffered a breakdown in 1958, retired from the CIA in 1962, and committed suicide in 1965 with his son's gun.[73] Wisner's work in Hungary certainly would have brought him into contact with Queen Geraldine's sister, Virginia, who was cooperating there with US military intelligence's G-2 unit during the war, and possibly with Geraldine herself.

One month after Ted Church's visit to the CIA offices, Colonel (later Major General) Robert A. Schow, who would become the US Army's chief intelligence officer, knew about Ted "and brought a letter over for the DCI's signature, addressed to Mr. Church. Director has reply to this letter which he will give to Col. Schow this afternoon."[74]

It seems highly unlikely that the attention and access given to Ted Church at that level would have been afforded to someone with whom they had no experience. Church was a longtime member of the Council on Foreign Relations, and, in 1953–1954, he participated in a "think tank" group to study the theory of international relations. When that report was finally published, the editor noted that he did not include any biographical information about Church and one other member "because of difficulties tracing their histories."[75] There remains a remarkable dearth of available information about Church and his professional career, leading to the speculation that it could only have been erased with covert assistance.

Regardless of whether Muriel's son-in-law ever worked for the OSS,[76] it is puzzling that he was so contemptuous of a family whose interests he represented in the United States, and even more so because of his wife's long family relationship with Queen Geraldine. One member of that family posits that Church may have been jealous of his wife's family, their social standing, and their affluence. His wife was a countess, and her grandfather was one of the nation's most respected diplomats. It would have been difficult to live up to that standard, even for someone who earned two degrees from Yale after graduating from the revered St. George's School in Newport that turned out Astors, Pells, and Vanderbilts. His apparent resentment and repeated insults throughout his report to the CIA seem designed to position himself as their best avenue to King Zog. As one CIA report asserted, "Church claims that Zogu has a lot of faith in him and is attentive to his advice and recommendations."[77]

Even allowing for his personal prejudices, several of Church's assertions are patently untrue and call into question the veracity of much of what he said. Yet his report was judged by the CIA to be "most likely true information." For example, he claimed that in 1947 Geraldine's sister,

Virginia, "made a personal visit to Rome and had an audience with the Pope." He gave two possible reasons:

> Either the Queen or the King wished to obtain a divorce, or it may be that the Queen was upset over the lack of Catholic education for her son in view of the King's strict Mohammedanism. I am inclined to think that should a divorce occur it would be more from the King's desire than those of his wife. I believe she feels that she is better off under the present circumstances as his wife than she would be as a divorced woman living in America on a small income.[78]

There is no evidence that the royal couple contemplated divorce—particularly as early as 1947—and the issue of religion had been satisfactorily addressed before the marriage. A different memo suggested that it was the king's sisters who were sent to Rome to meet with the pope on his behalf, despite the fact that they were Muslim. Had such an emissary been sent to the Vatican, it certainly would have been an official representative. Queen Geraldine had several prominent Catholics in her family, including a member of the prestigious Order of Malta, and they would have been far more likely emissaries if she were contemplating such a drastic course of action. Her friend and attorney, Dr. Imre Hunyor, who provided the Hungarian band for her wedding, was Catholic and would have been the logical choice.

Church's most scurrilous charges relate to sexual matters. He indicates that Count Alexander De Villa, the king's financial aide, "is used more or less as an attendant upon his wife [Geraldine]." The second and more blatant charge concerns one of the king's sisters: "I was told by the queen indirectly and by her sister, Virginia, very directly, that Xeneia [also spelled Senijé] has a very great influence on Zog indeed. It is quite obvious and apparent that Zog is living with his sister as man and wife." Later in his report, he notes that he was given by Queen Geraldine a personal tour of the new residence they were building and that "all of the sisters . . . with the exception of Xeneia, will live in another house approximately 300 yards away from this residence. As it is now arranged, Xeneia will occupy quarters immediately adjacent to Zog and the queen will occupy quarters somewhat removed from the king." At the time these documents were declassified by the CIA in 2007, the charge of incest was widely reported.

And what does Church report as Queen Geraldine's response to such an explosive charge? Ted claimed, "Geraldine knows about this [the alleged incestuous affair], but loves Zog deeply and laughs the situation off." Church would have had his handlers believe that Geraldine sent an emissary to the pope about a possible divorce and yet acknowledged that she "loves Zog deeply." Almost as an afterthought, Church also claimed that De Villa "is reputed to have been brought into the court to entertain and be a lover for Geraldine while Zog was having an affair with Zeneia. I do not believe this as Geraldine is . . . entirely devoted to Zog in spite of his infidelity."

Later that year, the CIA was still in direct communication with Ted Church. In response to further inquiries from the director, former OSS agent Lyman P. Kirkpatrick compiled a written report and summary about Church and Albania submitted to the director on September 19, 1949.[79] The Albania report was marked "EYES ALONE" and included handwritten notations and additions to Church's original report. One can assume they would not still have been in direct contact with him without reason.

Ted Church and Countess Margaret Seherr-Thoss divorced in 1959, and he married at least twice more. One of his stepsons from those years recalled him as

> just a terrible example of old-male misanthropic/homophobic/racist/xenophobic virus. Ted was a good embodiment of that last generation of men who didn't sense that their gender's time at the helm was ending. That he could feel completely secure in his role of societal villain speaks as much about where we were in his masculine post-war era as his own ethical compass.[80]

If Ted Church thought he would benefit financially from his peregrinations on behalf of King Zog, he was mistaken. There is no indication that Church was involved in Zog's purchase of an extensive estate on the Gold Coast of New York's Long Island. Knollwood was a sixty-room mansion on 260 acres of land located in Muttontown. King Zog purchased it in 1951 with what was reported to be "a bucket of diamonds and rubies" but actually was $105,000. The king intended to bring his extended family and entourage there, farming the land and living independently. The rumor that jewels were buried on the property brought scavengers and sightseers as soon as Zog's purchase was made public. He had great difficulty in securing more than one hundred visas he requested and refused to pay local property taxes because he believed his royal status gave him sovereign immunity as it had in Europe. When the property was listed for sale for an unpaid tax lien of $2,914, Zog paid the bill but never moved into the estate; it was eventually demolished because of safety concerns. Zog's attorney was listed as Borris M. Komar rather than Ted Church.[81] That same year, Zog hired a Boston press agent, William Frary von Blomberg, "to aid in meeting 'helpful' State Department officials . . . and others who might be 'helpful' to the monarch in exile."[82] There is no mention of Ted Church despite his claims to be the king's representative in the United States.

Zog's plans to recapture the Albanian throne came to naught. In fact, he never saw Albania again after his escape. He wanted to ensure his son's claims, however, and,

> in 1960, in the Bristol Hotel in Paris, Prince Leka was consecrated King before seventy representatives of Albanian groups throughout the world. Although Leka had spent only three days on Albanian soil, he had been brought up in an Albanian household, attended to by Albanian instructors and nurtured on the idea that he was of nobility, a prince who one day would ascend to the throne.[83]

As Leka's first cousin, Count André de Baghy, recalled, Zog "brought up his son as the future King of Albania. He was great friends with King Saud of Saudi Arabia who took care of him financially."[84]

While in exile in Egypt, the former king and queen of Italy lived in close proximity to the former king and queen of Albania. In fact, Geraldine became very dear to the former queen Giovanna of Bulgaria, who in 1930 had married Boris III in a ceremony attended by Mussolini. Boris died under suspicious circumstances just after a stormy meeting with Hitler, when Boris refused to send Bulgarian Jews to death camps in Poland and Germany and also declined Hitler's order to declare war against the Soviet Union. Giovanna was a daughter of the same King Victor Emmanuel III of Italy who overran Albania and forced King Zog into exile. Geraldine's nephew recalled, "Giovanna apologized to Geraldine for what her father had done and the two became close friends."[85] Ted Church agreed in his submission to the CIA, although, true to form, he had to add an insult at the end of his report:

> The Queen's closest non-family friend is the Queen of Bulgaria, Giovanna. The Queen of Bulgaria and the Queen of Albania generally have tea together at least three times a week, and I know from having talked to the Queen of Bulgaria that she is very fond of Geraldine. The Queen of Bulgaria, being older than Geraldine, is in a position to help her and advise her with respect to many personal problems that Geraldine is faced with as the wife of Zog. I received the distinct impression that Giovanna is more intelligent than she looks or appears to be.[86]

After King Zog's death in 1961, Queen Geraldine lived in South Africa until she was invited to return to Albania after the law that had previously blocked her entrance was changed. She died five months later, in 2002, at the age of eighty-seven, in Tirana's military hospital. Though Muriel did not live to see Geraldine's adult legacy, she would have been proud of her ward's accomplishments. Geraldine's grandson, Crown Prince Leka, in 2004, accepted on her behalf the Mother Teresa Medal awarded to her in recognition of her charitable work on behalf of Albania's people. In 2020, the crown prince's child, born in the Queen Geraldine Maternity Hospital in Tirana, was named Geraldine in her honor. Queen Geraldine's memory is still cherished in Albania. A successful exhibition about her life was held in 2017 and 2018 at the Hungarian National Museum, where she once worked. She was the only queen of Albania.[87] Her descendants have remained close to the family of Geraldine's sister, Virginia.

Chapter Eight

The count [Manni] must have known that his wife was hiding American pilots on the estate, whose planes crashed near Dobra. Was Muriel so independent that she did it regardless of her husband's opinion? But if the count tolerated all this, if he supported his wife's activities, why didn't he protect her from Gestapo pressure? Why didn't he prevent her suicide?[1]

—Jolanta Ilnicka

Muriel had always been liked by her staff and servants. Her renovations to Rosnochau and Dobrau made their work easier and more efficient, especially because they no longer had to carry water into the house from outside wells. She learned enough Polish to be able to speak with them in their language and allowed them to have access, with their families, to walk in the private park on weekends.[2]

Muriel became close to her head chef, Albina Jenek, who told her own granddaughter, Jolanta Ilnicka, "many stories about the war, and . . . to write down the specifics in detail . . . you must know what happened, and maybe someday some of the Countess's family will come, wanting to know the truth of what happened."[3] Jolanta recalled, "I remember from childhood the stories of my father's sister, Aunt Agnieszka, about the beautiful ballroom in the count's castle, where Christmas breakfasts were eaten, to which all the servants were invited. And how beautifully it was decorated about the large crystal chandelier hanging above the table."[4]

Albina at first worked on the farm, but one day Manni's mother, the dowager countess, "notices her and, delighted with the girl's beauty, ordered her to be transferred to work in the palace. 'Such a beautiful girl will not take care of cows,' said the Countess. This is how my grandmother Balbina's [the grandchildren's name for Albina] career in the court kitchen began. With time she became the boss. . . . The cruel times of the war brought together a 40 year-old cook and a 60 year-old Muriel."[5]

Manni "was not indifferent to [Albina's] beauty." In fact, "her relations with Count Seherr-Thoss were not only purely business."[6] Manni approached his stable groom, "saying, it is time that you marry, and I have chosen a good wife for you. Immediately after, the couple were wed."[7] Albina, pregnant at twenty-one, with her new husband "lived in a house next to the palace. She is liked by the Seherr-Thoss family and often receives gifts from the Count and his wife, Muriel. Balbina's children often stay in the palace kitchen and, like children, they roam the palace chambers."[8] Albina's oldest son, Jan, "is forced to go to war (my mother claimed that my grandmother said that it was the count who personally told him to join the army). He never returned to his mother."[9] As Jolanta Ilnicki explained, "Grandma received some kind of notification but I don't know if it said that he was dead or that he was missing. Grandma looked for him long after the war but didn't find him."[10]

Although Muriel's sons were safely out of harm's way in the United States, Manni was not. The medical deferment he had received either came to an end or was cancelled when more troops were needed, and he was ordered to report for service. Muriel had been living as his unpaid chatelaine since their divorce, and there is a strong possibility that the woman who would become his second wife was at Dobrau as well while her husband was away at war.[11] Despite the fraught relationship, Muriel's great-grandson recalled reading a letter describing "a respectful point of acceptance" between Muriel and Manni in their last days together. They were "sitting before the fire in the great Saal [great hall]—she is writing, he is reading. . . . Muriel wrote, 'It's as if we are living in the Book of Revelation.'"[12]

Boysie said that his mother's days were chiefly spent "writing letters to her friends. Politics was of great interest to her. Politics was discussed every day and the future of the world."[13] He recalled a particularly telling anecdote about his parents during the time they were divorced but both living at Dobrau. His mother wrote about it to him in one of the last letters he received before her death.

> This will tell you exactly how my mother felt. During the war, they were taking a walk with their dog, Mingo. My mother said to my father, "Put Mingo on the leash because we are going to pass the gardener's cottage and he has a bitch in heat and a very jealous mate." Your father said, "Mingo can take care of himself." Mingo went into the bushes and came back two hours later to the house bleeding and limping. My mother said to my father, "Another classical example of your father's and his countrymen's inability to deduce the possibilities from the existing facts."[14]

Muriel had certainly heard that opinion before. Her father had written to her as early as 1920, "It is a pity that Manni does not listen to you in respect to people and things but . . . he has not a good appreciation of cause and effect."[15]

Nevertheless, now it was left to Muriel to do for her former husband what she had done for their sons. Margaret told her own grandson that Muriel "devised a plan to get Hermann [Manni] out of Silesia to Krastowitz-Herzoghof to protect him from being forced into military service and to distract them from the SS. He was to be buried in a hay wagon with a supply of water, clothes, and food and driven over the Tatra mountains. This was successful. I believe Jolanta Ilnicka's grandfather had a direct role as at least one of the two drivers."[16]

But as Manni made his way to safety, due entirely to Muriel's efforts, she was left alone to protect and care for the estate and the families who depended on her. In Muriel's last year, she "barely went out of the house for months due to soldiers all surrounding the place, she wrapped herself in peasant clothes to go out to feed and pet the goats. . . . She couldn't leave and she cared deeply for the staff and stewards who cared for her."[17]

In 1941, she had helped two British pilots escape from Łambinowice, the prisoner-of-war camp built within sight of the castle. "To this day it is not known what their fate was."[18] That escape put Muriel directly in the crosshairs of the authorities. After she arranged for her sons to be sent to the United States, "the visits and threats addressed to her by Gestapo officers led her to extreme depression."[19]

Muriel's depression was not new. In 1925, she wrote to her aunt, "You were so cheerful and gay that I never would have thought you suffered from low spirits. I have the deepest sympathy for you & for anyone who suffers in that way since I had this nervous breakdown myself. Personally when I am with gay cheerful people I am all right but when I am lonely or dull then I feel like drowning myself."[20]

As the Gestapo noose tightened, she expended great time and effort in an attempt to regain her American citizenship, which she had lost due to her marriage to Manni. One advantage of her divorce was that it made it possible for her to begin the lengthy endeavor to do so. Early in the process,

> one friend feared I would, at no very future date, no longer be able to receive the protection of my own country and that it would be a good thing for me if I had another passport and nationality as well as Uncle Sam's. I thereupon confided to him that I had applied in May at the Albanian Ministry in Rome for recognition by the Italian government of the Albanian citizenship conferred on me by King Zog. Also for a new Albanian passport.[21]

Muriel's efforts to regain her US citizenship and passport would end in a Pyrrhic victory. She learned that her efforts to have Manni legally emigrate to the United States as her husband had been approved in 1940 (after their divorce, although American officials may not have known about it), but "the consulate and all its records were destroyed during the bombardment of Rotterdam on May 14, 1940," so she was instructed to begin again. Because applicants must show "financial means of subsistence" in order to emigrate to the United States, she had noted on her original application that her attorney, Lewis S. Morris, could confirm that he held "a trust by which Manni benefits in the event of my death."[22] The American embassy in Vienna issued her new passport on February 14, 1941, but it was subsequently "detained by the German authorities" and came too late.[23]

Cut off from her family in the United States, correspondence was rare and, even then, usually passed through a diplomatic pouch among the family's contacts. Muriel learned that her first grandchild, Alanson Church, was born on July 18, 1940, near the same date as Albina's younger son, Ginter. Muriel "never saw her grandson, because he was in the USA and the countess could not go there. So she came to grandma and looked after [Ginter]. She brought him clothes, toys, and went for walks. She often said it was her son and asked my mother to give him back to her. Granny, of course, didn't want to hear about it."[24]

Albina, her chef, became her close friend and ally. Muriel often told Albina "how afraid she was that the Gestapo would arrest her and take her to Auschwitz for hiding her sons and helping American prisoners of war. She was afraid to go out to the palace gardens because she claimed that someone was following her."[25] She did not want her sons to become soldiers of the Nazi army.[26]

Muriel had never met her cousin, Henry J. White. "Imagine my surprise when I received a letter from our cousin & the namesake of our dear father, Lt. Commander Henry White, who is now attached to the American Embassy in the Capital of this country [Berlin]. We have been corresponding & I should like to meet him,"[27] she wrote to her brother. A US Naval Academy graduate, White qualified as a pilot at the age of nineteen when his license was signed by Orville Wright. He also instructed Charles Lindbergh in seaplane operations. When White was appointed assistant naval air attaché at the US embassy in Berlin in April 1940, he wrote to Muriel, and even after he was interned as a prisoner, their correspondence flourished. He recalled, "She sent me 2 kilos of bacon and a complete set of Trollope. I might add that the former was considerably more to my taste than the latter."[28]

They discussed getting together, but Muriel responded "that she wouldn't dare to make any move, in view of the low regard with which the National Socialist authorities looked upon her and her husband. The same letter contained what seemed to me very indiscreet aspersions on the German Government." When he suggested that Manni should "feel out the authorities on the subject . . . [h]er answer . . . made it perfectly plain that he would be risking his life were he to intervene in a matter of that kind, and it left me the impression that he might be up to something which in the Nazi mind might well be skullduggery."[29]

As Muriel waited at Dobrau without any immediate family or support except her few remaining female servants, she knew she had done all she could. Her three children were safe in America, although on January 15, 1943, Germany officially seized the property of Marian and Boysie and revoked their citizenship.[30] Muriel had made arrangements for the escape of her ex-husband. She knew what was coming. "The Gestapo . . . threatened her with a concentration camp if her sons living in America were not brought to Germany."[31] Muriel told a friend,

> She was hounded by the Gestapo, which during the war visited her very often in the palace. Officers of the secret police demanded that she bring her children back to the Third Reich. The Countess claimed that she was being followed and that there were strangers in the garden—that's why she spent most of her time in the palace chambers. Her biggest fear was being deported to a concentration camp.[32]

"On the morning of the last day of her life, Muriel was agitated and asked those in Dobrau to review their strategies and drills with her for taking shelter in nearby places in the immediate surroundings. They assured her that they were ready if necessary. Muriel said she was likely to be leaving soon, that something was unfolding. They urged her not to worry."[33]

Muriel's instincts were correct. On March 13, 1943, the moment she had been dreading was literally at her door. She knew that even strong men were unable to survive their treatment at concentration camps, and she had no intention of seeing what would happen to a woman they suspected of treason against Germany. Her family would be spared their fear of knowing she was imprisoned. Everything had been left for her to shoulder alone. Other than Albina and a few loyal staff members, there was no one left to protect. Her decision was made, her conscience was clear. "Seeing the Gestapo men approaching, the countess threw herself from the highest floor of the palace. This event was witnessed by the personal governess and seamstress, who tried to resuscitate the countess, but to no avail."[34]

Muriel was sixty-two and had spent more than half her life in a country she came to despise. As she wrote, "I have never known a nation so undeservedly cried up as the Germans. They are hard workers but I consider them singularly devoid of altruism and any nobler sentiments! All they have is a certain sentimentality. God knows how bitterly I rue the day that I ever had anything to do with them."[35]

Muriel's great-grandson, who has visited the family schloss and the local church in Silesia, was told by locals that "the funeral was held at the family church at Dobrau with a small number of family members and staff. Many men were in service to the war or dead,"[36] so there were only women and children to mourn her passing. Gestapo officers "participated in the funeral preparations and ceremonies. They wanted a guarantee that the countess was officially dead."[37]

"The surrounding residents remembered Countess Muriel as a person sensitive to human needs. . . . During the funeral, the staff mourned the death of the Countess. On the day of the funeral the road from the palace to the church in the village was laid with red carpets."[38] Muriel was laid to rest at Johannes-der-Täufer-Kirche (Church of John the Baptist) in Dobrau, along with her husband's parents.

After the war, naval attaché Henry J. White read the published diaries of Ulrich von Hassell, a member of the German resistance against the Nazis, who was executed for his part in a plot to overthrow Hitler. White "somehow got the impression that [Manni] Seherr-Thoss might have been mixed up in the anti-Hitler activities, although he was not mentioned by name"[39] in the diaries. As a result of his "voluminous" correspondence with Muriel, White believed

> that both she and her husband were under grave suspicion of disloyalty to the Nazi government. . . . All in all, I was in no way surprised to hear that Muriel had suffered a violent and mysterious death, and it is a distinct surprise that her husband lived through the whole thing. More than likely, he was unable to take any active part in far-off Silesia and thus avoided the fate of von Hasselt [sic] by little more than a hair's breadth.[40]

With the perspective of several years, after the war, White's final analysis was that he could "certainly affirm that she was not only anti-Nazi, but of an almost incredible, though courageous indiscretion. She was also very kind to a distant cousin, and I'm sure this kindness may have contributed to her sad end. Her husband's survival I can only attribute to a larger measure of discretion on his part."[41] Of course Manni's escape was due much more to Muriel's actions in smuggling him out of the country than to his own discretion.

The official government report of Muriel's death was filed with the American Foreign Service on April 15, 1943, one month later, with the Swiss Legation in Berlin, who were "in charge of American interests" since there was no US embassy in Germany. The cause of death was listed as "fraction of the skull," and her personal effects were "in custody of divorced husband Count von Seherr-Thoss" at Dobrau. Manni requested that his daughter, Margaret, be informed, and he was again referred to in the document as Muriel's "divorced husband." Perhaps the most important detail was "the passport No. 12 of the deceased, issued on February 14, 1941, by the American Consulate General, Vienna, has been detained by the German authorities. Steps have, however, been taken to get hold of the passport which, if and when returned, will be forwarded in due course."[42] So Muriel died an American citizen. She should have been able to rely on her government's protection and leave at any time after her passport was reissued in 1941—had it not been withheld by the Germans.

Notifying relatives of Muriel's death would have been difficult from behind enemy lines without the diplomatic connections of her family. Evidently the first to hear was Margaret in New York City, who learned of it from "a friend resident in England." She then notified her uncle, Jack, who on May 3 wrote a letter to the family's attorney and trustee, Lewis S. Morris, advising him of Margaret's news. He continued, "I greatly regret to inform you that my sister Muriel is dead. . . . I learned that she died on March 13th, apparently at her home." White advised Morris that he should seek official confirmation, as "I should not think it would be sufficient by itself for legal purposes—the more so as I prefer not to mention my sources."[43]

On May 5, 1943, seven weeks after Muriel's death, US Secretary of State Cordell Hull sent to Muriel's brother, Jack, the ambassador to Haiti, the following telegram:

For the Ambassador: I deeply regret to inform you that the Department has received from the Legation at Bern a telegram dated 4 May which reports the death of your sister, Muriel Seherrthoss [*sic*], on March 13th. The Swiss representatives have given the cause of death as skull fracture and the Legation has requested them for further details. Please accept my sincere sympathy.[44]

Ambassador White replied the next day, "DEEPLY APPRECIATE KIND SYMPATHY AND DEPARTMENT'S EFFORTS TO OBTAIN FURTHER INFORMATION. WHITE."[45] That same day, Jack sent to Muriel's son-in-law, Edgar Church, a cable reading, "STATE DEPARTMENT ADVISES CAUSE SKULL FRACTURE AND IS ENDEAVORING ASCERTAIN FURTHER DETAILS. WHITE."[46] On May 12, an attorney at the New York law firm that represented the trust of Muriel's mother, Daisy, wrote to the Department of State seeking official confirmation of death. That letter specifically stated that Muriel "died an American citizen, having regained her citizenship after the last war." The trust's coexecutor was Muriel's brother, John C. White.[47] In seeking permission for Manni to emigrate to the United States several years earlier, Muriel had referred to "a trust by which Manni benefits in the event of my death."[48] Evidently this was the trust to which she referred, and there was no indication that Manni had been removed as a beneficiary. Finally, as a result of an official request for more information, on June 5, 1943, the American Legation in Bern notified the US government that they "learned from a private source that Countess von Seherr-Thoss committed suicide."[49] That was ruled the official cause of death.

Margaret wrote from her home in Sharon, Connecticut, a touching letter to her Uncle Jack in response to the news:

> I still can't grasp it and somehow refuse to believe it still, although I suppose that is extremely stupid and childish of me. If one only could know what happened to her! . . . It was the most frightful blow— because I had always believed so strongly that the day would come when—after the war—we could see her again and I could show her little Alan and our home here in the country. I have the feeling that—if at all—somebody must have done something to her. It is so awful not knowing anything![50]

Margaret also expressed concern for her father, saying, "Now we will never be able to help him get out or do anything for him, and I am convinced he will be needing help soon." She informed Jack that they "had a requiem mass said for dear Mama at St. Ignatius Loyola and all her old friends and very many relations were there." Most important, she told her uncle, "Mama was *never* a trying mother for me. Everything that I can remember of her is that she always wanted to help her children to have as much as she could possibly give us—even if it meant her own deprivation and I am very glad that I always tried to spare her as much unpleasantness and sorrow as I could."[51]

Margaret appreciated the fact that her mother had continued sending small family treasures, including jewelry and Fabergé, and other gifts disguised in packages of ordinary clothes. Muriel wrote in one letter to her daughter-in-law, Marian, "The rest of the contents of the safe I put in an envelope and put them in the pocket of one of the coats sent to Margaret in her trunk. You must please both of you be very careful in unpacking. One dozen of the towels are yours from the Herzoghof and one dozen (just like them only smaller) are mine which I sent to Margaret. I have written to Adelaide in which garment your lace is stitched."[52] Margaret's grandson would later be "astounded by the amount and beauty of the jewelry my grandmother had inherited. She was very modest about it and never wore much of it. She said it made her feel uncomfortable and vulnerable. . . . There were three Fabergé brooches, two of which were given to Marian Frelinghuysen. I was with my grandmother the day Marian's chauffeur came to pick the box up."[53]

Jack White proved to be a loyal and supportive uncle to Margaret and her brothers. Their families remain close more than eighty years after Muriel's death. Jack wrote to Margaret later that month that he found on his desk an envelope from the Haitian Red Cross that contained, "in your mother's script . . . a touching message in which she shows her solicitude for your welfare. . . . It is presumably the last she ever wrote me being less than one month before her death—and I shall treasure it accordingly."[54] He included a copy for her as well as two for her brothers.

And where was Manni during this period? As Albina's granddaughter asked, "Why didn't he protect her from Gestapo pressure? Why didn't he prevent her suicide?"[55] On July 8, 1943, he sent Jack in Haiti a Red Cross message thanking him for the Christmas greetings sent to him months earlier, as well as "Our deepest sympathies for you because of Muriel's death and your loneliness. We still do not know the cause of her fatal accident."[56] Two months later, Manni wrote to Jack, "Many thanks for condolence. Am profound [sic] sad. Lost all my happiness of life. Dear Muriel was best wife and mother. Can never forget her. Manni."[57] At some point, Manni later made his way back to Dobrau and reportedly lived in one of the small cottages on the estate.

The Germans took over Dobrau as a military facility after Muriel's death. On January 17, 1945, soldiers stationed at Dobrau and the town of Opole learned that Russian forces were approaching on their way to capture Berlin. "The command of the German units guarding the ammunition warehouse near the palace ordered Count Hermann [Manni] to evacuate. The count gathered servants and workers in the courtyard. He ordered the people to take horses and carts and run away . . . the inhabitants of Opole were evacuated."[58]

And what did Manni do? "He decided to flee to Austria. The family had a chic residence near Klagenfurt. He managed to get away just before the Soviet offensive." Between January 19 and January 22, units of the First Ukrainian Front captured Opole and surrounding towns.

> Soviet soldiers took over the palace in Dobra only two days after the owner escaped. Over the next two days, the local Wehrmacht troops successfully pushed the Red Army soldiers from the estate. As a result of the fighting and heavy artillery fire, there was a fire and most of the rooms were completely burned out. There was a theory that the fire was not because of the fighting, and that it was planted by German soldiers in retaliation for Count Hermann's anti-Nazi views.[59]

After the onslaught of the Red Army, "In the cellar of Dobrau Castle we found over 30 dead women and girls from Poland and Upper Silesia who the Russians had dragged along and slaughtered before their retreat. In the village several nuns, women and girls lay violated and dead in their own blood, often with whimpering children next to them."[60] Most were buried at Klein Strehlitz (now Strzeleczki) about three miles from Dobrau.

Several servants survived the onslaught and were able to return to Dobrau and learn what had happened.

> When the Russians were advancing they [Germans] doused the carpets with fuel and tossed in a flare so the place would be uninhabitable for the Russians' use. There is a 3" × 5" picture of Dobrau taken by Hermann [Manni]. On the back of it he wrote to Muriel's brother, "Dearest Jacko, In remembrance of better times. The last time I left Dobrau. 3 hours later she was completely destroyed."[61]

How did Manni escape, and with whom? He had a wagon, and "on the way to Austria, the count took a widow with two little boys on his wagon. After the war, this woman became his second wife." She was Ursula von Hirschfeld, since 1941 the widow of Caspar, Baron von Berlepsch, whom she had married in 1932.[62] Manni supposedly had room for a few other people in the wagon.

He went to Albina's house and, according to her granddaughter, said, "Take the kids and some blankets and get in. I'm leaving for my estate in Austria. Go with me!"[63] "Albina said she was caring for sick and wounded persons and the children of some others and would not leave them."[64] According to local historians, Manni "left in a carriage drawn by two pairs of horses, only in the company of the coachman Kowolik, says Piotr Miczka, who heard this story from the Count's descendants. Hermann [Manni] left behind a handwritten gothic diary with memories of escaping from the front. He only took oats for the horses and 11 pairs of shoes for himself because he liked shoes a lot."[65]

Albina's granddaughter wonders how things might have been different: "If Grandma Balbina had not been so honorable and responsible and had gone with the count, would her story have ended similarly to that of [second wife Ursula]? Would she have 'von' before her name? What would the fate of her children and grandchildren be like? And would she be happy?"[66]

Albina and the other families at Dobrau were left to fend for themselves. "Somehow Albina and others made it to adequate points of shelter in the Park. The night sky was aglow from the conflagration. When it appeared they could return, they saw how damaged the place was."[67]

Even in death, Muriel's strife was not over. On returning to Dobrau, "Albina went to the Church of St John the Baptist to see if it was destroyed. [There was] very little damage; however, the crypt Muriel was laid in had been opened, the body removed, her fingers and wrists broken and the jewelry she was buried with taken. Albina and some others cleaned up and restored the body."[68]

With Dobrau devastated by fire, Manni remained at Klagenfurt, Austria, where he had fled to the Seherr-Thoss estate at the foot of the Alps. Only a few months after their arrival, on May 3, 1945, in order to "avoid further destruction and bloodshed," Nazi General Alexander Löhr, commanding officer of the Wehrmacht's Army Group E, agreed to declare Klagenfurt an open city, "in case Anglo-American forces should attack the city."[69] Five days later, British troops of the Eighth Army entered Klagenfurt and were met by the new democratic city and state authorities. "All the strategic positions and important buildings were immediately seized, and Major General Horatius Murray was taken to General Noeldechen for the official surrender of the 438th German Division."[70] Manni's children urged him to move to the United States. "He replied, however, that he would never leave Europe."[71]

Manni's cousin, Count André de Baghy, was a nephew of Queen Geraldine. As a young man, after the war he worked harvesting Manni's fields at Klagenfurt. He would watch Manni leave home each morning carrying a briefcase. Manni would then walk to the village ice cream shop, where he would sit all day reading newspapers. In late afternoon, he would return home with his briefcase as though he had been working all day.[72]

After the war, Manni was partially compensated for his loss of property at Dobrau, but Jack White advised him, "I do not think it would be prudent to try and secure your return to one of the two chateaux. It was already an exception to allow you to remain in Austria, an exception due to the acquiescence of the English." Obviously Muriel's family was still making allowances for him. His brother-in-law generously said in the letter, "You are without a doubt right to have remarried, and I hope you will be happy."[73]

Manni's daughter and sons in America remained extremely generous to him although they had no legal obligation to do so. They ensured that he received Muriel's share of the family trust fund and approved his wish to bequeath his estate at Klagenfurt to his second wife's two sons, Christof and Nurmie, who often used Manni's family name although he did not adopt them. "Christof inherited Herzoghof, only because Boysie and Sunny [his second wife] financed Manni's and Ursula's life, and gave Christof the deed. I was present when that conversation took place in the States after Ursula's death. Muriel and her children were extremely generous and kind people. They took their Catholic faith seriously," recalled Muriel's great-grandson, Paul Church.[74]

Manni and Ursula made multiple trips to the United States in the 1950s. In September 1955, he and Ursula sailed on the SS *United States* and were guests of his daughter, Margaret, in Connecticut. In March 1959, they sailed as first-class passengers on the *Queen Mary* when they listed their destination as "Palm Beach." Only months after the visit to Palm Beach, Manni was back home walking at Klagenfurt when he wandered onto a major highway. He was hit by a speeding car and died on November 12, 1959.[75] He was buried just outside Saint Ulrich Church in Klagenfurt, Austria, beneath a tombstone that proclaims, "Far from his beloved Silesian homeland." Ursula would join him there at her death on December 5, 1974. She had continued to be financially supported by Manni's American family, and her oldest son, Christof, would become the owner of Klagenfurt in 1975.[76]

In the generations since Muriel's death, one alternate explanation of that fateful day in 1943 has come to light. Her close childhood friend, Gertrude Schley, told Muriel's great-grandson, Paul Church, "as you are [Margaret's] oldest grandson, it is time that you know and understand the reason for [Muriel's] mysterious death. Of course it was a very difficult experience for your family, it has been rarely discussed with the younger generations for valid reasons. Muriel's death was not actually a suicide, though it could be seen as such."[77] Gertrude then told Paul Church her version of the day Muriel died:

> She was apparently sitting near a window on the ground floor of the home when a car with seven or so SS officers in black coats got out and rang the bell. She opened the door. The butler and chefin, Albina, were

nearby in the hall with some others. The men had documents showing that her sons, and daughter, as well as Hermann [Manni] had been sent elsewhere. That she had conspired with these and other escape plans involving other persons. Muriel said her children had gone rightfully to America, she didn't know where her ex-husband was, and had nothing more to tell them, that they should leave. She said she was going upstairs and went to close the door. One of them apparently stuck his boot in the doorway and said "Very well Madame, go and think about all of this, collect yourself. If you don't come down shortly we will come up for you, on this day you are going to Auschwitz."[78]

"Muriel went to the third floor and tried to get out of one of the smaller windows which went onto part of the rather flat roof of the West wing."[79] "She tried to get out onto the roof . . . to gain access to the tower. They found her struggling to get out of a window; in that struggle Muriel was either pushed or fell."[80]

Gertrude was the godmother of Muriel's oldest grandchild, Alan, and had been a family friend for decades. It is likely she would have wished to lessen the trauma and stigma attached to Muriel's suicide. She certainly would not have wanted Muriel's descendants to believe she had been condemned to hell for taking her own life, no matter how noble the reason. Gertrude was being characteristically generous.

At the time, the Catholic Church considered suicide a grave sin, as one's life is the property of God and destroying that life wrongly asserts dominion over God's creation. The church would not conduct services for Catholics who killed themselves, nor could they be buried in a Catholic cemetery. Not until the 1990s did Pope John Paul II acknowledge the role that mental illness may play in suicide. The catechism was then changed to reflect that "grave psychological disturbances, anguish, or grave fear of hardship, suffering, or torture can diminish the responsibility of the one committing suicide."[81] Muriel's cousin, Henry J. White, wrote to her brother, Jack, after the war, "We heard that Muriel had either jumped or been pushed to her death from an upper storey at Dobrau. Because of the suspicion of suicide, I believe she was not buried in the cemetery—maybe on the outskirts thereof."[82]

Muriel's three children were all safely in the United States, and she had done the honorable thing by her husband, no matter what it cost her both emotionally and financially. Muriel's niece, Margaret White Bennett, told Paul Church, "Muriel had been extremely generous with the Seherr-Thoss family. Renovating the palaces, greatly improving the lives and working conditions of the servants, and that none of this was ever acknowledged by one Seherr-Thoss family member during her life, nor after her death."[83] When her children heard about their mother's death, they may have been comforted by a letter she sent to Boysie after his parents' divorce when they were living together at Dobrau.

> I can never begin to tell you how constantly I have felt the close help of Heaven in all the difficulties I have been helped through lately. I could almost *feel* my guardian angel leading me by the hand. All the time you thought I was so peaceful in my mind nearly 2 years ago, I kept praying to God, "Please save them, for my efforts have failed to do it." And you see I was answered. The Bible story of Daniel being saved in the Lion's Den seems far more *natural* to me now than it used to for I have been preserved from pitfalls in such a *wonderful* way that I have no doubt whatever that I am constantly receiving Heaven's help to fulfil the duty which kept me over here. If I hadn't had these wonderful experiences I should be perhaps afraid of what is coming, for myself and another, but now I am not afraid.[84]

Chapter Nine

Muriel's death has caused me great sadness. She was the victim of her devotion. In the end, her departure spared many a painful and difficult moment. One can say that it was a deliverance for her.[1]
—JOHN C. WHITE TO MANNI SEHERR-THOSS

URIEL HAD BEEN THE FAMILY MEMBER EVERYONE RELIED ON NO matter the issue at hand. She wouldn't have the privilege of those senior years when she might have enjoyed her grandchildren. She knew of the oldest, Alan, but never saw him and even fantasized that Albina's little boy, born at the same time, was hers.

Boysie, who "revered" his mother, knew he had to avenge her death and make something of her example. She had desperately tried to keep him out of Europe, and now he was even more desperate to return there on her behalf. He would do so in a US Army uniform. Boysie entered the army on July 20, 1943, less than four months after his mother's death, and was a private assigned to Company A, 15th Engineer Battalion. He began at Camp Ritchie in Maryland and completed his basic training at Camp Wheeler in Macon, Georgia, an infantry replacement training center, where he took the Oath of Renunciation and Allegiance on October 22, 1943.[2] Of course, the question was where to send him. "He found his way to alpine shooters because he was a great skier. When his comrades realized he was of German origin, they directed him to the Chancellery where he dealt with German prisoners of war."[3]

Obviously, Boysie could be of greatest use to the US Army back in Europe, but it would be difficult to hide his German double name, particularly when paired with his Aryan good looks and his accent. As a solution, he became Master Sergeant John Strutt "for the duration of my stay in Europe."[4] He wrote to his Aunt Betty and Uncle Jack that he was first sent to a camp in England, "which was most unpleasant," but after six weeks, he was reassigned to one much more to his liking. "First, the work is interesting. Second, I am stationed practically on a golf course where I can play during my off duty hours, which are very frequent. Third, Geraldine Apponyi Zog is not too far away, and for that matter some former friends in London. And last but not least, this is a very small and attractive British camp where everyone is extremely nice to us." He did not know how long he would remain at the base but hoped it might "continue for a couple of months. By that time the worst of the winter should be over and the prospect of going to the continent will appear less grim."[5] What he did not tell them was that he was assigned to interrogate German officers who understandably resented him. "It happened that he took friends prisoner. . . . Sometimes, when they were alone, he heard harsh words from prisoners: 'You traitor!'"[6]

Boysie's nephew, Alan Church, had a long conversation with him about his duties in England and his name change.

> Boysie was most likely attempting to shield his identity. My mother told us that Boysie, as a soldier, had not been allowed to go on the Continent. His duty had been the interrogation of higher ranking captured German officers. Boysie told me himself that he was disappointed that he hadn't been able to travel to the Continent. It was most likely the fact that higher ups didn't trust him. Also, having interrogated many higher-ranking captured officers, he had a great deal of information. Surely the GSP [Gestapo] knew that Boysie was in England and would have been watching for his appearance.[7]

Boysie was also concerned at having no news of his father. "Naturally, Boysie was anxious about his father, Manni; if he had been able to escape Silesia which was directly in the path of advancing Russians."[8]

On July 20, 1944,[9] there was a plot by the German resistance (mainly composed of Wehrmacht officers) to assassinate Adolf Hitler.[10] Through Manni's brother, Theobald (whom Alan Church calls admiringly "the real deal"), the Seherr-Thoss family, including Manni, would be drawn into that fray.

Theobald had long warned against the rising tide of Germany's National Socialist Party (the Nazis). Theo joined the Prussian army in 1902 as an ensign in the 2nd Silesian Dragoon Regiment, known as the "King Friedrich III Regiment." After rising through the ranks, during World War I, he was a first lieutenant and then captain in the 1st Guards Uhlan Regiment. For his service, he was awarded a Knight's Cross of the Royal Prussian House Order of Hohenzollern. With other postings, he rose to major, then lieutenant colonel, and in 1932 he was appointed commander of his own regiment. On February 1, 1933, Count Theobald Seherr-Thoss declared to his regiment at Breslau:

> The National Socialists, who are now in a crucial position of govern-
> ment responsibility, have repeatedly emphasized that they developed
> their ideology from the spirit of the front-line soldiers. If that were true,
> we soldiers could only be happy about it. But I don't want to hide my
> skepticism from you. I will also tell you why: In my opinion, this Hitler
> is not a gentleman, but just a guy. And sooner or later his movement
> will perish because of this.[11]

The following January, he gave up his command of the 7th Prussian Cavalry Regiment in Breslau and retired from active service in 1935 as a major general.[12] At the time, Hitler had been chancellor of Germany for a year, the Nazis had already established their first concentration camp at Dachau, and the party had organized the first nationwide boycott of Jewish-owned businesses. Theo wanted no part of it all.

In 1944, a heavily decorated German army officer, Count Claus von Stauffenberg, led a conspiracy to assassinate Adolf Hitler. His father was the last Oberhofmarschall (Chief Court Marshal) of the Kingdom of Württemberg. The son was a veteran of several decisive battles who had lost his left eye, his right hand, and two fingers on his left hand in April 1943. While recuperating at home, Stauffenberg's strong Catholic faith led him to question the growing ill treatment of Jews and sup-pression of religion.

After the Allies landed in France on D-Day, June 6, 1944, most German officers thought the war was lost and only an armistice could prevent more damage to the nation. Stauffenberg began considering a plot to assassinate Hitler even though he knew his actions were treasonous. On July 20, 1944, Stauffenberg attended a briefing for Hitler carrying a briefcase containing two bombs. The assigned room had been changed at the last moment, and, missing one hand and several fingers, Stauffenberg had difficulty arming the bombs. Because of an interruption, he was able to arm only one of the two, which he placed underneath the table as close to Hitler as he could manage. Taking a pre-planned call, Stauffenberg left the room without knowing that, seconds later, an officer moved the brief-case behind a heavy conference table leg. When the blast happened, four people were killed and most of the other attendees were injured, but Hitler, shielded by the table, was only slightly wounded. Stauffenberg hurried to Berlin to lead the second half of the planned coup, not realizing that Hitler had survived. The next day, he and several of his coconspirators were executed by firing squad after an announcement that only a "very small clique" of traitors were involved. In total, an estimated 7,000 people would be arrested, of whom approximately 4,980 were executed, some slowly strangled with piano wire on Hitler's insistence. Some were anti-Nazi but had not necessarily been involved in the Stauffenberg plot.

It was important there be no public comprehension of how many officers had been involved in the plot. In the ensuing investigation, those in charge

> were by no means able to uncover all contacts and networks of relation-ships or did not include them in the investigation—whether for tactical reasons or due to misjudgment. Failure to make arrests is more likely to suggest the latter. . . . Others were classified as accomplices, even though they were actively involved—but this did not prevent the Nazi courts from sentencing them to death.[13]

While it was estimated that approximately two hundred people were actually involved in some way, "the Nazi sources came up with 132 people with 650 contacts between them. . . . In addition, many more people probably knew about the plans without revealing their knowledge. Many were probably only willing to participate as soon as the assassination attempt had succeeded."[14] Only the first trial of the conspirators on August 7–8, 1944, before the People's Court was reported in detail in the controlled press. "The more names, faces and fates of those involved in the coup attempt had emerged, the more likely the constructed image might have been questioned. The Nazi leadership did not want to risk this and almost stopped reporting on the further trials."[15]

One of those arrested for questioning was Theo Seherr-Thoss, then living in Berlin.[16] It was logical, given his stated opposition to the Nazis and his voluntary retirement from the military, that he was suspected in the plot to assassinate Hitler. Also arrested were his brothers, Manni, Roger, and Wolfgang (Hans had died in 1918), most likely to determine whether they might have any information that implicated their brother.[17] "In many cases, however, despite long and grueling interrogations, the detainees kept their mouths shut, did not betray those who they knew were already dead, or only named people they knew were already dead."[18] None of the Seherr-Thoss brothers was implicated or executed.

Theo also testified in the Nuremberg trials.[19] He signed an affidavit on May 31, 1946, that Franz von Papen had tried to talk Hitler out of the Anschluss (annexation of Austria).[20] He and his brother, Roger, heard Papen declare at the Union Club late in the evening, "I am just coming from the Reichskanzlei [the chancellor's office]. I tried to talk Hitler out of the march into Austria and strongly advised against it. But he is committing the madness and just gave order for the Einmarsch [invasion]."[21] The court acquitted Papen, stating that while he had committed a number of "political immoralities," these actions were not punishable under the "conspiracy to commit crimes against peace" written in Papen's indictment. The Soviets wanted to execute him.[22]

The long and brutal war finally ended. D-Day had taken place in Normandy on June 6, 1944, and Paris was liberated on August 25, only months before Boysie's letter from London. In 1945, Hitler committed suicide on April 30, and Germany surrendered unconditionally on May 7. The Japanese surrendered on August 14, having had atomic bombs dropped on both Hiroshima and Nagasaki.

With the war over, Boysie was back in the States in early 1946, when he and Marian were overjoyed to learn she was pregnant. On October 31, 1946, their only child was born and named Henry White Seherr-Thoss for his great-grandfather, Ambassador Henry White, and called "Harry." The couple had no money, so their son was born in New York City's Foundling Hospital, established in 1869 by the Sisters of Charity "for abandoned infants."[23] Another family member confirms that Boysie didn't have enough money to pay for their hospital release.

Baby Harry with his parents, Marian and Boysie. CREDIT: ELIZABETH SEHERR-THOSS

Obviously, the young family could not continue with such bleak financial prospects. In 1947, Marian and Boysie divorced very amicably and remained friends. Two family members said the Kingsland fortune "wasn't sufficient" for their needs. Marian then married a wealthy long-time suitor, Henry Osborne Havemeyer Frelinghuysen, usually called "H.O.H." by his family. He had proposed to Marian even before her marriage to Boysie, and their families were old friends. His twin brother, Peter Hood Ballantine Frelinghuysen Jr., served for more than twenty years in the US House of Representatives, where he spoke out publicly against the Communist witch hunt of Senator Joseph McCarthy. Peter's wife, Beatrice Sterling Procter, had been mentioned in newspapers as the "best gal" and possible fiancée of Cincie Seherr-Thoss, Boysie's younger brother,[24] and she had served as a bridesmaid at Marian and Boysie's wedding. It was an intersecting and complex group.

Marian Kingsland Seherr-Thoss and H.O.H. Frelinghuysen married in New York City on August 28, 1947. They lived principally in Far Hills, New Jersey, and had one son, George, in 1951. George was close to his half-brother, Harry, and they served as one another's best man at their respective weddings. Marian remained close to her first son and his children. She accompanied Harry and his oldest son, Christopher, on an extended visit to Silesia and Germany. While there, she provided a plaque to commemorate Muriel's life and death and arranged and paid for the ruins of Dobrau Castle to be reinforced so that it would not continue to deteriorate. Several decades later, when someone bought the castle to restore it, the new owner confirmed that it would have been impossible to do so if Marian had not expended such an effort to save it.[25] On one of Marian's trips to Dobrau, "seeing the state of the palace now, she wept. Some parts of the palace could not even be entered."[26]

The following spring after Marian's wedding, Boysie married Sonia "Sunny" Phipps, a granddaughter of steel industrialist and philanthropist Henry Phipps, closest partner and childhood friend of Andrew Carnegie. The wedding took place on March 3, 1948, at the home of the bride's parents in Palm Beach, a resort principally developed by the Phipps family.[27] Sunny had earlier been married to Herbert Farrell Jr., with whom she had two children before divorcing in 1946. Sunny's mother,

Gladys Livingston Mills,[28] was from the same rarefied family circle as Daisy White. Gladys's twin sister, Beatrice, was an important link to the British peerage as the wife of the eighth Earl of Granard. Gladys and Beatrice's brother, Ogden Livingston Mills, was a member of Congress before becoming US secretary of the Treasury in 1933. In fact, his first wife, Margaret Stuyvesant Rutherfurd, was Daisy's niece and namesake.

Boysie with Sunny Phipps, his second wife. CREDIT: BRUCE FARRELL

The families were long associated with one another and belonged to many of the same clubs and social circles. Both Sunny and Daisy were descendants of the first Lord of Livingston Manor in colonial America, so perhaps Daisy would have approved of the marriage.

While the couples remained amicable after their remarriages, the fact that Boysie remained in almost daily telephone communication with Marian caused some understandable "strain" on the relationships. Harry spent one month each summer and one week at Christmas with Sunny and his father. Alan Church recalled, "As a young man I worked on the farm for my uncle [Boysie] in Litchfield, Connecticut. He and his second wife Sonia had been most kind to me, enabling me to build a home for my family."[29]

Sunny's son by her first marriage, Bruce Farrell, was particularly close to Boysie. He recalls, "At the age of seven Boysie . . . became my father and brought so much into my life. At 21 I changed my middle name to Christoph in his honor and at 23 I asked him to be the best man at my wedding. That gives you an idea of the relationship I had with him."[30]

Manni, Boysie, and Henry at the Litchfield farm. CREDIT: BRUCE FARRELL

Sunny established, in 1991, a foundation for the benefit of citizens and organizations in Litchfield, Connecticut, where in 1948 she and Boysie bought three hundred acres of farmland to raise Jersey cows. In 1994, she added another charitable trust in the couple's name. The two combined entities distribute more than $1 million each year to nonprofit organizations in Litchfield. Sunny was an active member of the board of Phipps Houses, established by her grandfather, the oldest and largest not-for-profit developer, owner, and manager of affordable housing in New York City. Sunny and Boysie traveled extensively throughout the world; he took photographs as she made extensive notes. In 1968, the Smithsonian Institution Press published a book, *Design and Color in Islamic Architecture: Afghanistan, Iran, Turkey*, written by her with photos by Boysie. After his death in 1992, she wrote four more books and died in 2006. They had no children together and are buried in Litchfield's East Cemetery.

Harry, the only child of Marian and Boysie, enlisted in the US Marine Corps before graduating from Columbia University Business School. He enjoyed a successful career in commercial real estate, and, although proudly an American, he retained great appreciation for his father's German heritage but did not use his title as a count. On February 9, 1973, in New York City, he married Consuelo Vanderbilt Hutton, a descendant of Commodore Cornelius Vanderbilt and of Senator James G. Fair, one of the famous "silver kings" in the Comstock Lode. Consuelo and Harry had five children. After their protracted divorce, Harry married Elizabeth Hanlon in a civil ceremony at Gstaad, Switzerland, in 1995, with a church wedding the next year in Alford, Massachusetts, followed by a reception at Blueberry Hill. They had one son, and Harry died in Manhattan on March 11, 2022.

Boysie's brother, Cincie, realized his dream of becoming a successful rancher. His first wife, Virginia "Virgie" DeLoney, while perfectly suited to the life Cincie wanted, kept waiting for him to take responsibility for their future. Muriel had been aware of her youngest son's lack of direction, writing to their family attorney in 1941, "C. [Cincie] always has been quite helpless regarding legal or official matters!"[31] Virgie wrote of her husband, "Poor fellow, his mind is always in such a turmoil, and I never seem to be able to give him the reassurance he seems to require."[32] Cincie had filed a petition for naturalization in New York in 1939, before he was married, and according to Virgie's letters, the file was lost. After their marriage, when she was their sole source of income, Virgie refiled on his behalf in Miami on December 15, 1943, and he gained US citizenship.

Virgie's warm letters to his family contained many examples of Cincie's restlessness and his emotional mistreatment of her, but she remained supportive as long as she could. She wrote to Betty and Jack, "Right now it is the same old story—either I get out of the army and come with him, or he wants a divorce. And he has even gone one step further this time! If I *do* get out, and *he* isn't completely happy, I must let him go. Seems to me as if he's taking out a little insurance on the success of his operations."[33] Finally, her patience exhausted, she divorced Cincie on March 18, 1947. There were no children, and she returned to service in the Women's Army Corps and later in the National Forest Service. Virgie died at her ranch at Jackson, Wyoming, in 1999, having never remarried.

On November 10, 1947, at Jackson, Cincie married Constance "Connie" Fleischmann, whose family owned the Bar-B-Bar Ranch on the Snake River in view of the Tetons. The Fleischmanns eventually purchased several other ranches in the area. Cincie and his wife had a son and a daughter. On September 2, 1953, the couple separated, and on September 15, Cincie brought suit for divorce against Connie, charging "intolerable indignities." The uncontested divorce was immediately granted, and neither party was ordered to pay alimony. Perhaps the reason for the divorce can be understood by Connie's marriage the next day to Paul Theodor Edward von Gontard, an heir to the Anheuser-Busch fortune through his grandmother, Clara Busch. To make matters a bit more convoluted, eight months later, Cincie was married on May 18, 1954, in a grand New York City wedding to Clara Hazel "Baby" von Gontard, a first cousin of Connie's new husband. By then Anheuser-Busch was quickly becoming the largest brewery in the world, a title it would attain in 1957. St. Louis newspapers covered Cincie's wedding in detail because of the family's business headquartered there.

Not only was "Baby" a great-granddaughter of Adolphus Busch and Elizabeth Anheuser, but her grandfather was Baron Paul T. E. von

Gontard, president of the Mercedes Motor Car Company in Germany, while her mother was Baroness Susanne Schilling von Canstatt.[34] In an unusual move, Kaiser Wilhelm II had created Susanne, an American citizen, a baroness on the same day he elevated her husband to the Prussian House of Lords.[35] The Busch family had experienced a great deal of anti-German sentiment during both world wars, so they would have welcomed Cincie as one of their own. After the wedding service, the reception was held at the bride's grandmother's Fifth Avenue apartment. Cincie's sister, Margaret, attended.

The handsome young couple appeared in a flashy *Life* magazine article about the Busch family, photographed by Margaret Bourke-White.[36] They would have two children before she divorced him on January 29, 1963. At one point, Cincie owned the Riverview Ranch but eventually sold it and bought the Albert Nelson Ranch. Boysie's stepson, Bruce Farrell, worked on Cincie's ranch in the summer of 1962. After he married, he took his wife there for another visit. He recalls it as a beautiful place, and he was impressed by Cincie's operations there.[37] Cincie died at Jackson on August 24, 1992, and was buried there in South Park Cemetery. His and Connie's son, Roger, has continued to operate the ranch.

Muriel's grandson, Alan Church, is particularly complimentary about Cincie's side of the family. Cincie's oldest son, Roger, was Alan's godson. Alan recalled of them, "That part of the family is to my liking . . . smart and clever to a high degree, work with their hands; ranching, sand, gravel, trucking, building. They work hard and play hard."[38]

And what of Boysie and Cincie's only sister, Margaret Seherr-Thoss, and her marriage to Ted Church? "My siblings and I have come to the conclusion that our grandfather was a fortune hunter and a rather troubled person," their grandson Paul Church says.[39] "They both said more than a few times how much they loved one another, yet could not bear one another. I feel our grandfather was jealous of his wife's lineage and talents."[40]

Margaret and Ted had three sons: Alanson (always called Alan), Christopher, and Edgar III (Teddy). "My mother paid for the farm in Sharon [Connecticut] in 1940. . . . I believe my father paid for our education at the best possible schools," Alan Church said.[41] Grandson

Paul Church recalled, "My understanding has always been that our grandmother's money was largely involved with the real estate, land, and lifestyle we grew up with. . . . The children's home life was disrupted due to arguments, and they were often at boarding schools and camp."[42]

At home, Alan, Chris, and Teddy Church had a governess who had been with the Seherr-Thoss family in Germany.

> The lady, Elisabeth Elbin, who mostly raised us boys was born and raised on the Dobrau estate. Her father was the overseer of the place. She had left her home in 1919 after witnessing the horrendous events in Germany resulting from the "Treaty" and from the occupation of the country and the influx into Germany of beginning communism. The tales she told us boys about killings of Catholics and school teachers, we thought she related into frightening us into submission when we were "boys being boys," and came in late for supper for example. It was clear that she observed the future more visually than anyone else and acted upon it. It was only after reading Muriel's letters, translated from the French by Margaret White Bennett, I believe, that I came to understand what our care giver was relating.[43]

Ted had graduated from top-tier schools and expected his sons and grandsons to do the same. Paul Church recalled, "Our grandfather was a rather insecure person and victim of aberrant personality traits. We children didn't get to know him at all. The few times we spent with him towards the end of his life, his demeanor was acerbic and condescending. Ted put our grandmother and her brothers down frequently."[44] Ted and Margaret "argued often and at the dinner table in front of us, beginning in English [and], as the conversation heated, switching to French. It may have been jealousy. It's difficult to answer. They played the stupid game of one-upmanship," Alan Church said.[45] As the oldest of Margaret's grandchildren, Paul recognized how "that energy prevailed in my father, his brother [Teddy], and was quietly referenced as similar to Pappa's behavior at times by our grandmother. This anger and unkindness was an integral part of [Ted]; his three sons have said their father was a snob."[46]

Alan had been told by his father, "Gentlemen don't work with their hands,"[47] but he found much more to interest him outside the strictures imposed on his family. "There seemed to be much pretense in our family. 'We are who we are, and that is how you are being *brought up* and must comport yourselves accordingly.'... Having grown up among farm workers and other laborers, we *knew* that there was more *wisdom* among those folks than among our parents and their contemporaries!"[48]

Alan would not be surprised to learn for certain that his father was in the CIA's predecessor, the OSS. "Both my parents spoke multiple European languages. As a Yale grad with much time spent on the Continent and with many people contacts, he was surely valued by the OSS. My father was a legion of honor [recipient]. He was CFR [Council on Foreign Relations]. I met strange characters at times when I was in his company."[49] He also mentioned "spooky characters who seemed to know and be comfortable with my father."[50]

Paul Church confirmed that the marriage of his Church grandparents had similarities to that of his Seherr-Thoss great-grandparents: "A slice of the Seherr-Thoss men were very harsh and selfish. They lacked empathy and excelled in righteous indignation. Margaret married that part of her father in [Ted]."[51]

"There are many parallels to the marriage of Muriel and Manni. Ted was physically and mentally abusive with our grandmother. At the time of their divorce in 1959–1960, my grandmother's attorney was able to [secure] a decree that Ted could not legally live within 100 miles of her."[52] Whereas Muriel had been limited by her lack of finances and passport, "Margaret maintained her own life, finances, and stood her ground. After many difficulties she filed for divorce."[53] It was a contentious and lengthy process, and Ted sought to end payment of child support earlier than the divorce specified.[54]

The women in the Rutherfurd/White/Seherr-Thoss/Church line were never shrinking violets. They were fiercely independent and never ceased trying to escape from the constraints placed upon them by society. They made mistakes, but it is highly doubtful that their immediate families could have achieved what they did without the strength of character that sometimes led others to view the women as difficult and even overbearing. They are traits that would have been applauded in men as virtuous.

A contemporary wrote of Muriel's grandmother, "Mrs. Rutherfurd was a law-giver in her circle and no weak one; she invited whom she pleased, as she pleased, and an offender against her exactions came never any more. But she had the prettiest way in the world of putting people in the appropriate place."[55]

The Four Hundred of New York Society had a favorite "extra man," Frederick Townsend Martin, who was a great admirer of Daisy's success as a hostess. He wrote,

> I think Mrs. Henry White carried off the palm for tact and under-standing. She knew exactly who were the *right* people, and her dinners and teas illustrated the parable of the sheep and the goats. The sheep were invited to dinner and the goats browsed contentedly through the teas. Happily, they never suspected why they were asked to these informal gatherings, and such was Mrs. White's savoir faire that nobody felt neglected.[56]

Yet Daisy did not receive universal accolades even within her own family. Her grandson, Boysie, said of her, "Daisy was always sickly. She had certain problems."[57] While he didn't specify what those problems were, Muriel worked directly with writer Allan Nevins, who wrote the authorized biography of her father, Ambassador Henry White. After-ward, she wrote to her brother, "I think it remarkable how he [Nevins] has visualized both our parents having seen neither of them. I kept my promise to Betty & never put him wise about Mother but he seems to have sized her up pretty correctly as beautiful, reserved & ambitious with the very reverse of Papa's impulsiveness."[58] And when Muriel complained to her brother about Daisy's roadblocks to her marriage prospects, she wrote, "Mother I blame less than Papa because she wasn't properly balanced."[59]

Paul Church's assessment of Daisy is that she "was a remarkable beauty and force. Her personal ambitions would lead to much unhappi-ness in her daughter's life."[60] However, she was given deserved thanks for having led her husband into the diplomatic service and then ensuring his success there. As Paul Church recalled, Daisy "had an ambitious plan for her husband which he carried out. No gentleman-farmer-huntsman life for Henry White."[61] "My instincts tell me Daisy was an astute listener, and a most ambitious socialite."[62] She was always plagued by ill health, and he "wondered if her own great aims depleted her very life force. Maintaining her physique, social, political, and dynastic ambitions."[63]

As for Muriel, Boysie's stepson confirmed that "Boysie absolutely revered his mother. It was painful for him to know the way her life ended."[64] "Muriel's decisions were clearly of her own making. She was not the entirely good, subservient wife of Hermann, [she] navigated around him, used her own resources, bought her own real estate, helped protect and hide [others] from the Nazis."[65]

As a daughter of a well-known ambassador, Muriel was thrust onto the stage earlier than expected because of her mother's declining health. But she wasn't merely a substitute hostess. Her observations were acute, her loyalty constant, and her generosity unparalleled. She overcame adversity that would have crushed someone less capable. Muriel worked closely with her father's official biographer to shape and develop his record and legacy. President Wilson told her personally that she had informed her father's position on the Silesian Uprising, and he, in turn, had been able to affect the official US policy on that issue.[66] Although her brother became a respected ambassador in his own right, Muriel was not afforded that privilege. Not until 1949, well after Muriel's death, would the United States appoint a female ambassador.[67]

Muriel's daughter, Margaret, seemed to learn from her mother's missteps, although Alan Church recognizes his mother's blind spots: "My mother, on recollection, seemed to have narcissistic tendencies. Her will needed to be done. She needed to be *right*, even when obviously wrong."[68] Yet this was a woman of enormous accomplishments. In 1927, she won the mixed doubles tennis cup at the Lenox Club in Berkshire Hills,[69] and twenty years later she gave a well-reviewed solo vocal performance at Carnegie Hall to "a large and appreciative audience."[70] At the time, she had two toddlers at home and one more son yet to be born. Her grandson, Paul, to whom she was particularly close, said admiringly of her, "She spoke five languages fluently, Russian and Greek well, was a

MARGARET SEHERR - THOSS
DRAMATIC SOPRANO

CARNEGIE CHAMBER
MUSIC HALL

Friday evening

February 28th

at 8:30

SAMUEL QUINCY
at the Steinway Piano

CONCERT MANAGEMENT VERA BULL HULL
101 West 55th Street - - - Circle 7-2837 - - - New York 19, N. Y.

Program for a solo recital by Margaret at Carnegie Hall. CREDIT: PAUL CHURCH

talented Wagnerian soprano, marvelous ballroom dancer, tennis player, equestrienne, well-connected round the world. Despite her wealth, she lived relatively simply and helped many people discreetly."[71]

Her youngest son, Teddy, said at her memorial service:

> Perhaps least known to many of us even in the family was the fact that during the cold war days in the 1960's, especially after the construction of the Berlin wall, our dear mother managed to get about 20 relatives and friends out from behind the Iron Curtain. On several occasions she herself went through Check Point Charlie in Berlin to go into East Germany to fight for people's freedom. Ma was just picking up where her mother left off while living as an American in Silesia during WWII and helping people escape the Nazis. The loss of her home, Dobrau, and her mother devastated her.[72]

In a world that seems ever more divided, it seems a rare accomplishment for Muriel's descendants (including those of her niece, Margaret White Bennett) to remain close more than eighty years after Muriel's death. Paul Church attested, "One striking feature of the second and first cousins is a shared will and resolve individually to be as independent as possible. Reserved, eccentric, and not in the least interested in the social limelight. The Bennetts are much the same, but dare I say more refined across the board."[73]

Muriel's tempestuous life was multilayered and emotionally tortured. When she walked up those stairs at Dobrau, aware she was going to her death, she had the satisfaction of knowing all three of her children were married and safely in America. She had helped several prisoners of war to escape and several others to receive more humanitarian care. Most of those would not have even known her name, but that was fine with her. As her grandson said, "Many were able to get away because of her help."[74] The Jewish Lederer family was prospering in Australia, where she had helped them escape and establish a new life. She had used much of her fortune for the benefit of her husband's family and forced herself to be kind and forgiving to a husband who badly misused her. She even ensured his safety by smuggling him out of harm's way, knowing she

Boysie and his second wife, Sunny Phipps. Her son recalls, "To see them waltz was to see beauty and grace in motion. Boysie knew how to waltz, and my mother knew how to follow. No better picture of their marriage!" CREDIT: BRUCE FARRELL

Muriel was buried just outside the church at Dobrau along with several other Seherr-Thoss family members, but not her husband. CREDIT: ROBERT WINIARZ

was left behind to answer for it all. Although she never heard a word of appreciation for those actions, her son finally did. After his mother's death, when Boysie went back to see his father in Germany, Manni said to him, "Your mother was right after all."[75]

ACKNOWLEDGMENTS

I BEGAN MY QUEST FOR MURIEL'S STORY WITH A PHONE CALL ON November 8, 2021, to Harry and Elizabeth Seherr-Thoss. They kindly referred me to Allan Nevins's 1930 biography of Ambassador Henry White and from there my circle kept expanding. My first debt of gratitude is to Paul Church, Muriel's great-grandson. He made necessary introductions, explained family real estate, shared intimate details about his grandmother and her mother, made travel arrangements, and recognized that a hagiography that did nothing but praise Muriel would not be authentic. He particularly appreciates the long-standing encouragement of Paula Smith Cotter. Paul's father, Alan Church, was very helpful, writing to me at one point, "This work is yours, whether or not it gladdens or saddens us, we wholeheartedly support your thorough effort." Elizabeth Seherr-Thoss, by then widowed, very generously hosted me at Blueberry Hill, which gave me a special insight into her late husband's family. We were joined by their very gracious cousin, Anne B. Bennett, who shares my Georgia heritage, and enjoyed a great treat by calling her mother, Muriel's niece, still active and vital at age 102. Elizabeth also provided photographs and retrieved old audiotapes Boysie recorded, had them copied, and made available to me. Their first-person account adds a great deal to the narrative. Boysie's stepson, Bruce Farrell, was very kind and helpful, as was Manni's cousin and Queen Geraldine's nephew, Count André de Baghy. While all those family members have contributed, they should not be assumed to agree with all of my conclusions, and I gratefully respect any of their opinions that may differ from my own.

Krzysztof (Christoph) Bialas, whose great-grandfather was the overseer of the Rosnochau estate, was an incredible source of data and never seemed to tire of my incessant questions. I could have written another chapter using his sources alone. He also uncovered excellent photographs and sought permission for their use. Similarly, Jolanta Ilnicka, whose grandmother, Albina Jenek, was the chef at Dobrau and Muriel's friend, generously allowed me to use information her grandmother asked her to preserve for future generations.

For personal correspondence, photographs, diaries, and family records, my greatest source was the William Tapley Bennett, Jr., Papers at the University of Georgia Special Collections Library given by Margaret White Bennett, Muriel's niece. They are extensively catalogued and administered by Sheryl Vogt and Jill Severn at the Richard B. Russell Library for Political Research and Studies. Julia Lehnert at the National Park Service's Hampton National Historical Site at Towson, Maryland, is intimately familiar with Ambassador Henry White's family records and correspondence there and was extremely helpful over a long period of time. There are also various family papers at the Library of Congress, where Patrick Kerwin was helpful, and at Columbia University.

I am likewise indebted to Joséphine Dedet (Queen Geraldine's biographer), Inger Sheil at the Australian National Maritime Museum, Cortni Merritt for her technical assistance, Elisabeth Basford, Alex Beam, Scott Clemons, Hubert Hering, Janet and Bob Katz, Donna Lucey, Harry Musselwhite, Andrew Nagorski, Dr. Christine D. Reskowski-Santos, Peter Richmond, Robert Winiarz, and especially Hugo Vickers, whose friendship I value as much as I do his professional opinion. My editor, Brittany Stoner, made this project a true collaborative effort, and I hope to work again with her as well as Assistant Managing Editor Patricia Stevenson and their team at Lyons Press. I am particularly grateful to my wife, Katherine, who generously allows me to continue living in the past. Our daughter, Katy, rescued and formatted several photographs used in the book.

NOTES

INTRODUCTION

1. Henry James White to John C. White, November 15, 1948, the William Tapley Bennett, Jr. Papers, Richard B. Russell Library for Political Research and Studies, University of Georgia Libraries.

2. H. J. White to J. C. White, November 15, 1948, Bennett Papers.

3. Alanson Church, email to the author, September 17, 2022.

4. Theodore Roosevelt, *The Autobiography of Theodore Roosevelt* (New York: Scribners, 1926), 388.

5. Edith Wharton, *A Backward Glance* (New York: D. Appleton-Century Company, 1934), chapter 3.

6. Paul Church, email to the author, November 11, 2021.

7. Silesia is a region of central Europe that now lies mainly within Poland, with smaller parts in the Czech Republic and Germany. It became part of Prussia in the 1700s and, eventually, the German Empire in 1871.

8. Muriel Seherr-Thoss at Krastowitz to John C. White, January 27, 1941, Bennett Papers.

9. Andrew Nagorski, *Hitlerland* (New York: Simon & Schuster, 2012), 231; quoting an unpublished manuscript by Jacob Beam, former US ambassador to Russia.

10. "Work Camps," Pegasus Archive, accessed August 13, 2022, https://www.pegasus archive.org/pow/Work_camps.htm. "E" denotes English for British prisoners.

11. Dagmara Spolniak, "The Extraordinary Story of an American Woman in Dobrau," Turystyka, August 30, 2023, 1.

12. Erwin Filipczyk, Fr. Norbert Zawilak, et al., *Good for Seven Centuries* (Opole, Poland: Litar Sp. Zoo, 2002), 40.

13. Muriel Seherr-Thoss at Scheveningen, Holland, to John C. White, July 29, 1919, Hampton National Historic Site (National Park Service), Maryland.

CHAPTER 1

1. Auchincloss, *Vanderbilt Era*, 73.

2. Henry White, "Memoirs" (unpublished), Hampton National Historic Site, National Park Service, 9–10. By the will of Henry White's maternal grandfather, all enslaved people were freed before the war—the men at twenty-eight and the women at twenty-five.

3. White, "Memoirs" (unpublished), 8.

4. Auchincloss, *Vanderbilt Era*, 74.

5. White, "Memoirs" (unpublished), 29–30.

6. White, "Memoirs" (unpublished), 39.

7. Margaret White Bennett to Paul Church, undated note, Paul Church private collection.

8. Auchincloss, *Vanderbilt Era*, 73.

9. Allan Nevins, *Henry White* (New York: Harper & Row, 1930), 3.

10. Auchincloss, *Vanderbilt Era*, 74–75.

11. Auchincloss, *Vanderbilt Era*, 92.

12. Auchincloss, *Vanderbilt Era*, 74.

13. White, "Memoirs" (unpublished), 63.

14. Auchincloss, *Vanderbilt Era*, 75.

15. George Templeton Strong, *The Diary of George Templeton Strong*, 4 vols. (New York: Macmillan, 1952).

16. His claim to the earldom was initially granted by a Scottish court in 1759, and he was allowed to vote in the election of the Scottish representative peers; however, the House of Lords ultimately overruled Scottish law and denied the title in 1762 because of his support for the American colonies. He continued to hold himself out as "Lord Stirling" nonetheless, and his wife, "Lady Kitty," was a celebrated hostess of her day. The wife of the present author is also their descendant.

17. Constance Cary Harrison, *Recollections Grave and Gay* (New York: Scribners, 1911), 281.

18. Wharton, *A Backward Glance*, 356.

19. Emily Katherine Bibby, "Making the American Aristocracy: Women, Cultural Capital, and High Society in New York City, 1870–1900," master's thesis, Virginia Polytechnic Institute, June 10, 2009, p. 11.

20. Wharton, *A Backward Glance*, 356.

21. Wharton, *A Backward Glance*, 356. They were Lewis Morris Rutherfurd Jr. and Winthrop Chanler Rutherfurd.

22. Nevins, *Henry White*, 33.

23. Nevins, *Henry White*, 33.

24. Mrs. Richard Aldrich, *Family Vista*, quoted in Nevins, *Henry White*, 35.

25. Donna M. Lucey, *Archie and Amélie: Love and Madness in the Gilded Age* (New York: Harmony Books, 2006), 128.

26. Daisy White to Elizabeth Chanler, December 29, 1879, Chapman Papers, Rokeby, New York. Quoted in Donna M. Lucey, *Sargent's Women: Four Lives Behind the Canvas* (New York: W. W. Norton, 2017), 276.

27. White, "Memoirs" (unpublished), 80.

28. Nevins, *Henry White*, 36. She was twenty-eight.

29. Nevins, *Henry White*, 35.

30. In 1902, Morton's daughter, Alice, married Daisy's brother Winthrop Rutherfurd, who had been secretly engaged to Consuelo Vanderbilt before her mother forced her to marry the ninth Duke of Marlborough. After his wife's death in 1917, he married Lucy Mercer in 1920; she was best known for her lengthy affair with President Franklin D. Roosevelt.

31. Now the Château de Pourtalès.

32. Nevins, *Henry White*, 41–42.

33. Morgan Friedman, "The Inflation Calculator," accessed January 8, 2024, https://westegg.com/inflation/.

34. Ben Taylor, email to the author, September 6, 2022. Ben Taylor is assistant records manager and archivist at Waddesdon Manor.

35. White (unpublished memoirs), 93. The duchess, after her husband's death in 1890, would then marry her longtime lover, the Duke of Devonshire, and forever be known as "the Double Duchess." She would invite Daisy and Henry White to her famous costume ball in 1897.

36. Nevins, *Henry White*, 44.

37. Former secretary of war and US attorney general and father of the future president and chief justice William Howard Taft.

38. Nevins, *Henry White*, 45.

39. Nevins, *Henry White*, 46–47.

40. Lucey, *Archie and Amélie*, 127.

41. Lucey, *Sargent's Women*, 133–34.

42. Paul Church, Zoom conversation with the author, July 31, 2022.

43. Lucey, *Archie & Amélie*, 127.

44. National Gallery of Art, "Margaret Stuyvesant Rutherfurd White (Mrs. Henry White)," accessed October 23, 2023, https://www.nga.gov/collection/art-object -page.166470.html.

45. Henry James to Alice James, May 3, 1884, *The Complete Letters of Henry James,* vol. 2, *1883–1884* (Lincoln: University of Nebraska Press, 2019), 106.

46. Nevins, *Henry White*, 227.

47. Nevins, *Henry White*, 49.

48. Wilson Sullivan, *New England Men of Letters* (New York: Macmillan, 1972), 219.

49. Nevins, *Henry White*, 51.

50. Auchincloss, *Vanderbilt Era*, 76.

51. Nevins, *Henry White*, 52.

52. Nevins, *Henry White*, 57.

53. Nevins, *Henry White*, 72.

54. Richard Jay Hutto, *A Poisoned Life: Florence Chandler Maybrick, the First American Woman Sentenced to Death in England* (Jefferson, NC: McFarland, 2018).

55. Nevins, *Henry White*, 76.

56. Lucey, *Archie & Amélie*, 130.

57. David Gilmour, *Curzon: Imperial Statesman* (New York: Farrar, Straus & Giroux, 2006), 101.

58. Lady Wemyss, *A Family Record* (London: Curwen Press, 1932), 52–53.

59. Wemyss, *A Family Record*, 47–48.

60. Margaret "Lolly" White Bennett conversation, February 15, 2024.

61. Muriel White to Daisy White, April 20, 1893. Queen Mary I of England married King Philip II of Spain.

62. *Daily Globe*, St. Paul, MN, February 1, 1889, 1.

63. Nevins, *Henry White*, 77.

64. Nevins, *Henry White*, 80.

65. Nevins, *Henry White*, 80.

66. Nevins, *Henry White*, 80.

67. Consuelo, Duchess of Marlborough, *The Glitter and the Gold* (New York: Harper & Brothers, 1952), 273. Her stepmother, Anne Harriman Sands Rutherfurd Vanderbilt, married as her second husband Daisy's brother, Lewis Morris Rutherfurd Jr., and named her oldest daughter for Daisy.

68. Larz Anderson, *Letters and Journals of a Diplomat* (Grand Rapids, MI: Fleming H. Revell Co., 1940), 88.

69. Anderson, *Letters*, 72.

70. Alfred Allan Lewis, *Ladies and Not So Gentle Women* (New York: Viking, 2000), 128.

71. Lewis, *Ladies*, 128.

72. Lewis, *Ladies*, 156.

73. Nevins, *Henry White*, 76.

74. Nevins, *Henry White*, 77.

75. Nevins, *Henry White*, 81.

76. Henry White, "Personal Diary," October 12, 1892; Henry White Papers, Library of Congress.

77. Henry White, "Personal Diary," October 12, 1892, Henry White Papers, Library of Congress.

78. Nevins, *Henry White*, 97.

79. Nevins, *Henry White*, 95.

80. Lucey, *Archie & Amélie*, 159.

81. Lucey, *Archie & Amélie*, 159.

82. Muriel White to Henry White, September 4, 1892, Hampton.

83. Nevins, *Henry White*, 100.

84. Ruth 1:16.

85. Friedman, "Inflation Calculator," https://westegg.com/inflation/.

86. Nevins, *Henry White*, 122.

87. Julia Lehnert at Hampton NHS, email to the author, June 23, 2022. "Mrs. Morton" was the wife of his friend and mentor, Levi P. Morton. Kate Brice came as an infanta from a Velasquez painting and wore the most striking costume of the evening. It was shipped from Worth in Paris, and she had to be lowered into it the night of the ball.

88. Nevins, *Henry White*, 89. An aigrette is a headdress including a white egret's feather or spray of gems.

89. Nevins, *Henry White*, 90–91.

90. Nevins, *Henry White*, 90–91.

91. Henry White, "Diary," unpublished manuscript, April 15, 1898, Henry White Papers. Harriet S. Blaine was the daughter of James G. Blaine, US senator, speaker of the House of Representatives, and secretary of state under three presidents. Harriet married, in 1894, Truxton Beale. They were divorced, and their son, Walker Blaine Beale, was killed in action in 1918.

92. Henry White to Senator H. Cabot Lodge, February 4, 1901, Bennett Papers.

93. Henry White to Mrs. Theodore Roosevelt, June 13, 1902, Bennett Papers. President Roosevelt's two sisters, "Bamie" Cowles and Corinne Robinson, were guests at the dinner.

94. White to Mrs. Roosevelt, June 13, 1902, Bennett Papers.

95. White to Mrs. Roosevelt, June 13, 1902, Bennett Papers.

CHAPTER 2

1. *The Evening World*, March 8, 1909, 1.

2. Nevins, *Henry White*, 242.

3. Ruth and Ogden Mills's granddaughter, Sonia "Sunny" Phipps, would marry, in 1948, Muriel's oldest son, Hans Christoph "Boysie," Count Seherr-Thoss.

4. Nevins, *Henry White*, 243.

5. Henry White in Borca di Cadore, Italy, to President Theodore Roosevelt, August 29, 1906, Bennett Papers.

6. https://nypl.getarchive.net/media/dinner-farewell-to-honhenry-white-usminister-to-italy-held-by-dowager-queen-3324d1, accessed February 21, 2024.

7. *San Francisco Call*, September 20, 1903, 1.

8. Nevins, *Henry White*, 247.

9. Undated letter from Muriel Seherr-Thoss at Rome to Sophie White.

10. Lilian Whiting, *Italy, the Magic Land* (Glasgow: Good Press, 2019), 165.

11. Nevins, *Henry White*, 248.

12. Vienna Salonblatt, March 21, 1908, Österreichische Nationalbibliothek, accessed August 24, 2022, https://anno.onb.ac.at/cgi-content/annoshow?text=wsb%7C19051223%7Cx.

13. "Americans Who Marry Italians," *New York Times*, May 5, 1907, 3.

14. *Time* magazine, August 22, 1932.

15. *The North American Review*, September 1937.

16. Richard Jay Hutto, *Crowning Glory: American Wives of Princes and Dukes* (Macon, GA: Henchard Press, 2007), 38.

17. Vittoria Colonna, Duchess of Sermoneta, *Things Past* (London: Hutchinson & Co., 1929), 184.

18. M. Seherr-Thoss to H. White, November 30, 1925, Hampton NHS.

19. Elizabeth Basford to the author, January 29, 2023; Basford is the author of *Princess Mary: The First Modern Princess* (London: History Press, 2021).

20. Basford, *Princess Mary*, 389. Citing Geoffrey Hall, *Fifty Years Gardening at Harewood* (Wakefield: EP Publishing, 1978), 24.

21. *New York Times*, September 19, 1880. This is approximately $290 million in today's currency (https://westegg.com/inflation/).

22. M. Seherr-Thoss to H. White, November 30, 1925, Hampton NHS.

23. Lady Margaret "Peggy" Crewe-Milnes, Marchioness of Crewe (née Primrose, daughter of the fifth Earl of Rosebery), second wife of the first Marquess of Crewe (1881–1967). Her mother was a member of the extremely wealthy Rothschild family and Peggy inherited a fortune. Muriel was a bridesmaid at her 1899 wedding, which was attended by the then-Prince and Princess of Wales, later King Edward VII and Queen Alexandra.

24. "Sex Scandal behind Brideshead Revisited," *The Times*, London, August 10, 2009; *The Irish Independent*, June 7, 2008.

25. Adrian Tinniswood, *The Long Weekend: Life in the English Country House Between the Wars* (Jonathan Cape, London, 2016), 260.

26. *Omaha Daily Bee*, July 19, 1903.

27. *Wyoming Derrick* 14, no. 23 (August 13, 1903).

28. Henry White to John Hay, September 4, 1903, Hampton NHS.

29. *New York World*, July 16, 1903, 1. With photos of Muriel and Austen Chamberlain. Austen Chamberlain's future wife would be neither.

30. Paul Church, email to the author, September 5, 2022.

31. Paul Church, email to the author, September 5, 2022.

32. Lucey, *Sargent's Women*, 143.

33. Muriel White to Sophie White, May 15, 1906, Hampton NHS.

34. Muriel Seherr-Thoss to Austen Chamberlain, May 15, 1921, Parliamentary Archives, LG/F/7/4/3.

35. Muriel Seherr-Thoss in Rome to Henry White, January 27, 1926, Hampton NHS.

36. D. J. Dutton, *Oxford Dictionary of National Biography*.

37. Muriel Seherr-Thoss in New York City to John C. White, December 20, 1928; Bennett Papers. A possible candidate is the ninth Duke of Northumberland, who never married and was killed in action in 1940. His secondary courtesy title before he inherited the dukedom in 1930 was Lord Percy.

38. *The Evening World*, March 8, 1909, 1; *East Liverpool Evening Review*, March 19, 1909, 35; *Washington Herald*, March 21, 1909, 7.

39. Audiotape of Boysie Seherr-Thoss, Elizabeth Seherr-Thoss collection.

40. *New York Times*, April 17, 1938. Hitt would eventually be appointed US minister to Panama and Guatemala after serving in several posts with Henry White. His daughter, Elizabeth Hitt, married Andor Hertelendy de Hertelend, who was secretary of the legation of Hungary. At their wedding, the best man was Count László Széchenyi, who married Gladys Vanderbilt. In 1905, White suggested Hitt as second secretary for the embassy in Rome.

41. *The Butte Daily Post*, March 9, 1909, 9; *The Oshkosh Northwestern*, March 9, 1909, 1; *San Francisco Call*, March 10, 1909, 2.

42. *Los Angeles Herald* 36, no. 160 (March 10, 1909).

43. *New York Times*, March 14, 1909. About $93,000 in the current equivalent. https://westegg.com/inflation/.

44. *The Pittsburgh Index* 20, no. 14 (April 3, 1909): 5.

45. His father, George L. Rives, US assistant secretary of state, was a first cousin of novelist Amelie Rives, who married John Armstrong Chanler, the oldest of the Astor orphans for whom Daisy served as guardian. Her second husband was artist Prince Pierre Troubetzkoy.

46. Muriel Seherr-Thoss in Rome to Jack White, April 1927, Hampton NHS.

47. *New York Times*, April 18, 1909.

48. M. White to S. White, March 2, 1909, Hampton NHS.

49. M. White to S. White, March 2, 1909, Hampton NHS.

50. M. White to S. White, March 2, 1909, Hampton NHS.

51. M. White to S. White, March 2, 1909, Hampton NHS.

52. *New York Times*, May 2, 1909.

53. *Los Angeles Herald*, April 29, 1909.

54. *Los Angeles Herald*, April 29, 1909.

55. *New York Times*, May 2, 1909.

56. *Los Angeles Herald* 36, no. 210 (April 29, 1909): 6.

57. *New York Times*, May 2, 1909.

58. One of his brothers, Hans, died on August 8, 1918, at Fauconcourt, France, in the waning days of World War I. His widow married the father of Princess Michael of Kent.

59. "Paqui" Rutherfurd was married six times to four husbands, including Sir Paul Dukes and Prince Charles Murat. Lucy Buckler wrote a history of nursing and married Major Vivian Home Seymer.

60. *New York Times*, May 2, 1909.

61. *Los Angeles Herald*, August 29, 1909.

62. *The Boston Globe*, January 16, 1911. The pearls are visible in this book's cover photo. Jane Norton Grew's first cousin, future ambassador and undersecretary of state Joseph C. Grew, was the father of Lilla C. Grew, who married future ambassador Jay Pierrepont Moffat, brother of Betty Moffat, wife of John C. "Jack" White, only brother of the bride, Muriel. Jay Pierrepont Moffat Jr. would become the US ambassador to Chad.

63. *The Daily Record*, May 1, 1909, 2.

64. Joséphine Dedet, email to the author, September 25, 2022.

65. In 1909, they owned seven estates: Dobrau, Friedersdorf, Körnitz, Rosnochau, Zwiastowice, Stöblau, and Walzen.

66. *The Daily Journal* (Telluride, CO), April 28, 1909. A spouse can manage, use, and dispose of his/her property without the spouse's consent and is responsible for his/her own debts.

67. Muriel Seherr-Thoss at Rome, Italy, to John W. White, March 22, 1926, Hampton.

68. Muriel Seherr-Thoss at Rome, Italy, to John W. White, March 22, 1926, Hampton.

CHAPTER 3

1. Muriel Seherr-Thoss at Rosnochau to "Chère Amie" at Kreis Neustadt, May 15, 1921, trans. from French by Krzysztof Bialas, Henry White Papers, Library of Congress.

2. "Muriel White Married to a German Count," *Daily Journal* (Telluride, CO), April 28, 1909.

3. "Heinrich Leopold von Seherr-Thoss," Wikipedia, accessed December 14, 2023, https://de.wikipedia.org/wiki/Heinrich_Leopold_von_Seherr-Tho%C3%9F.

4. In 1936, Dobrau was renamed Burgwasser by the Nazis to erase traces of Polish origin. After World War II, the name Dobrau was restored when the village again became part of Poland.

5. *The Andalusia Star* (Andalusia, AL), November 5, 1926, 6.

6. Jan Szczurek, "This Land Is Very Interesting," Pisarze PL, No. 457, 2020, accessed September 9, 2022.

7. "Norddeutsche allgemeine Zeitung" (Berlin), April 27, 1892. "Parish of St. Barlomiej in Glogowek," Wikipedia, accessed December 13, 2023, https://pl.wikipedia.org/wiki/Parafia_%C5%9Bw._Bart%C5%82omieja_w_G%C5%82og%C3%B3wku.

8. *Chicago Tribune*, August 14, 1909. Wilhelmshöhe was the kaiser's summer residence in Kassel.

9. *New York Times*, April 3, 1910.

10. *New York Times*, January 16, 1911.

11. *Boston Globe*, January 16, 1911.

12. Nevins, *Henry White*, 323.

13. Nevins, *Henry White*, 323.

14. Theodore Roosevelt to Henry White, January 22, 1915, Theodore Roosevelt Papers, Library of Congress Manuscript Division, https://www.theodorerooseveltcenter .org/Research/Digital-Library/Record?libD=o211502.

15. T. Roosevelt to H. White, January 22, 1915, Roosevelt Papers.

16. Nevins, *Henry White*, 327.

17. Bright's Disease/nephritis is an inflammation of the kidneys caused by toxins, infection, or autoimmune conditions. It may not always be curable but today can be managed with proper care or dialysis or kidney transplant.

18. Muriel Seherr-Thoss in Karlsbad, to John C. White, July 16, 1916. They had gone to Karlsbad seeking a cure for Manni's illness.

19. Winthrop Chanler Rutherfurd Sr. (1862–1944). After the death of his first wife, Alice, a daughter of US Vice President Levi P. Morton, he married Lucy Mercer, who had been the acknowledged mistress of US President Franklin D. Roosevelt.

20. *Baltimore Sun*, September 3, 1916.

21. *New York Times*, September 3, 1916.

22. Henry White papers, Library of Congress.

23. Daisy White to Henry White, Hindhead Beacon Hotel, Haslemere, December 3, 1906, Henry White Papers, https://lccn.loc.gov/mm78045328.

24. Muriel Seherr-Thoss in Washington, DC, to John C. White, September 16, 1916, Hampton.

25. Sculptor Daniel Chester French, who designed the statue of Abraham Lincoln in the Lincoln Memorial.

26. Henry White to Muriel Seherr-Thoss, September 2, 1917, Bennett Papers.

27. Through his mother, born Mathilde Saurma von Jeltsch.

28. Timothy Leo Lohof, "Berlin Embassy of James Watson Gerard: Reflections of a Diplomatic Paradigm Shift 1913–1917" (master's thesis, University of Montana, 1997), 107–108, https://scholarworks.umt.edu/etd/4713.

29. Ludwig H. Dyck, "Panzer General Strachwitz," Warfare History Network, accessed November 8, 2023, https://warfarehistorynetwork.com/article/unstoppable-strachwitz/.

30. Schierstaedt and Patrouille Schierstaedt, *Selbsterzähltes aus französischer Gefangenschaft* [Self-narrated Stories from French Captivity] (Berlin: O. Elsner Verlagsgesellschaft m.b.H, 1918).

31. Emily's aunt, Emily Thorn Vanderbilt Sloane, was Henry White's second wife.

32. The Silesian-born General Moritz von Bissing was governor-general of occupied Belgium.

33. Henry White to Muriel Seherr-Thoss, January 31, 1919, Bennett Papers. He would be awarded by the US president the Army Distinguished Service Medal for "his loyalty and friendship for the United States and the American Army."

34. *Baltimore Sun*, August 21, 1923, 22.

35. Henry White to John C. White, March 6, 1919, Bennett Papers. The countess's sister, Anita, married Baron Louis de la Grange.

36. Henry White to Muriel Seherr-Thoss, January 31, 1919, Bennett Papers. Henry White had purchased for her a private home in Holland held only in her name.

37. Mathilde Elizabeth Frelinghuysen Davis; her sons were senator and ambassador Henry Cabot Lodge Jr. and governor and ambassador John Davis Lodge.

38. *New York Times*, September 18, 1920. In 1921, she married Adolph Pavenstadt.

39. Henry White to Muriel Seherr-Thoss, Washington, DC, January 22, 1920, Bennett Papers.

40. H. White to J. C. White, March 6, 1919, Hampton.

41. H. White to J. C. White, March 6, 1919, Hampton.

42. Auchincloss, *Vanderbilt Era*, 66.

43. *New York Times*, November 4, 1920.

44. *New York Times*, November 4, 1920. Today's equivalent would be $6.2 billion (https://westegg.com/inflation/).

45. Muriel Seherr-Thoss at The Hague to John C. White, November 8, 1920, Bennett Papers.

46. "Silesia," *The American Heritage Dictionary of the English Language*, 5th ed. (New York: HarperCollins, 2012).

47. Margaret MacMillan, *Paris 1919* (New York: Random House, 2001), 219.

48. Anna M. Cienciala, "The Rebirth of Poland," Centre for Military and Strategic Studies, accessed October 24, 2023, http://www.conflicts.rem33.com/images/Poland/rebirth.html.

49. Manni Seherr-Thoss at Gravenhage to Henry White, February 22, 1919, Henry White Papers, Hampton.

50. Tim Wilson, *Frontiers of Violence: Conflict and Identity in Ulster and Upper Silesia, 1918–1922* (Oxford: Oxford University Press, 2010).

51. Christian Raitz von Frentz, *A Lesson Forgotten: Minority Protection Under the League of Nations: The Case of the German Minority in Poland, 1920–1934* (New York: LIT Verlag Berlin-Hamburg-Münster, 1999), 76.

52. M. Seherr-Thoss to "Chère Amie," May 15, 1921, trans. K. Bialas, Henry White Papers.

53. M. Seherr-Thoss to "Chère Amie," May 15, 1921, trans. K. Bialas, Henry White Papers.

54. M. Seherr-Thoss to "Chère Amie," May 15, 1921, trans. K. Bialas, Henry White Papers.

55. M. Seherr-Thoss to "Chère Amie," May 15, 1921, trans. K. Bialas, Henry White Papers.

56. M. Seherr-Thoss to "Chère Amie," May 15, 1921, trans. K. Bialas, Henry White Papers.

57. M. Seherr-Thoss to "Chère Amie," May 15, 1921, trans. K. Bialas, Henry White Papers. Victor, third Duke von Ratibor and second Fürst von Corvey, married Princess Elizabeth of Oettingen-Oettingen und Oettingen-Spielbeg in 1910.

58. M. Seherr-Thoss to "Chère Amie," May 15, 1921, trans. K. Bialas, Henry White Papers.

59. M. Seherr-Thoss to "Chère Amie," May 15, 1921, trans. K. Bialas, Henry White Papers.

60. *Capital Journal*, Salem (OR), May 20, 1921, 5.

61. M. Seherr-Thoss to "Chère Amie," May 15, 1921, trans. K. Bialas, Henry White Papers.

62. Ray Stannard Baker, *Woodrow Wilson and World Settlement* 11 (Gloucester, MA: P. Smith, 1960), 60.

63. *The North American Review's War Weekly* ("Harvey's Weekly") 1, no. 49, December 7, 1918, 4.

64. Nevins, *Henry White*, 423.

65. Nevins, *Henry White*, 423.

66. Nevins, *Henry White*, 423.

67. Nevins, *Henry White*, 421.

68. Nevins, *Henry White*, 421.

69. Nevins, *Henry White*, 423.

70. Nevins, *Henry White*, 332.

71. Nevins, *Henry White*, 332.

72. Nevins, *Henry White*, 332. After Germany's defeat, General Erich Ludendorff played an integral part in the Nazis' rise to power.

73. Nevins, *Henry White*, 332.

74. Wilhelm II, *My Early Life* (London: Methuen & Co., trans. ed. 1926), 133.

75. Elizabeth Moffat White, "Elizabeth Moffat White," interview by Jewell Fenzi, *The Association for Diplomatic Studies and Training: Foreign Affairs Oral History Program, Foreign Service Spouse Series*, 25, July 26, 1988, https://www.adst.org/OH%20TOCs/White,%20Elizabeth%20Moffat.toc.pdf.

76. Paul Church, email to the author, November 30, 2022. Hermann Göring was one of the most powerful figures in the Nazi Party. He oversaw the creation of the Gestapo. After the war, he was sentenced to death by hanging but died by suicide, having ingesting cyanide the night before his scheduled execution. He and Manni were friends from their military service.

77. Paul Church, email to the author, December 14, 2022.

78. Muriel Seherr-Thoss to Henry White, from Rosnochau, January 15, 1922.

79. Roger's son, Hans Christoph (1918–2011), an inventor and automobile engineer named for his uncle, was a great favorite in the family, who called him "Uncle Mu."

80. Christoph Bialas, email to the author, December 26, 2023.

81. Paul Church, email to the author, December 24, 2023.

82. Paul Church, email to the author, December 24, 2023.

83. E. M. White interview by Fenzi, 1988, https://www.adst.org/OH%20TOCs/White,%20Elizabeth%20Moffat.toc.pdf.

84. Henry White at Elm Court to Muriel Seherr-Thoss, July 24, 1922.

CHAPTER 4

1. G. S. Messersmith to William Phillips, undersecretary of state, June 26, 1933, 5, George S. Messersmith Papers, University of Delaware Library, http://udspace.udel.edu/handle/19716/6176; http://udspace.udel.edu/handle/19716/6679.

2. Muriel White in Loseley, Guilford, UK, to Jack White, September 1894, Hampton NHS.

3. Muriel White in Reigate, Surrey, to Jack White, October 20, 1895, Muriel White Seherr-Thoss Papers, Hampton NHS.

4. Muriel White onboard the RMS *Teutonic* to Jack White, May 14, 1895, Muriel White Seherr-Thoss Papers, Hampton NHS.

5. Muriel White to Daisy White, April 20, 1893, Hampton NHS.

6. Muriel White to Daisy White, March 11, 1895, Hampton NHS. In 1904, Mary's sister, Daisy Leiter, married the nineteenth Earl of Suffolk and twelfth Earl of Berkshire. Mary Curzon, as vicereine of India, would hold the highest official title in the Indian Empire that a woman could claim. Yet several British duchesses, who considered their rank superior, refused to curtsey to her at the Delhi Durbar as protocol required. She died before Curzon was raised to a marquess, leaving him with her fortune and three daughters. The characters in *Downton Abbey* were based on the Leiter and Curzon marriage and offspring.

7. Betty White's brother, Abbot Low Moffat, was elected to the New York legislature before joining the foreign service and helping to administer the Marshall Plan in Europe. Serving as head of the State Department's Southeast Asian Affairs office, his was an early voice warning against US involvement in the quagmire that became the Vietnam War.

8. Muriel Seherr-Thoss from Rosnochau to Betty Moffat, March 26, 1921 (Easter Sunday), Muriel White Seherr-Thoss Papers, Hampton NHS.

9. *Annener Zeitung*, "verbunden mit der Annener Volkszeitung: Anzeigenblatt für Witten-Annen und die Stadtteile Rüdinghausen, Stockum und Düren," July 14, 1925.

10. Nevins, *Henry White*, 493.

11. The Beatitudes, Matthew 5:9, the Bible. In 1967 and 1993, he would be joined by their son, Jack, and their daughter-in-law, Betty, in the lower-level crypt of Saint Joseph's Chapel.

12. David M. Kennedy, *Freedom from Fear: The American People in Depression and War* (Oxford: Oxford University Press, 1999), 412.

13. Arnold A. Offner, "William E. Dodd: Romantic Historian and Diplomatic Cassandra," *Historian* 24, no. 4 (1962): 68.

14. William E. Dodd, *Ambassador Dodd's Diary, 1933–1938* (London: Victor Gollangz, 1945).

15. His son, J. P. Moffat Jr., would serve as US ambassador to Chad from 1983 to 1985. They were Barclay cousins.

16. Jack White's son-in-law, William Tapley "Tap" Bennett Jr., would become the longest-serving officer in the American Foreign Service and was ambassador to the Dominican Republic, Portugal, and NATO.

17. Fred Arthur Bailey, "A Virginia Scholar in Chancellor Hitler's Court: The Tragic Ambassadorship of William Edward Dodd," *The Virginia Magazine of History and Biography* 100, no. 3 (1992): 338.

18. J. Pierrepont Moffat to John C. White, January 12, 1935, White Papers, Digital Library of the Commons, Library of Congress. Ambassador Dodd's daughter, Martha, first supported the Nazis and had an affair with Hitler's aide, Ernst Hanfstaengl, but later she became a spy for the Soviet Union. She also had an affair with Kaiser Wilhelm's

grandson, Prince Louis Ferdinand, and "considers herself a Communist and claims to accept the party's program." See Erik Larson's superb book, *In the Garden of Beasts.*

19. Muriel Seherr-Thoss in Rome to Emily White, January 18, 1926, Hampton NHS.

20. Muriel Seherr-Thoss in Rome to Emily White, January 18, 1926, Hampton NHS.

21. E. M. White interview by Fenzi, 1988.

22. E. M. White interview by Fenzi, 1988. Crown Prince Wilhelm was the oldest son and heir of Kaiser Wilhelm II.

23. Der Stahlhelm, Bud der Frontsoldaten, operated as the paramilitary wing of the monarchist German National People's Party.

24. E. M. White interview by Fenzi, 1988. Joseph Goebbels was the Nazi district leader for Berlin and the chief propagandist for the Nazi party. After Hitler's suicide, he was chancellor for one day. Then he and his wife committed suicide after poisoning their six children with cyanide.

25. Margaret White Bennett, "Margaret White Bennett," interview by Jewell Fenzi, *The Association for Diplomatic Studies and Training Foreign Affairs Oral History Program, Foreign Service Spouse Series,* November 21, 1988, https://adst.org/OH%20TOCs/Bennett,%20Margaret%20White.toc.pdf.

26. M. White Bennett interview by Fenzi, 1988.

27. "Sent to Coventry" is to ostracize someone deliberately and no one is to speak to them; it is taken from the English Civil War punishment when Coventry was a Parliamentary stronghold.

28. E. M. White interview by Fenzi, 1988, 25–26.

29. G. S. Messersmith in Vienna to Jay Pierrepont Moffat, June 6, 1934, Messersmith Papers, http://udspace.udel.edu/handle/19716/6348.

30. G. S. Messersmith in Vienna to Cordell Hull, secretary of state, in Washington, July 31, 1936 (marked Confidential), 6–7, Messersmith Papers, http://udspace.udel.edu/handle/19716/6679.

31. Henry White to John C. White, March 6, 1919, Bennett Papers. "Delie" was Cordelia Schermerhorn Jones, wife of John Steward, a second cousin of Ambassador Henry White. They lived in Switzerland, where Muriel often visited them, calling them Aunt Delie and Uncle Johnnie. When he died, in 1923, he left Muriel $100,000 from his estate of $2,357,046. According to family members, she had been told to expect to be the majority beneficiary.

32. Muriel Seherr-Thoss from Scheveningen, Holland, to John C. White, July 29, 1919, Hampton NHS.

33. Henry White to Muriel Seherr-Thoss, January 31, 1919, Bennett Papers.

34. Muriel Seherr-Thoss to John C. White, July 29, 1919, Bennett Papers.

35. Muriel Seherr-Thoss to John C. White, July 29, 1919, Bennett Papers.

36. Muriel Seherr-Thoss to John C. White, July 29, 1919, Bennett Papers.

37. Muriel Seherr-Thoss to John C. White, July 29, 1919, Bennett Papers.

38. Muriel Seherr-Thoss to John C. White, July 29, 1919, Bennett Papers.

39. Muriel Seherr-Thoss to John C. White, July 29, 1919, Bennett Papers.

40. Baron Willem Gevers (1911–1994) competed in the 1930 Olympics in bobsledding. He became the Dutch ambassador to the United Kingdom.

41. Evelyn, Princess Blücher, *An English Wife in Berlin* (New York: E. P. Dutton, 1921), 194.

42. Muriel Seherr-Thoss to John C. White, July 29, 1919, Bennett Papers.

43. Margaret White Bennett to Paul Church, undated note on a copy of a letter dated June 14, 1928, from Muriel Seherr-Thoss to John C. White, Paul Church private collection.

44. Muriel Seherr-Thoss to John C. White, Vienna, January 6, 1932, Paul Church private collection.

45. Muriel Seherr-Thoss to John C. White, Dobrau, April 15, 1931, Paul Church private collection.

46. Muriel Seherr-Thoss to "Ella" (Elizabeth Moffat White), Jagdhaus Oberhof, Post Metniz Kamten, October 20, 1931, Paul Church private collection.

47. Muriel Seherr-Thoss to "Ella" (Elizabeth Moffat White), Jagdhaus Oberhof, Post Metniz Kamten, October 20, 1931, Paul Church private collection.

48. Paul Church, email to the author, August 3, 2022.

49. Where he succeeded Count László Széchenyi, husband of American heiress Gladys Vanderbilt. They would have five daughters.

50. *New York Times*, April 4, 1937.

51. Muriel Seherr-Thoss at Krastowitz to John C. White, January 27, 1941, Bennett Papers.

52. The basic monetary unit of Hungary from 1927 until 1946, when it was replaced by the forint.

53. Muriel Seherr-Thoss at Krastowitz to John C. White, January 27, 1941, Bennett Papers.

54. Muriel Seherr-Thoss at Krastowitz to John C. White, January 27, 1941, Bennett Papers.

55. Dr. Konstantin von Masirevich, an ethnic Serb who served in several posts as an Austro-Hungarian diplomat.

56. Possibly Pál, Count Teleki, future prime minister of Hungary, and Baron Mihály Prónay, lord lieutenant of Nógrád County.

57. Muriel Seherr-Thoss to Betty White, April 5, 1937, Hampton NHS.

58. Prince György Festetics, Duke de Tolna (1882–1941), diplomat. His mother was Lady Mary Douglas-Hamilton, formerly the crown princess of Monaco; his half-brother succeeded as Prince Louis II of Monaco.

59. Muriel Seherr-Thoss to Betty White, April 5, 1937, Hampton NHS.

60. Daughter of broker Grant Barney Schley Jr. and Jane Seney Plummer Schley. She was the godmother of Margaret's son, Alan Church, and never married.

61. Paul Church, email to the author, November 20, 2023, et seq.

62. National Archives at New York, "Arriving Passenger and Crew Lists (including Castle Garden and Ellis Island), 1820–1957, Year: 1937," microfilm T715, p. 24, line 14.

63. Muriel Seherr-Thoss to John C. White, Oldebarneveldtlahn, Holland, January 18, 1920, Paul Church private collection.

64. Muriel Seherr-Thoss to John C. White, Oldebarneveldtlahn, Holland, January 18, 1920, Paul Church private collection.

65. Dagmara Spolniak, "The Extraordinary Story of an American Woman in Dobra," Turystyka; [Turkish], published August 30, 2023, accessed December 10, 2023, https://turystyka.wp.pl/s/dagmara-spolniak/niezwykla-historia-amerykanki-w-dobrej-mieszkancy-ja-kochali-a-gestapo-zastraszalo-6936060113549824a.

66. Muriel Seherr-Thoss to Henry White, Dobrau, November 30, 1925, White Papers.

67. Muriel Seherr-Thoss at Dobrau, to John C. White, August 9, 1928, Paul Church private collection.

68. M. Seherr-Thoss, to J. C. White, August 9, 1928, Paul Church private collection.

69. M. Seherr-Thoss, to J. C. White, August 9, 1928, Paul Church private collection.

70. M. Seherr-Thoss, to J. C. White, August 9, 1928, Paul Church private collection.

71. M. Seherr-Thoss, to J. C. White, August 9, 1928, Paul Church private collection.

72. Muriel Seherr-Thoss to John C. White in New York City, December 20, 1928, Paul Church private collection.

73. Muriel Seherr-Thoss to Ellen Pierrepont Moffat at Grand Hotel Karlsbad, July 28, 1933, Paul Church private collection.

74. M. Seherr-Thoss to E. P. Moffat, July 28, 1933, Paul Church private collection.

75. M. Seherr-Thoss at Grand Hotel, Karlsbad to John C. White, August 5, 1933, Paul Church private collection.

76. M. Seherr-Thoss at Grand Hotel, Karlsbad to John C. White, August 5, 1933, Paul Church private collection.

77. Andrew Nagorski, *Hitlerland* (New York: Simon & Schuster, 2012), 231; quoting an unpublished manuscript by Jacob Beam, former US ambassador to Russia.

78. Nagorski, *Hitlerland*, 231.

79. "Dragon Lady: The Life of Sigrid Schultz," Westport Museum, accessed December 18, 2023, https://westporthistory.org/dragon-lady-the-life-of-sigrid-schultz/.

80. Muriel Seherr-Thoss on the *Isle-de-France* to John C. White, June 14, 1928.

81. Jean Lederer (daughter-in-law of Arthur Lederer), "Waves of Migration," *Signals Quarterly* (Australia National Maritime Museum) 102 (May 2013): 6, https://issuu.com/anmmuseum/docs/signals_102/1.

82. Esther Han, *The Sydney Morning Herald*, January 20, 2013. Archduke Otto von Habsburg (1912–2011) was the last crown prince of Austria-Hungary until the 1918 dissolution of the empire, when he became head of his royal house. He was openly anti-Nazi and anti-Fascist.

83. Lederer, "Waves of Migration," May 2013.

84. "Handwritten Testimonial for Arthur Lederer by the Aide-de-camp to the Emperor," 1904, *Five Handwritten Testimonials for Arthur Lederer*, Powerhouse Collection, accessed December 3, 2023, https://collection.powerhouse.com.au/object/327734.

85. Nicole Cama and Penny Edwell, "Object of the Week: The Importance of Doors, the Lederer Collection," Australia National Maritime Museum, accessed October 19, 2023, https://www.sea.museum/2012/05/08/object-of-the-week-the-importance-of-doors-the-lederer-collection.

86. Giles McDonough, "Philip de László in the Great War," The de László Archive Trust, accessed October 19, 2023, https://www.delaszlocatalogueraisonne.com/media/_file/imported/article-giles-macdonogh-with-images-final.pdf. De László painted her portrait, but his wife struck through the name in his sitters' book, writing across it

"Manifestation of Perfidy," after Lady Max Muller betrayed his confidence by repeating his conversation with her husband. She accused de László of being "to all intents and purposes an enemy alien and I did not regard him as a loyal British subject."

87. Nathan Pike, "The Lederer's Journey to Australia," Prezi, accessed October 19, 2023, https://prezi.com/fnxel0ghucld/lederers-journey-to-australia/.

88. Arthur Lederer to Lady Max-Muller, February 14, 1939, Australia National Maritime Museum.

89. Lederer, "Waves of Migration," 2013. The Maharajah had been a client.

90. Lederer, "Waves of Migration," 2013.

91. "Lederer Family," Australia National Maritime Museum, accessed October 19, 2023, https://www.sea.museum/explore/online-exhibitions/waves-of-migration/immigration-stories/lederer-family.

92. "Lederer Family," Australia National Maritime Museum, accessed October 19, 2023, https://www.sea.museum/explore/online-exhibitions/waves-of-migration/immigration-stories/lederer-family.

93. "Lederer Family," Australian Maritime History Museum, accessed December 3, 2023, https://www.sea.museum/2012/05/08/object-of-the-week-the-importance-of-doors-the-lederer-collection.

94. Muriel Seherr-Thoss to Arthur Lederer [postcard], trans. Christine Reskowski-Santos, December 27, 1939, Lederer Collection, Australia National Maritime Museum.

CHAPTER 5

1. Jason Tomes, *King Zog: Self-Made Monarch of Albania* (Gloucestershire: History Press, 2007), 208.

2. Csaba Katona, "Geraldine Apponyi, the Sold Bride," *Acta Balcano Hungarica* 1 (2019): 204, https://www.academia.edu/40294836/Geraldine_Apponyi_the_Sold_Bride.

3. Antoinette de Szinyei-Merse, *Ten Years, Ten Months, Ten Days* (London: Hutchinson & Co., 1940), 32.

4. de Szinyei-Merse, *Ten Years, Ten Months, Ten Days*, 32.

5. "Certificate of Registration of American Citizen," vol. 95, RG 47200–47699, August 8, 1914, National Archives.

6. *Neenah Daily Times* (Neenah, WI), July 30, 1914.

7. Count André de Baghy, nephew of Queen Geraldine, email to the author, June 30, 2022: "She and my mother were seldom separated, this was true to their deaths."

8. de Szinyei-Merse, *Ten Years, Ten Months, Ten Days*, 33.

9. Tomes, *King Zog*, 197.

10. Joséphine Dedet, email to the author, September 25, 2022.

11. Gwen Robyns, *Geraldine of the Albanians* (London: Muller, Blond & White, 1987), 20.

12. Tomes, *King Zog*, 197.

13. de Szinyei-Merse, *Ten Years, Ten Months, Ten Days*, 35.

14. Tomes, *King Zog*, 197.

15. Tomes, *King Zog*, 197.

16. Tomes, *King Zog*, 139.

17. Muriel Seherr-Thoss, "Memoirs" (unpublished manuscript, Henry White Family Collection, Hampton National Historic Site, National Park Service), 1.

18. Tomes, *King Zog*, 197. Muriel was born in Paris to two American parents and was legally American.

19. Seherr-Thoss, "Memoirs" (unpublished), 1–2.

20. Robyns, *Geraldine of the Albanians*, 23.

21. Count André de Baghy, email to the author, June 19, 2022. The aunt was Franciska (not Madeleine) Karolyi.

22. Muriel Seherr-Thoss from Dobrau to Margaret Apponyi, June 28, 1930; Magyar Nemzeti Levéltár, National Archives of Hungary. Countess Karl Rumerskirch was born Maria Theresia, Countess of Khevenhuller Metsch (1877–1968).

23. From 1939, more than one hundred children and young people with disabilities were housed in the Sacre Coeur in Pressbaum, which was occupied by the Nazis. All were eventually murdered at Am Spiegelgrund in 1941. "Sacre Coeur Is Reminiscent of a Dark Chapter," published June 5, 2019, https://noe.orf.at/v2/news/stories/2985512/.

24. Seherr-Thoss, "Memoirs" (unpublished), 3.

25. Tomes, *King Zog*, 197–98.

26. *New York Times*, November 23, 1928, 24.

27. Seherr-Thoss, "Memoirs" (unpublished), 1–2. Muriel's husband was also descended from Sofie of Thuringia.

28. Seherr-Thoss, "Memoirs" (unpublished), 2.

29. de Szinyei-Merse, *Ten Years, Ten Months, Ten Days*, 46–47.

30. Tomes, *King Zog*, 198.

31. de Szinyei-Merse, *Ten Years, Ten Months, Ten Days*, 49.

32. de Szinyei-Merse, *Ten Years, Ten Months, Ten Days*, 54.

33. Robyns, *Geraldine of the Albanians*, 16–17.

34. Robyns, *Geraldine of the Albanians*, 17.

35. Robyns, *Geraldine of the Albanians*, 27–28.

36. Joséphine Dedet, *Geraldine—A Hungarian Woman on the Throne of Albania* (Libri, 2017), 98.

37. Dedet, 98.

38. Dedet, *Geraldine*, 98.

39. Dedet, *Geraldine*, 98.

40. Joscphine Dedet, email to the author, September 25, 2022.

41. Other Nightingale students included Gloria Morgan Vanderbilt, Millicent Fenwick, and Mandy Grunwald, as well as the daughters of Bette Midler and Billy Joel.

42. Paul Church, email to the author, November 30, 2022.

43. Paul Church, email to the author, November 30, 2022.

44. Joséphine Dedet, email to the author, September 25, 2022: "In fact these friends were Wehrmacht high officers opposed to the Nazi regime."

45. Joséphine Dedet, email to the author, September 25, 2022.

46. Robyns, *Geraldine of the Albanians*, 20–21. King Zog purchased it in 1938 as a wedding present for his wife.

47. Robyns, *Geraldine of the Albanians*, 20–21. Their cousin was Countess Theresa "Resy" Apponyi (1913–1944); she died unmarried.

48. Robyns, *Geraldine of the Albanians*, 22.

49. "Baghy-Szinyei Merse Manor," Cserkeszőlői Borászati Élményközpont, accessed May 18, 2022, http://www.cserkeszolokastely.hu/.

50. "Baghy-Szinyei Merse Manor," Cserkeszőlői Borászati Élményközpont, accessed May 18, 2022, http://www.cserkeszolokastely.hu/. He died October 25, 1941.

51. Muriel Seherr-Thoss to John Campbell White, November 2, 1941, Henry White Family Collection, Muriel White Seherr-Thoss Papers, Box 62A/Folder 12.

52. de Szinyei-Merse, *Ten Years, Ten Months, Ten Days*, 52.

53. Seherr-Thoss, "Memoirs" (unpublished), 3.

54. de Szinyei-Merse, *Ten Years, Ten Months, Ten Days*, 57.

55. Seherr-Thoss, "Memoirs" (unpublished), 3.

56. de Szinyei-Merse, *Ten Years, Ten Months, Ten Days*, 58.

57. Dedet, *Geraldine*, 129–35.

58. Robyns, *Geraldine of the Albanians*, 13.

59. *Pittsburgh Sun-Telegraph*, February 11, 1939, 16.

60. de Szinyei-Merse, *Ten Years, Ten Months, Ten Days*, 58.

61. Robyns, *Geraldine of the Albanians*, 28.

62. Árpád Hornyák, "Magyarország Balkán-politikája a két világháború között és Albánia függet-lensége," in *Kelet-európai sorsfordulók: Tanulmányok a 80 éves Palotás Emil tiszteletére*, edited by József Juhász (Budapest: ELTE BTK Kelet-Európa Történeti Tanszék–L'Harmattan, 2016), 249.

63. Robyns, *Geraldine of the Albanians*, 29.

64. Within three months of her marriage, she would deliver a radio address in Albanian. A 1947 CIA document states that Queen Geraldine spoke "perfect English, perfect French, perfect German, perfect Hungarian, perfect Albanian, and a few Arabic languages."

65. Count André de Baghy, email to the author, July 13, 2022.

66. Robyns, *Geraldine of the Albanians*, 31.

67. Robyns, *Geraldine of the Albanians*, 31.

68. Robyns, *Geraldine of the Albanians*, 35.

69. de Szinyei-Merse, *Ten Years, Ten Months, Ten Days*, 98–99.

70. Robyns, *Geraldine of the Albanians*, 39.

71. Tomes, *King Zog*, 198.

72. *Pittsburgh Sun-Telegraph*, February 11, 1939, 16.

73. *Pittsburgh Sun-Telegraph*, February 11, 1939, 16.

74. Tomes, *King Zog*, 199.

75. András D. Bán, "Barcza, György: Naplórészletek, 1938–1944," *2000* 8, no. 3 (1996): 36. The author's information was not totally valid. He incorrectly referred to King Zog's sisters as "obese Mohammedan women," even though they subsisted mainly on cigarettes and black coffee.

76. Seherr-Thoss, "Memoirs" (unpublished), 4.

77. *New York Times*, March 10, 1938, 9.

78. *Pittsburgh Sun-Telegraph*, February 11, 1939, 16.

79. Tomes, *King Zog*, 200. A Te Deum is a hymn to God normally sung on occasions of public rejoicing.

80. Seherr-Thoss, "Memoirs" (unpublished), 3. It had been the home of his half-brother.

81. Seherr-Thoss, "Memoirs" (unpublished), 3.

82. Robyns, *Geraldine of the Albanians*, 41–42.

83. de Szinyei-Merse, *Ten Years, Ten Months, Ten Days*, 100.

84. Tomes, *King Zog*, 202.

85. *New York Times*, May 26, 1938, 28.

86. Michael O'Sullivan, *Patrick Leigh Fermor: Noble Encounters between Budapest and Transylvania* (Budapest and New York: Central European Press, 2018), 123. Hunyor was also the attorney for Geraldine's sister, Virginia. He would later be arrested and imprisoned by the Nazis in 1944. His name was on a blacklist because he objected to the anti-Jewish laws that prohibited Jews from practicing law in Hungary, and he resigned from the bar in protest. He survived the war and died in poverty in Budapest in 1971, having survived a suicide attempt.

87. *Manchester (CT) Evening Herald*, April 27, 1938, pp. 1, 13. Other sources insisted that Geraldine's mother did not attend the wedding.

88. Prince and Princess Michael of Kent attended the 2016 wedding of Geraldine's grandson, Leka, in Tirana.

89. "Geraldine of the Albanians," *Royalty* magazine, May 29, 2015, https://www.royalty-magazine.com/royal-history-and-heritage/geraldine-of-the-albanians.html.

90. Tomes, *King Zog*, 206.

91. Tomes, *King Zog*, 206.

92. *Daily Telegraph*, April 26, 1938.

93. Seherr-Thoss, "Memoirs" (unpublished), 4.

94. Robyns, *Geraldine of the Albanians*, 56.

95. Robyns, *Geraldine of the Albanians*, 55–56.

96. Tomes, *King Zog*, 203.

97. Robyns, *Geraldine of the Albanians*, 54–55.

98. Ray Moseley, *Mussolini's Shadow: The Double Life of Count Galeazzo Ciano* (New Haven, CT: Yale University Press, 1999), 51.

99. Tomes, *King Zog*, 208.

100. Tomes, *King Zog*, 207.

101. Muriel Seherr-Thoss to Henry White, November 24, 1925.

102. Paul Church, email to the author, August 21, 2022.

103. Draft letter for John C. White's signature written by Muriel Seherr-Thoss. Manni had insisted her funds be deposited in Germany but also stipulated that the money she paid to him be deposited outside Germany. The letter may not have been sent. In 1931, an eviction notice was published in the "Deutscher Reichsanzeiger and Prussian State Gazette" for unpaid bills at Dobrau that were eventually settled.

CHAPTER 6

1. Muriel Seherr-Thoss to Henry White, November 30, 1925.

2. Muriel Seherr-Thoss to Betty White, April 5, 1937, Hampton National Historic Site NHS.

3. Hubert Hering at Benediktinergymnasium Ettal, email to the author, February 27, 2024.

4. Boysie Seherr-Thoss, audiotape interviews by Julia Scott, 1987–1988, Elizabeth Seherr-Thoss private collection.

5. Boysie Seherr-Thoss, audiotape.

6. Duncan's mother was also an American, the pharmaceutical and chemical heiress Helen Pfizer.

7. His mother, Helen Schermerhorn Welles, was a daughter of Katharine Schermerhorn Welles, who was Mrs. Astor's sister.

8. In an unusual departure from the practice of foreign-titled husbands marrying wealthy American wives, George's first cousin, Walter Frederick Kingsland Jr., married, in 1928, Princess Marie Louise, a daughter of the Duc de Vendome and a great-granddaughter of King Leopold I of Belgium.

9. He was born on February 6, 1912.

10. *Brooklyn Daily Eagle*, May 29, 1938, 14.

11. *New York Times*, June 26, 1938.

12. Alan Church, email to the author, September 26, 2022.

13. Bruce Farrell, personal communication, December 20, 2023.

14. Boysie Seherr-Thoss, audiotape.

15. Alanson Church, email to the author, February 25, 2024.

16. Boysie Seherr-Thoss, audiotape.

17. Muriel Seherr-Thoss to Henry White, August 6, 1926.

18. Boysie Seherr-Thoss, audiotape.

19. Natalie Livingstone, *The Women of Rothschild* (New York: St. Martin's Press, 2021), 289, quoting Kathleen "Nica" de Rothschild, Baroness de Koenigswarter.

20. Boysie Seherr-Thoss, audiotape. The first job was at J. Stirling Getchell Agency. After the principal's death, the firm closed, and Boysie moved to Young & Rubicam, which assumed some of Getchell's clients.

21. H. C. "Boysie" Seherr-Thoss to J. C. White, January 23, 1943, Bennett Papers.

22. Tea dance; copy of invitation at Hampton.

23. Muriel Seherr-Thoss to Henry White, November 30, 1925.

24. Muriel Seherr-Thoss to John C. White, The Westbury Hotel, New York City, January 15, 1929. A *whiskerando* is a man with extravagant whiskers. Don Ferolo Whiskerandos was a character in Sheridan's play *The Critic*.

25. Muriel Seherr-Thoss to John C. White, Dobrau, April 15, 1931. Count Franz Deym von Střítež was the Austro-Hungarian ambassador to the United Kingdom, 1888–1903.

26. Muriel Seherr-Thoss at Rome to Henry White, 9 (month obscured) 1925.

27. The American-born Elizabeth "Bessie" Hickson Field married in 1870 the first Prince Brancaccio, fifth Duke of Lustra. She was so accepted in Roman society that she served as a lady-in-waiting to Queen Margherita.

28. Muriel Seherr-Thoss to her father, Henry White, in Rome, June 9, 1925.

29. Muriel Seherr-Thoss to her father, Henry White, in Rome, June 9, 1925.

30. Muriel Seherr-Thoss to her father, Henry White, in Rome, June 9, 1925. At the time, Margaret was sixteen.

31. Muriel Seherr-Thoss to her father, Henry White, in Rome, January 27, 1926.

32. *Swedish Men and Women: Biographical Reference Book (1942–1948)*, vol. 4, I–Linder (Project Runeberg, 2023), 420. https://runeberg-org.translate.goog/smok/4/0464.html ?_x_tr_sch=http&_x_tr_sl=sv&_x_tr_tl=en&_x_tr_hl=en&_x_tr_pto=sc.

33. Caroline Russell Lagergren's sister, Joanna, married John W. Auchincloss, and their grandson was the writer Louis Auchincloss.

34. *Who's Who in American Sports* (Washington, DC: National Biographical Society, Inc., 1928), 142.

35. *New York Times*, October 22, 1939. Many cousins and in-laws were referred to as *aunt* and *uncle* no matter their level of familial relationship.

36. He served as a volunteer ambulance driver at the American Ambulance Hospital in Paris.

37. Muriel Seherr-Thoss to John C. White, October 20, 1939.

38. *New York Daily News*, June 15, 1940, 10. Beatrice Procter, a descendant of the founder of Procter & Gamble, married Peter H. B. Frelinghuysen, who was a member of Congress, as was their son, Rodney. She was a bridesmaid at the wedding of Marion Kingsland to Boysie Seherr-Thoss.

39. *New York Times*, March 3, 1943.

40. Alanson Church, email to the author, September 27, 2022.

41. Women's Army Auxiliary Corps created in 1942 as an auxiliary unit and converted to active duty status in the army of the US as the Women's Army Corps (WAC) on July 1, 1943.

42. H. C. "Boysie" Seherr-Thoss to J. C. White, January 23, 1943.

43. Muriel Seherr-Thoss to Lewis Spencer Morris, April 21, 1941, Bennett Papers.

44. Muriel Seherr-Thoss to Lewis Morris, April 21, 1941, Bennett Papers.

45. Boysie Seherr-Thoss, audiotape.

46. "US Petition for Naturalization," October 22, 1943, US District Court, Macon, GA, RG 1845. The author's father had his basic training at the same camp and fought in the Pacific.

47. Muriel Seherr-Thoss to Lewis Morris, April 21, 1941.

48. Muriel Seherr-Thoss to Lewis Morris, April 21, 1941.

49. Muriel Seherr-Thoss to Lewis Morris, April 21, 1941.

50. Muriel Seherr-Thoss to Lewis Morris, April 21, 1941.

51. Cornelius Vanderbilt Jr., *Queen of the Golden Age* (New York: McGraw-Hill, 1956), 44.

52. Elizabeth Shoumatoff, *FDR's Unfinished Portrait* (Pittsburgh: University of Pittsburgh Press, 1990), 120.

53. Elizabeth Seherr-Thoss, personal communications, February 14, 2024, and February 25, 2024.

54. Boysie Seherr-Thoss, audiotape.

55. Boysie Seherr-Thoss, audiotape.

56. Muriel Seherr-Thoss to Marian Seherr-Thoss, Hotel Kontinental, Yugoslavia, 1939, Elizabeth Seherr-Thoss collection.

57. Muriel Seherr-Thoss to Marian Seherr-Thoss, Hotel Cecil, Kifissia, Greece, October 8, 1939. Elizabeth Seherr-Thoss collection.

58. Alanson Church, email to the author, September 26, 2022.

59. Muriel Seherr-Thoss to Marian Seherr-Thoss, Hotel Cecil, Kifissia, Greece, October 8, 1939.

60. Muriel Seherr-Thoss to Marian Seherr-Thoss, Hotel Cecil, Kifissia, Greece, October 8, 1939.

61. Muriel Seherr-Thoss to Sophie Beylard White, October 21, 1925 (written on her coroneted stationery).

62. Muriel Seherr-Thoss to Jack White, Rome, ca. April 1927.

63. Undated draft letter by Muriel Seherr-Thoss for her father and brother's signature (Elm Court stationery).

64. Jolanta Ilnicka, blog, May 17, 2015.

65. Boysie Seherr-Thoss, audiotape.

66. Boysie Seherr-Thoss, audiotape.

67. Boysie Seherr-Thoss, audiotape.

68. Muriel Seherr-Thoss to John C. White, February 14, 1926.

69. Alanson Church, email to the author, September 26, 2022.

70. Paul Church, email to the author, November 30, 2022. "I attest to having read this written in Muriel's hand in the collection of her personal letters."

71. Muriel Seherr-Thoss to Marian Seherr-Thoss, Hotel Kifissia, Greece, October 8, 1939.

72. Muriel Seherr-Thoss to John C. White, New York City, December 20, 1928. At Newbold Morris's death in 1928, he left an estate of more than $7 million. His wife, Helen Schermerhorn Kingsland Morris, was a niece of Mrs. Astor. Her niece, Marian Kingsland, was the first wife of "Boysie" Seherr-Thoss.

73. Undated note from Margaret White Bennett to Paul Church.

74. Paul Church, email to the author, November 19, 2021.

75. Boysie Seherr-Thoss, audiotape.

76. Muriel Seherr-Thoss to Jack White, October 4, 1941.

77. Muriel Seherr-Thoss to Jack White, October 4, 1941.

Chapter 7

1. Muriel Seherr-Thoss to Henry White, January 15 (year illegible).

2. Muriel Seherr-Thoss, "Memoirs" (unpublished), 4.

3. Muriel Seherr-Thoss, "Memoirs" (unpublished), 4.

4. Muriel Seherr-Thoss, "Memoirs" (unpublished), 4.

5. Muriel Seherr-Thoss, "Memoirs" (unpublished), 5.

6. Muriel Seherr-Thoss, "Memoirs" (unpublished), 5.

7. Tomes, *King Zog*, 225.

8. Muriel Seherr-Thoss, "Memoirs" (unpublished), 5. On February 20, 1931, after attending a performance of *Pagliacci* at the Vienna State Opera, Libohova was injured in an assassination attempt against King Zog. The king and their chauffeur returned fire. Libohova was shot in the leg and a bullet went through his hat; the king was unharmed. Libohova was an Axis collaborator who would serve twice as the puppet prime minister during the Italian occupation. When Germany invaded Albania to replace the Italians, he fled to Rome, where he died in 1948.

9. Muriel Seherr-Thoss, "Memoirs" (unpublished), 6.

10. After Italy's annexation of Albania, he headed the German mission as consul general. After Germany's surrender, he was sent to a US internment camp near Hof, where he died in 1945.

11. Muriel Seherr-Thoss, "Memoirs" (unpublished), 6.

12. Muriel Seherr-Thoss, "Memoirs" (unpublished), 6–7.

13. Count André de Baghy, Zoom conversation with the author, July 7, 2022.

14. Muriel Seherr-Thoss, "Memoirs" (unpublished), 7.

15. Muriel Seherr-Thoss, "Memoirs" (unpublished), 7.

16. Tomes, *King Zog,* 225.

17. G. Bernard Noble and E. R. Perkins, eds., *Foreign Relations of the United States 1939,* vol. 2 (Washington, DC: Office of the Historian, 1956), 373, https://history.state.gov/historicaldocuments/frus1939v01.

18. Tomes, *King Zog,* 226.

19. Tomes, *King Zog,* 226.

20. Szinyei-Merse, *Ten Years, Ten Months, Ten Days,* 244.

21. Muriel Seherr-Thoss, "Memoirs" (unpublished), 8.

22. *New York Times,* April 5, 1939, 8.

23. *New York Times,* April 5, 1939, 8.

24. Tomes, *King Zog,* 228.

25. Muriel Seherr-Thoss, "Memoirs" (unpublished), 7.

26. *New York Times,* April 10, 1961, 31.

27. Muriel Seherr-Thoss, "Memoirs" (unpublished), 8–9.

28. Robyns, *Geraldine of the Albanians,* 91.

29. Lloyd Jones, *Biografi: A Traveller's Tale* (Toronto: Vintage Canada, 2010).

30. Robert Elsie, "1947 Galeazzo Ciano: Diary of Events on Albania," *Texts and Documents of Albanian History,* accessed May 28, 2022, http://www.albanianhistory.net/1947_Ciano/index.html.

31. Jay Nordlinger, "Good King Michael," *The National Review,* January 16, 2018, https://www.nationalreview.com/2018/01/michael-romania-monarch-and-mensch/.

32. Bernd J. Fischer, *Albania at War, 1939–1945* (West Lafayette, IN: Purdue University Press, 1999), 5.

33. Mirela Bogdani and John Loughlin, *Albania and the European Union: The Tumultuous Journey Towards Integration and Accession* (London: I. B. Tauris, 2007), 230.

34. *Lexico UK English Dictionary,* s.v. "Hoxha, Enver," Oxford University Press, accessed September 14, 2019.

35. C. L. Sulzberger, *A Long Row of Candles* (New York: McMillan, 1969), 479; quoted in Stephen Dorril, *MI6: Inside the Covert World of Her Majesty's Secret Intelligence Service* (Washington, DC: Free Press, 2002). The second Viscount Harcourt was the son of an American heiress mother, Mary Ethel Burns, a niece of J. P. Morgan.

36. *New York Times,* April 23, 1939.

37. *New York Times,* April 15, 1939.

38. Robyns, *Geraldine of the Albanians,* 157.

39. Joséphine Dedet, email to the author, September 25, 2022.

40. Katona, "The Sold Bride," 205. Rohan's wife was a daughter of Albert Apponyi. Mauthausen Concentration Camp in Austria was liberated by US troops on May 5, 1945. Out of approximately 190,000 people imprisoned there over seven years, at least 90,000 died. Wallenberg saved thousands of Jews during the Holocaust. Virginia's son, born in 1941, recalls that Wallenberg lived with them, but he was too young to know details.

41. Count André de Baghy, email to the author, August 2, 2022. "One thing I am sure of is that Mother was never deported to a concentration camp."

42. Central Intelligence Agency, "Office Memorandum: BGFIEND Operations, 16 September 1949" (declassified), 2007, page 9, https://tetovalajm.blogspot.com/2014/01/cia-incesti-dhe-arkat-me-flori-ne.html.

43. "Blackburn, Joseph," *US Consular Reports of Marriages 1910–1949*, RG 59 (Washington, DC: National Archives), 133.

44. "Naturalization Records Created by the US District Court in Colorado, 1877–1952," *Naturalization Records, Colorado, 1876–1990*, M1192 (Washington, DC: National Archives).

45. Count André de Baghy, Zoom conversation with the author, July 7, 2022.

46. Count André de Baghy, Zoom conversation with the author, July 7, 2022.

47. Central Intelligence Agency, "Office Memorandum: BGFIEND Operations, 16 September 1949" (declassified), 2007, page 2, OBOPUS BGFIEND VOL. 14 (BGFIEND OPERATIONS)_0039.pdf (cia.gov).

48. *Sunday Pictorial*, January 3, 1943, https://www.ucl.ac.uk/library/ssees-archives/nac3.htm. The king sued the magazine for libel for this article.

49. Douglas Saltmarshe, *Identity in a Post-Communist Balkan State: An Albanian Village Study* (Farnham, UK: Ashgate Pub Ltd, 2001), 56.

50. Count André de Baghy, Zoom conversation with the author, July 7, 2022.

51. Count André de Baghy, Zoom conversation with the author, July 7, 2022.

52. Muriel Seherr-Thoss to John Campbell White, September 14, 1940, Muriel White Seherr-Thoss Papers: Personal Correspondence, Henry White Family Collection.

53. Muriel Seherr-Thoss to John Campbell White, July 17, 1941, Henry White Family Collection.

54. Muriel Seherr-Thoss to John Campbell White, March 28, 1941, Henry White Family Collection.

55. Muriel Seherr-Thoss to John Campbell White, October 4, 1941, Henry White Family Collection. Her brother, who was born in London, was at that time US ambassador to Haiti.

56. Central Intelligence Agency, "Office Memorandum: BGFIEND Operations, Day September 1949" (declassified), 2007, page 2, OBOPUS BGFIEND VOL. 14 (BGFIEND OPERATIONS)_0037.pdf (cia.gov).

57. Central Intelligence Agency, "HR 70-14" (declassified), May 2, 2012, 6, https://www.cia.gov/readingroom/docs/1949-05-02.pdf.

58. So many society figures and upper-class agents were recruited (e.g., film director John Ford, chef Julia Child, actor Sterling Hayden, baseball player Moe Berg, Supreme Court Justice Arthur Goldberg, historian Arthur Schlesinger Jr.) that the agency was sometimes called "Oh So Social."

59. Major Robert E. Mattingly, USMC, *Herringbone Cloak—GI Dagger: Marines of the OSS* (Quantico, VA: Marine Corps University, 1989), 87, https://www.ibiblio.org/hyperwar/USMC/USMC-OSS/USMC-OSS-6.html.

60. John Pearson, *The Life of Ian Fleming* (London: Jonathan Cape, 1966), 105.

61. Albert Lulushi, *Operation Valuable Fiend* (New York: Arcade, 2014), 21.

62. Lulushi, *Operation*, 21.

63. Mattingly, *Herringbone Cloak*, 360.

64. James D. Callanan, "The Evolution of the CIA's Covert Action Mission, 1947–1963" (doctoral thesis, Durham University, 1999), 116, https://etheses.dur.ac.uk/4481/.

65. Central Intelligence Agency, "Scope of BGFIEND Operation" (declassified), 2007, https://gjonmarkagjoni.files.wordpress.com/2017/08/obopus-bgfiend-vol-13-bg fiend-operations_0056-scope-of-bgfiend.pdf.

66. Callanan, "CIA's Covert Action Mission," 119.

67. CIA, "Office Memorandum: BGFIEND Operations, 16 September 1949," 2–3.

68. CIA, "Office Memorandum: BGFIEND Operations, 16 September 1949," 1, OBOPUS BGFIEND VOL. 14 (BGFIEND OPERATIONS)_0037.pdf (cia.gov).

69. CIA, "Office Memorandum: BGFIEND Operations, 16 September 1949," 2.

70. CIA, "Office Memorandum: BGFIEND Operations, 16 September 1949," 2.

71. CIA, "HR 70-14" (declassified), May 2, 2012, 1, 58, https://cia.gov/readingroom/docs/1949-05-02.pdf.

72. Gary Ginzberg, "A Complicated Life: Frank G. Wisner, Sr.," *Advisors* magazine, accessed August 7, 2022, https://www.advisorsmagazine.com/trending/23537-a-compli cated-life-frank-g-wisner-sr.

73. Evan Thomas, *The Very Best Men: Four Who Dared* (New York: Touchstone, 1995). His biographer said of his reasons for taking his life, "He was manic-depressive . . . he tried to do too much. He tried to create this fantastic covert operation capability to fight the Soviet Union in the 1950s. We were up against a very tough foe: the KGB. And he had, at best, limited success and he had some tragic setbacks, particularly the Hungarian revolution in 1956. And it got to him. He went mad on the job."

74. CIA, "HR 70-14" (declassified), May 2, 2012, 58. "DCI" and "Director" refer to the director of central intelligence.

75. David M. McCourt, "American Hegemony and International Theory at the Council on Foreign Relations, 1953–1954," *International History Review* 42, no. 3 (2020), https://www.tandfonline.com/doi/abs/10.1080/07075332.2019.1608283?jour nalCode=rinh20.

76. There is no official record that he was in the OSS; however, a catastrophic fire in St. Louis in 1973 destroyed 16–18 million official military personnel files for 1912–1960 that would have included military intelligence records, and there are no duplicates or microfilm, according to Suzanne Zoumbaris at National Archives, email to the author, April 12, 2024.

77. Skopje Press, "CIA: Incest and the Chests of Gold in Zog's Rooms," *Top Tetova News*, accessed April 7, 2024, https://tetovalajm.blogspot.com/2014/01/cia-incesti-dhe-arkat-me-flori-ne.html.

78. Skopje Press, "Incest and the Chests of Gold," accessed August 8, 2022.

79. CIA, "Office Memorandum: BGFIEND Operations, 21 September 1949," 1.

80. Peter Richmond, *New York Times* best-selling author, email to the author, August 8, 2022.

81. *New York Times*, November 29, 1952.

82. *New York Times*, September 21, 1951.

83. Lloyd Jones, *Biografi: An Albanian Quest*, ebook (Toronto: Vintage Canada, 2010; repr., Wellington, New Zealand: Victoria University Press, 1993).

84. Count André de Baghy, Zoom conversation with the author, July 7, 2022. Saud was crown prince of Saudi Arabia 1933–1953 and king 1953–1964.

85. Count André de Baghy, Zoom conversation with the author, July 7, 2022.

86. CIA, "Office Memorandum: BGFIEND Operations, 21 September 1949," 4.

87. Although Queen Elena of Italy—wife of King Victor Emmanuel III of Italy, who overran the country and claimed the Albanian throne for himself—was also called "queen of Albania," she never actually served.

CHAPTER 8

1. Jolanta Ilnicka (whose grandmother was Muriel's chef and friend), "'Good Lady'—Meeting of Great-Grandchildren," *My Skirmishes with Genealogy* (blog), May 17, 2014, https://potyczkizgenealogia.blogspot.com/2017/10/dobra-pani-spotkanie-prawnukow.html. Other sources say the pilots were British, which seems more likely.

2. Jan Szczurek, "This Land Is Very Interesting," *Pisarze* (blog), June 9, 2020, https://pisarze.pl/2020/06/09/jan-szczurek-wielce-interesujaca-to-kraina/.

3. Paul Church, email to the author, November 19, 2023.

4. Ilnicka, "Good Lady," October 20, 2013.

5. Ilnicka, "Good Lady," October 20, 2013.

6. Ilnicka, "Good Lady," October 20, 2013.

7. Paul Church, email to the author, March 10, 2024.

8. Ilnicka, "Good Lady," October 20, 2013. He was "a groom (equerry) of the same count. Sometimes he also served as a coachman when the lord of the castle went to visit, e.g., nearby Moszna."

9. Ilnicka, "Good Lady," October 20, 2013.

10. Jolanta Ilnicka, email to the author, March 22, 2024.

11. He was killed in Austria on December 2, 1941.

12. Paul Church, email to the author, November 19, 2023.

13. Boysie Seherr-Thoss, audiotape.

14. Boysie Seherr-Thoss, audiotape.

15. Henry White at Washington, DC, to Muriel Seherr-Thoss, March 3, 1920.

16. Paul Church, email to the author, November 19, 2023. The Tatra mountains are the highest in the Carpathians. They form a natural border between Slovakia and Poland.

17. Paul Church, email to the author, November 19, 2023.

18. Szczurek, "This Land Is Very Interesting," 4. Although there is no written documentation (perhaps due to fires and destruction at the end of the war), many sources refer to this event.

19. Szczurek, "This Land Is Very Interesting," 4.

20. Muriel Seherr-Thoss to Aunt Sophie (Mrs. Julian White), October 2, 1925, Hampton NHS.

21. Muriel Seherr-Thoss to John C. White, at Dobrau, October 9, 1940.

22. Muriel Seherr-Thoss to John C. White, October 9, 1940, quoting John H. Lord at the US consulate in Rotterdam, letter dated August 19, 1940. In 1964, Austria returned to the United States $50,295.76 in trust funds for Manni established by Muriel. "Treaties and International Agreements Registered or Filed and Recorded with the Secretariat of the United Nations," *Treaty Series*, vol. 511 (New York: United Nations, 1966), https://treaties.un.org/doc/Publication/UNTS/Volume%20511/v511.pdf.

23. "Report of the Death of an American Citizen, Form 192," US Foreign Service, April 15, 1943. It was not received until it was sent to her family after her death.

24. Ilnicka, "Good Lady," October 20, 2013. In Communist Poland, his name was officially changed to Franciszek, but his family still called him "Ginter." Ilnicka, email to the author, March 22, 2024.

25. Ilnicka, "Good Lady," October 20, 2013.

26. Ilnicka, "Good Lady," October 20, 2013.

27. Muriel Seherr-Thoss to John C. White, October 4, 1941.

28. Henry J. White to John C. White, Baltimore, November 15, 1948; Bennett, UGA. Ambassador Henry White, Muriel's father, was a second cousin of Harry White, father of the naval attaché. They grew up together in Baltimore.

29. Henry J. White to John C. White, Baltimore, November 15, 1948.

30. "Deutscher Reichsanzeiger und Preußischer Staatsanzeiger" (Berlin), June 25, 1943, citing Section 2 Paragraph 1 of the law on the revocation of naturalization and the revocation of German nationality of July 14, 1933 (RGBM. I p. 480).

31. "Silesian Castles and Palaces," ADAN publishing, 2000.

32. Filipczyk, Zawilak, et al., *Good for Seven Centuries*, 40.

33. Paul Church, email to the author, November 19, 2023.

34. Szczurek, "This Land Is Very Interesting," 4–5.

35. Muriel Seherr-Thoss at the Anglo-American Hotel in Florence, Italy, to Henry White, February 14, 1926; Hampton, NPS.

36. Paul Church, email to the author, May 17, 2022.

37. Szczurek, "This Land Is Very Interesting," 5.

38. Spolniak, "Niezwykła historia Amerykanki," 2.

39. Henry J. White to John C. White, in Baltimore, November 15, 1948.

40. Henry J. White to John C. White, in Baltimore, November 15, 1948.

41. Henry J. White to John C. White, in Baltimore, November 15, 1948.

42. "Seherr, Muriel von Thoss: Report of the Death of an American Citizen, Form 192" (Berlin: Swiss Legation), US Foreign Service, April 15, 1943.

43. John C. White to Lewis S. Morris, from Port-au-Prince, Haiti, May 3, 1943.

44. Secstate Code: Brown/48/JCW, No. 95; received May 5, 6:00 p.m., 1943.

45. John C. White to Secretary of State Hull, All America Cables and Radiograms, Port-au-Prince, 95A, May 6, 1943.

46. John C. White to Edgar Church, All America Cables and Radiograms, Port-au-Prince, 95A, May 6, 1943.

47. Allen T. Klots to James C. Watts, May 12, 1943, stamped "Received" May 19, 1943.

48. Muriel Seherr-Thoss to John C. White, October 9, 1940, quoting John H. Lord at the US consulate in Rotterdam, letter dated October 9, 1940.

49. "Seherr-Thoss, #5267," Federal Political Department, American Legation at Bern, June 5, 1943. Translation of information received May 27, 1943.

50. Margaret Church to John C. White, Sharon, CT, June 20, 1943.

51. Margaret Church to John C. White, Sharon, CT, June 20, 1943.

52. Muriel Seherr-Thoss to Marian Seherr-Thoss, undated letter. Margaret's grandson would eventually wonder how all those valuable items made their way to Margaret in the United States.

53. Paul Church, email to the author, November 20, 2023.

54. John C. White to Margaret Church, in Port-au-Prince, June 29, 1943.

55. Ilnicka, "Good Lady," October 20, 2013.

56. Hermann (Manni) Seherr-Thoss to John C. White, Haiti Red Cross written message form, July 8, 1943.

57. Hermann (Manni) Seherr-Thoss to John C. White, Haiti Red Cross written message form, September 19, 1943.

58. Szczurek, "This Land Is Very Interesting," 6.

59. Szczurek, "This Land Is Very Interesting," 6. There is also the possibility that the retreating German soldiers knew Manni had been spirited away and did not fight when his country needed him, and, in retaliation, they started the fires.

60. "The End of Hitlerism in Klein Strehlitz" (trans. "Das Ende des Hitlerismūs in KleinStrehlitz") (Berlin) *Neustädter Heimatbrief* 1952, https://www.digishelf.de /objekt/010078045_1952/8/, accessed May 18, 2024.

61. Paul Church, email to the author, November 19, 2023.

62. Berlepsch was a son of Frances, Baroness von Berenberg-Gossler, whose family owned Berenberg Bank in Hamburg. Frances was a granddaughter of Mary Elizabeth Bray, whose grandfather was the immensely wealthy Boston banker Samuel Eliot.

63. Ilnicka, "Good Lady," October 20, 2013.

64. Ilnicka, "Good Lady," October 20, 2013.

65. Krzysztof Strauchmann, "Muriel's Children, or the Post-War Fate of the Owners of the Palace in Dobrau," *NTO* (blog), February 23, 2016, 6, https://nto.pl/dzieci-mu riel-czyli-powojenne-losy-wlascicieli-palacu-w-dobrej/ar/9428464.

66. Ilnicka, "Good Lady," October 20, 2013.

67. Paul Church, email to the author, November 19, 2023.

68. Paul Church, email to the author, November 30, 2023.

69. August Walzl, *Kärnten 1946. Vom NS-Regime zur Besatzungsherrschaft im Alpen-Adria-Raum* (Klagenfurt: Universitätsverlag Carinthia, 1985), 117. In 1947, General Löhr, an Austrian, was executed as a war criminal in Yugoslavia for his role in the bombing of Belgrade in 1941.

70. Walzl, *Kärnten 1946*, 194.

71. Strauchmann, "Muriel's Children."

72. Count André de Baghy, Zoom conversation with the author, July 7, 2022; Count André de Baghy, email to the author, August 2, 2022.

73. John C. White in Maryland to Manni Seherr-Thoss at Krastowitz, April 7, 1946.

74. Paul Church, email to the author, August 3, 2022. The estate was a castle on 240 hectares of land.

75. "Neustädter Heimatbrief" 11th year, issue 1, January 1960; obituary written by his lifelong friend and neighbor, Wilhelm Hans, Graf von Oppersdorff. "He knew how to decorate castles and, like his father, was an enthusiastic hunter who knew how to bring joy to many."

76. "Klagenfurt—Herzoghof," *Burgen-Austria* (archive), accessed March 30, 2024, https://www.burgen-austria.com/archive.php?id=1713.

77. Paul Church, email to the author, November 19, 2023.

78. Paul Church, email to the author, November 19, 2023.

79. Paul Church, email to the author, November 30, 2022.

80. Paul Church, email to the author, November 19, 2023.

81. "What Is the Catholic Church's Position on Suicide and Physician-Assisted Suicide?" *Institute of Clinical Bioethics, Saint Joseph's University* (blog), accessed March 22, 2024, https://www.sju.edu/centers/icb/blog/catholic-churchs-position-suicide-physician-assisted-suicide-declaration-euthanasia.

82. Henry J. White to John C. White, in Baltimore, November 15, 1948.

83. Paul Church, email to the author, November 19, 2021.

84. Muriel Seherr-Thoss to Boysie Seherr-Thoss, at The Hague, Holland, March 20, 1940.

CHAPTER 9

1. John C. White to Manni Seherr-Thoss, in Washington, DC, April 7, 1946.

2. "US Petition for Naturalization," October 22, 1943, RG 1845.

3. Strauchmann, "Muriel's Children," 7.

4. Boysie Seherr-Thoss (writing as John Strutt) in England to Mrs. John C. White in Lima, Peru, December 5, 1944. His draft card has "name changed to: John Strutt" written above his birth name.

5. Boysie Seherr-Thoss (writing as John Strutt) in England to Mrs. John C. White in Lima, Peru, December 5, 1944.

6. Strauchmann, "Muriel's Children," 7.

7. Alan Church, email to the author, September 26, 2022.

8. Alan Church, email to the author, September 26, 2022.

9. "Documentation of the Reichssicherheitshauptamt (RHSA), 1939–1945," *EHRI*, Bundesarchiv, Berlin R58 Collection, https://portal.ehri-project.eu/units/il-002798-m_29-bundesarchiv_berlin_r_58.

10. Perhaps some of those officers were at the secret meeting at the Seherr-Thosses' Gruben Palace during the 1936 Olympics.

11. "Generalmajor Theobald Graf von Seherr-Thoß," *Lexikon der Wehrmacht*, accessed March 4, 2024, https://lexikon-der-wehrmacht.de.

12. When Theo sailed to the Port of Miami, Florida, in 1937, he listed his occupation as "Ex-General."

13. Lars-Broder Keil, "This Enabled the Conspirators to Cover Up Many Traces," *Die Welt* magazine, published March 18, 2021, https://www.welt.de/geschichte/zweiter-weltkrieg/article197285955/Hitler-Attentat-So-gross-war-die-Verschwoerung-vom-20-Juli-wirklich.html.

14. Keil, "Conspirators," accessed March 4, 2024.

15. Keil, "Conspirators," accessed March 4, 2024.

16. "Arrest list No. 22—Hermann von Seherr-Thoss; Roger von Seherr-Thoss; Theobald von Seherr-Thoss; Wolfgang von Seherr-Thoss," *Compilation by the IV Special Commission at the RSHA*, RG 242, National Archives, accessed April 26, 2024, https://www.archives.gov/iwg/declassified-records/rg-242-seized-foreign-records.

17. "Document Book III (Documents 86–96) for the Defense of the Defendant Franz von Papen," Nuremberg Archives: International Court of Justice, accessed April 4, 2024, https://stacks.stanford.edu/file/kd270md6345/kd270md6345.pdf.

18. Keil, "Conspirators," accessed March 4, 2024.

19. "Document Book III," Nuremberg Archives, accessed April 4, 2024.

20. Papen served as the chancellor of Germany in 1932 and then as the vice chancellor under Adolf Hitler from 1933 to 1934.

21. "Document Book III," Nuremberg Archives, accessed April 4, 2024.

22. Papen was given a sentence of eight years' imprisonment at hard labor but was released on appeal in 1949.

23. Elizabeth Seherr-Thoss, personal communication, February 15, 2024.

24. *New York Daily News*, June 15, 1940, 10. Beatrice Procter, a descendant of the founder of Procter & Gamble, married Peter H. B. Frelinghuysen, who was a member of Congress, as was their son, Rodney. The Frelinghuysen family sent four members to the US Senate.

25. In 2017, Paul Church and his wife Linda visited Dobrau and saw the impressive restoration of the castle. Their visit was widely reported in local newspapers.

26. Strauchmann, "Muriel's Children," 6.

27. *Forbes* magazine lists the Phipps family as the fortieth wealthiest in the United States, just ahead of the Rockefellers, with $8.6 billion. Kerry A. Dolan, Chase Peterson-Withorn, and Jennifer Wang, eds., "Billion-Dollar Dynasties: These Are the Richest Families in America," *Forbes*, published December 17, 2020, https://www.forbes.com/sites/kerryadolan/2020/12/17/billion-dollar-dynasties-these-are-the-richest-families-in-america/?sh=47d1bcba772c. At one point, the Phipps family owned one-third of Palm Beach, including twenty-eight miles of oceanfront property. Among the many beneficiaries of Henry Phipps's philanthropy, he funded the Henry Phipps Psychiatric Clinic at Johns Hopkins Hospital, the first inpatient facility in the United States for the mentally ill as part of an acute care hospital.

28. Known as the "first lady of the turf," she was a highly successful horse owner and breeder.

29. Alan Church, email to the author, September 17, 2022.

30. Bruce Farrell, email to the author, April 9, 2024.

31. Muriel Seherr-Thoss to Lewis Morris, April 21, 1941.

32. Virginia Seherr-Thoss to Betty White, March 28, 1944.

33. Virginia Seherr-Thoss in Denver to Betty and John White, September 25, 1944.

34. Susanne's grandmother, Augusta, Countess von Waldeck-Pyrmont, was a cousin of Queen Emma of the Netherlands.

35. "American A German Peeress," *New York Times*, January 28, 1912, 1.

36. "The Baronial Busches," *Life* magazine, May 2, 1955, photographed by Margaret Bourke-White.

37. Bruce Farrell, conversations with the author, December 20, 2023, and April 9, 2024.

38. Alan Church, email to the author, September 17, 2022.

39. Paul Church, email to the author, July 18, 2022.

40. Paul Church, email to the author, August 21, 2022.

41. Alan Church, email to the author, September 27, 2022.

42. Paul Church, email to the author, August 21, 2022.

43. Alan Church, email to the author, September 17, 2022.

44. Paul Church, email to the author, August 21, 2022.

45. Alan Church, email to the author, September 17, 2022.

46. Paul Church, email to the author, August 22, 2022.

47. Alan Church, email to the author, September 17, 2022.

48. Alan Church, email to the author, September 17, 2022.

49. Alan Church email to the author, September 17, 2022.

50. Alan Church email to the author, September 27, 2022.

51. Paul Church, email to the author, March 13, 2024.

52. Paul Church, email to the author, August 21, 2022.

53. Paul Church, email to the author, August 21, 2022.

54. *Church v. Church*, 23 Misc.2d 189, 201 (N.Y. Sup. Ct. 1960), https://casetext.com/case/church-v-church-4.

55. Constance Cary Harrison, *Recollections Grave and Gay* (New York: Scribners, 1911), 281.

56. Frederick Townsend Martin, *Things I Remember* (London: Eveleigh Nash, 1913), 101.

57. Boysie Seherr-Thoss, audiotape.

58. Muriel Seherr-Thoss to John C. White, in New York City, December 20, 1928.

59. Muriel Seherr-Thoss in Rome, Italy, to John W. White, March 22, 1926, Hampton NHS.

60. Paul Church, email to the author, November 11, 2021.

61. Paul Church, email to the author, August 21, 2022.

62. Paul Church, email to the author, November 17, 2021.

63. Paul Church, email to the author, November 17, 2021.

64. Bruce Farrell, personal communication, December 20, 2023.

65. Paul Church, email to the author, November 19, 2021.

66. Nevins, *Henry White*, 423.

67. Helen Eugenie Moore Anderson was appointed US ambassador to Denmark in October 1949. In 1962, she was appointed US minister to Bulgaria.

68. Alan Church, email to the author, September 27, 2022.

69. *New York Times*, September 7, 1927.

70. *New York Times*, March 1, 1947.

71. Paul Church, email to the author, August 23, 2022.

72. Eulogy at Margaret Church's funeral by her son, Ted Church III, January 2, 1995.

73. Paul Church, email to the author, May 5, 2022.

74. Alan Church, email to the author, September 22, 2022.

75. Boysie Seherr-Thoss, audiotape.

BIBLIOGRAPHY

ARCHIVE COLLECTIONS

Australia National Maritime Museum, Online Exhibitions, Lederer Collection.

———. Cama, Nicole, and Penny Edwell. "Object of the Week: The Importance of Doors, the Lederer Collection." Accessed December 3, 2023. https://www.sea.museum/2012/05/08/object-of-the-week-the-importance-of-doors-the-lederer-collection.

———. "Lederer Family." Accessed October 19, 2023. https://www.sea.museum/explore/online-exhibitions/waves-of-migration/immigration-stories/lederer-family.

———. Lederer, Jean. "Waves of Migration." *Signals Quarterly*, May 2013. https://issuu.com/anmmuseum/docs/signals_102/1.

Central Intelligence Agency. Freedom of Information Act Electronic Reading Room, Historical Collections.

———. "HR 70-14" (declassified). May 2, 2012. https://www.cia.gov/readingroom/docs/1949-05-02.pdf.

———. "Office Memorandum: BGFIEND Operations, 16 September 1949" (declassified). OBOPUS BGFIEND vol. 14, 2007. https://tetovalajm.blogspot.com/2014/01/cia-incesti-dhe-arkat-me-flori-ne.html.

———. "Scope of BGFIEND Operation" (declassified). 2007. https://gjonmarkagjoni.files.wordpress.com/2017/08/obopus-bgfiend-vol-13-bgfiend-operations_0056-scope-of-bgfiend.pdf.

Church, Paul, private collection.

European Holocaust Research Infrastructure. "Documentation of the Reichssicherheitshauptamt (RHSA), 1939–1945." Bundesarchiv, Berlin R58 Collection. https://portal.ehri-project.eu/units/il-002798-m_29-bundesarchiv_berlin_r_58.

Henry White Family Collection, Hampton National Historic Site (NHS), Maryland, National Park Service.

———. Henry White Papers.

———. Muriel Seherr-Thoss, "Memoirs" (unpublished manuscript).

———. Muriel White Seherr-Thoss Papers, Box 62A/Folder 12.

Messersmith, George S. Papers. Special Collections, University of Delaware Library.

———. G. S. Messersmith in Vienna to Cordell Hull, secretary of state, in Washington, July 31, 1936 (marked confidential). http://udspace.udel.edu/handle/19716/6679.

———. G. S. Messersmith in Vienna to Jay Pierrepont Moffat, June 6, 1934. http://udspace.udel.edu/handle/19716/6348.

———. G. S. Messersmith to William Phillips, undersecretary of state, June 26, 1933. http://udspace.udel.edu/handle/19716/6176; http://udspace.udel.edu/han dle/19716/6679.

National Archives of the United States, Washington, DC.

———. "Arrest List No. 22—Hermann von Seherr-Thoss; Roger von Seherr-Thoss; Theobald von Seherr-Thoss; Wolfgang von Seherr-Thoss." *Compilation by the IV Special Commission at the RSHA*, RG 242. Accessed April 26, 2024. https://www .archives.gov/iwg/declassified-records/rg-242-seized-foreign-records.

———. "Blackburn, Joseph." *US Consular Reports of Marriages 1910–1949*, RG 59.

———. "Certificate of Registration of American Citizens," vol. 95, RG 47200–47699. August 8, 1914.

———. "Naturalization Records Created by the US District Court in Colorado, 1877– 1952." *Naturalization Records, Colorado, 1876–1990*, M1192.

———. "US Petition for Naturalization." October 22, 1943, US District Court, Macon, GA, RG 1845.

National Archives of Hungary. Muriel Seherr-Thoss from Dobrau to Margaret Apponyi, June 28, 1930.

National Archives at New York. "Arriving Passenger and Crew Lists (including Castle Garden and Ellis Island), 1820–1957, Year: 1937," microfilm T715, p. 24, line 14.

Nuremberg Archives: International Court of Justice. "Document Book III (Documents 86–96) for the Defense of the Defendant Franz von Papen." Accessed April 4, 2024. https://stacks.stanford.edu/file/kd270md6345/kd270md6345.pdf.

Parliamentary Archives, LG/F/7/4/3.

Pegasus Archive. "Work Camps." Accessed August 13, 2022. https://www.pegasusar chive.org/pow/Work_camps.htm.

Powerhouse Collection. "Handwritten Testimonial for Arthur Lederer by the Aide-de-camp to the Emperor." 1904. *Five Handwritten Testimonials for Arthur Lederer.* Accessed December 3, 2023. https://collection.powerhouse.com.au/object/327734.

Roosevelt, Theodore Papers. Library of Congress Manuscript Division, Washington, DC. https://www.theodorerooseveltcenter.org/Research/Digital-Library/Record?libD =o211502.

Seherr-Thoss, Elizabeth, private collection, Lenox, MA.

White Bennett, Margaret Papers. W. Tapley Bennett Papers, Richard B. Russell Library for Political Research and Studies, Special Collections Library, University of Georgia Libraries, Athens, GA.

White, Henry Papers. Digital Library of the Commons, Library of Congress, Washington, DC. https://lccn.loc.gov/mm78045328.

ARTICLES

András, Bán D. "Barcza, György: Naplórészletek, 1938–1944." *2000* 8, no. 3 (1996): 36.

"Baghy-Szinyei Merse Manor." Cserkeszőlői Borászati Élményközpont. Accessed May 18, 2022. http://www.cserkeszolokastely.hu/.

Bailey, Fred Arthur. "A Virginia Scholar in Chancellor Hitler's Court: The Tragic Ambassadorship of William Edward Dodd." *The Virginia Magazine of History and Biography* 100, no. 3 (1992): 338.

Cienciala, Anna M. "The Rebirth of Poland." Centre for Military and Strategic Studies. Accessed October 24, 2023. http://www.conflicts.rem33.com/images/Poland/rebirth.html.

Dolan, Kerry A., Chase Peterson-Withorn, and Jennifer Wang, eds. "Billion-Dollar Dynasties: These Are the Richest Families in America." *Forbes*. December 17, 2020. https://www.forbes.com/sites/kerryadolan/2020/12/17/billion-dollar-dynasties-these-are-the-richest-families-in-america/?sh=47d1bcba772c.

"Dragon Lady: The Life of Sigrid Schultz." Westport Museum. Accessed December 18, 2023. https://westporthistory.org/dragon-lady-the-life-of-sigrid-schultz/.

Dyck, Ludwig H. "Panzer General Strachwitz." Warfare History Network. Accessed November 8, 2023. https://warfarehistorynetwork.com/article/unstoppable-strachwitz/.

Elsie, Robert. "1947 Galeazzo Ciano: Diary of Events on Albania." *Texts and Documents of Albanian History*. Accessed May 28, 2022. http://www.albanianhistory.net/1947_Ciano/index.html.

"The End of Hitlerism in Klein Strehlitz" (trans. "Das Ende des Hitlerismus in Klein-Strehlitz"). *Neustädter Heimatbrief* (Berlin), 1952. Accessed May 18, 2024. https://www.digishelf.de/objekt/010078045_1952/8/.

Fenzi, Jewell. "Elizabeth Moffat White (interview)." *The Association for Diplomatic Studies and Training: Foreign Affairs Oral History Program, Foreign Service Spouse Series*. July 26, 1988. https://www.adst.org/OH%20TOCs/White,%20Elizabeth%20Moffat.toc.pdf.

———. "Margaret White Bennett (interview)." *The Association for Diplomatic Studies and Training: Foreign Affairs Oral History Program, Foreign Service Spouse Series*. November 21, 1988. https://adst.org/OH%20TOCs/Bennett,%20Margaret%20White.toc.pdf.

Friedman, Morgan. "The Inflation Calculator." WestEgg. https://westegg.com/inflation/.

"Generalmajor Theobald Graf von Seherr-Thoß." *Lexikon der Wehrmacht*. Accessed March 4, 2024. https://lexikon-der-wehrmacht.de.

"Geraldine of the Albanians." *Royalty*. May 29, 2015. https://www.royalty-magazine.com/royal-history-and-heritage/geraldine-of-the-albanians.html.

Ginzberg, Gary. "A Complicated Life: Frank G. Wisner, Sr." *Advisors*. Accessed August 7, 2022. https://www.advisorsmagazine.com/trending/23537-a-complicated-life-frank-g-wisner-sr.

Han, Esther. *The Sydney Morning Herald*, January 20, 2013.

"Heinrich Leopold von Seherr-Thoss." Wikipedia. Accessed December 14, 2023. https://de.wikipedia.org/wiki/Heinrich_Leopold_von_Seherr-Tho%C3%9F.

Ilnicka, Jolanta. "'Good Lady'—Meeting of Great-Grandchildren." *My Skirmishes with Genealogy* (blog). May 17, 2014. https://potyczkizgenealogia.blogspot.com/2017/10/dobra-pani-spotkanie-prawnukow.html.

Katona, Csaba. "Geraldine Apponyi, the Sold Bride." *Acta Balcano Hungarica* 1 (2019): 204. https://www.academia.edu/40294836/Geraldine_Apponyi_the_Sold_Bride.

Keil, Lars-Broder. "This Enabled the Conspirators to Cover Up Many Traces." *Die Welt* (Berlin), March 18, 2021. https://www.welt.de/geschichte/zweiter-weltkrieg

/article197285955/Hitler-Attentat-So-gross-war-die-Verschwoerung-vom-20 -Juli-wirklich.html.

"Klagenfurt—Herzoghof." *Burgen-Austria* (archive). Accessed March 30, 2024. https:// www.burgen-austria.com/archive.php?id=1713.

Mattingly, Robert E., Major USMC. *Herringbone Cloak—GI Dagger: Marines of the OSS* (Quantico, VA: Marine Corps University, 1989), 87. https://www.ibiblio.org /hyperwar/USMC/USMC-OSS/USMC-OSS-6.html.

McCourt, David M. "American Hegemony and International Theory at the Council on Foreign Relations, 1953–1954." *International History Review* 42, no. 3 (2020). https://www.tandfonline.com/doi/abs/10.1080/07075332.2019.1608283?journal Code=rinh20.

McDonough, Giles. "Philip de László in the Great War." The de László Archive Trust. Accessed October 19, 2023. https://www.delaszlocatalogueraisonne.com/media /_file/imported/article-giles-macdonogh-with-images-final.pdf.

National Gallery of Art. "Margaret Stuyvesant Rutherfurd White (Mrs. Henry White)." Accessed October 23, 2023. https://www.nga.gov/collection/art-object -page.166470.html.

"Norddeutsche allgemeine Zeitung" (Berlin). April 27, 1892. "Parish of St. Barlomiej in Glogowek." Wikipedia. Accessed December 13, 2023. https://pl.wikipedia.org /wiki/Parafia_%C5%9B._Bart%C5%82omieja_w_G%C5%82og%C3%B3wku.

Nordlinger, Jay. "Good King Michael." *The National Review.* January 16, 2018. https:// www.nationalreview.com/2018/01/michael-romania-monarch-and-mensch/.

Offner, Arnold A. "William E. Dodd: Romantic Historian and Diplomatic Cassandra." *Historian* 24, no. 4 (1962): 68.

Pike, Nathan. "The Lederer's Journey to Australia." Prezi. Accessed October 19, 2023. https://prezi.com/fnxel0ghucld/lederers-journey-to-australia/.

"Sacre Coeur Is Reminiscent of a Dark Chapter." June 5, 2019. https://noe.orf.at/v2 /news/stories/2985512/.

Salonblatt, Vienna. March 21, 1908, Österreichische Nationalbibliothek. Accessed August 24, 2022. https://anno.onb.ac.at/cgi-content/annoshow?text=wsb %7C19051223%7Cx.

"Silesian Castles and Palaces." ADAN publishing, 2000.

Skopje Press. "CIA: Incest and the Chests of Gold in Zog's Rooms." *Top Tetova News.* Accessed April 7, 2024. https://tetovalajm.blogspot.com/2014/01/cia-incesti-dhe -arkat-me-flori-ne.html.

Spolniak, Dagmara. "The Extraordinary Story of an American Woman in Dobra," Turystyka; [Turkish]. Accessed December 10, 2023. https://turystyka.wp.pl/s /dagmara-spolniak/niezwykla-historia-amerykanki-w-dobrej-mieszkancy-ja-koch ali-a-gestapo-zastraszalo-6936060113549824a.

Strauchmann, Krzysztof. "Muriel's Children, or the Post-War Fate of the Owners of the Palace in Dobrau." *NTO* (blog). February 23, 2016. https://nto.pl/dzieci-muriel -czyli-powojenne-losy-wlascicieli-palacu-w-dobrej/ar/9428464.

Szczurek, Jan. "This Land Is Very Interesting." *Pisarze PL,* No. 457 (blog). June 9, 2020. Accessed September 9, 2022. https://pisarze.pl/2020/06/09/jan-szczurek-wielce -interesujaca-to-kraina/.

"What Is the Catholic Church's Position on Suicide and Physician-Assisted Suicide?" *Institute of Clinical Bioethics, Saint Joseph's University* (blog). Accessed March 22, 2024. https://www.sju.edu/centers/icb/blog/catholic-churchs-position-sui cide-physician-assisted-suicide-declaration-euthanasia.

BOOKS

Anderson, Larz. *Letters and Journals of a Diplomat.* Grand Rapids, MI: Fleming H. Revell, 1940.

Auchincloss, Louis. *The Vanderbilt Era: Profiles of a Gilded Age.* New York: Charles Scribner's Sons, 1989.

Baker, Ray Stannard. *Woodrow Wilson and World Settlement* 11. Gloucester, MA: P. Smith, 1960.

Basford, Elisabeth. *Princess Mary.* Cheltenham, Gloucestershire: History Press, 2021.

Bibby, Emily Katherine. "Making the American Aristocracy: Women, Cultural Capital, and High Society in New York City, 1870–1900." Master's thesis, Virginia Polytechnic Institute, June 10, 2009.

Bogdani, Mirela, and John Loughlin. *Albania and the European Union: The Tumultuous Journey Towards Integration and Accession.* London: I. B. Tauris, 2007.

Callanan, James D. "The Evolution of the CIA's Covert Action Mission, 1947–1963." Doctoral thesis, Durham University, 1999. https://etheses.dur.ac.uk/4481/.

Colonna, Vittoria, Duchess of Sermoneta. *Things Past.* London: Hutchinson, 1929.

Consuelo, Duchess of Marlborough. *The Glitter and the Gold.* New York: Harper & Brothers, 1952.

Dedet, Joséphine. *Geraldine—A Hungarian Woman on the Throne of Albania.* Libri, 2017.

de Szinyei-Merse, Antoinette. *Ten Years, Ten Months, Ten Days.* London: Hutchinson, 1940.

Dodd, William E. *Ambassador Dodd's Diary, 1933–1938.* London: Victor Gollangz, 1945.

Dorril, Stephen. *MI6: Inside the Covert World of Her Majesty's Secret Intelligence Service.* Washington, DC: Free Press, 2002.

Dutton, D. J. *Oxford Dictionary of National Biography.*

Evelyn, Princess Blücher. *An English Wife in Berlin.* New York: E. P. Dutton, 1921.

Filipczyk, Erwin, Fr. Norbert Zawilak, et al. *Good for Seven Centuries.* Opole, Poland: Litar Sp. Zoo, 2002.

Fischer, Bernd J. *Albania at War, 1939–1945.* West Lafayette, IN: Purdue University Press, 1999.

Gilmour, David. *Curzon: Imperial Statesman.* New York: Farrar, Straus & Giroux, 2006.

Harrison, Constance Cary. *Recollections Grave and Gay.* New York: Scribners, 1911.

Hornyák, Árpád. "Magyarország Balkán-politikája a két világháború között és Albánia függet-lensége." In *Kelet-európai sorsfordulók: Tanulmányok a 80 éves Palotás Emil tiszteletére*, edited by József Juhász. Budapest: ELTE BTK Kelet-Európa Történeti Tanszék–L'Harmattan, 2016.

Hutto, Richard Jay. *Crowning Glory: American Wives of Princes and Dukes.* Macon, GA: Henchard, 2007.

———. *A Poisoned Life: Florence Chandler Maybrick, the First American Woman Sentenced to Death in England.* Jefferson, NC: McFarland, 2018.

James, Henry. *The Complete Letters of Henry James,* vol. 2, *1883–1884.* Edited by Michael Anesko and Greg W. Zacharias. Lincoln: University of Nebraska Press, 2019.

Jones, Lloyd. *Biografi: An Albanian Quest,* ebook. Toronto: Vintage Canada, 2010. First published 1993 by Victoria University Press (Wellington, New Zealand).

———. *Biografi: A Traveller's Tale.* Toronto: Vintage Canada, 2010.

Kennedy, David M. *Freedom from Fear: The American People in Depression and War.* Oxford: Oxford University Press, 1999.

Lewis, Alfred Allan. *Ladies and Not So Gentle Women.* New York: Viking, 2000.

Lexico UK English Dictionary, s.v. "Hoxha, Enver." Oxford University Press. Accessed September 14, 2019.

Livingstone, Natalie. *The Women of Rothschild.* New York: St. Martin's Press, 2021.

Lohof, Timothy Leo. "Berlin Embassy of James Watson Gerard: Reflections of a Diplomatic Paradigm Shift 1913–1917." Master's thesis, University of Montana, 1997. https://scholarworks.umt.edu/etd/4713.

Lucey, Donna M. *Archie and Amélie: Love and Madness in the Gilded Age.* New York: Harmony Books, 2006.

———. *Sargent's Women: Four Lives Behind the Canvas.* New York: W. W. Norton, 2017.

Lulushi, Albert. *Operation Valuable Fiend.* New York: Arcade, 2014.

MacMillan, Margaret. *Paris 1919.* New York: Random House, 2001.

Martin, Frederick Townsend. *Things I Remember.* London: Eveleigh Nash, 1913.

Moseley, Ray. *Mussolini's Shadow: The Double Life of Count Galeazzo Ciano.* New Haven, CT: Yale University Press, 1999.

Nagorski, Andrew. *Hitlerland.* New York: Simon & Schuster, 2012.

Noble, G. Bernard, and E. R. Perkins, eds. *Foreign Relations of the United States 1939,* vol. 2. Washington, DC: Office of the Historian, 1956. https://history.state.gov/historicaldocuments/frus1939v01.

O'Sullivan, Michael. *Patrick Leigh Fermor: Noble Encounters between Budapest and Transylvania.* Budapest and New York: Central European Press, 2018.

Pearson, John. *The Life of Ian Fleming.* London: Jonathan Cape, 1966.

Raitz von Frentz, Christian. *A Lesson Forgotten: Minority Protection Under the League of Nations: The Case of the German Minority in Poland, 1920–1934.* New York: LIT Verlag Berlin-Hamburg-Münster, 1999.

Robyns, Gwen. *Geraldine of the Albanians.* London: Muller, Blond & White, 1987.

Roosevelt, Theodore. *The Autobiography of Theodore Roosevelt.* New York: Scribners, 1926.

Saltmarshe, Douglas. *Identity in a Post-Communist Balkan State: An Albanian Village Study.* Farnham, UK: Ashgate, 2001.

Schierstaedt, Patrouille. *Selbsterzähltes aus französischer Gefangenschaft* [Self-Narrated Stories from French Captivity]. Berlin: O. Elsner Verlagsgesellschaft m.b.H, 1918.

Shoumatoff, Elizabeth. *FDR's Unfinished Portrait.* Pittsburgh: University of Pittsburgh Press, 1990.

"Silesia." *The American Heritage Dictionary of the English Language.* 5th ed. New York: HarperCollins, 2012.

Strong, George Templeton. *The Diary of George Templeton Strong*, 4 vols. New York: Macmillan, 1952.

Sullivan, Wilson. *New England Men of Letters*. New York: Macmillan, 1972.

Swedish Men and Women: Biographical Reference Book (1942–1948). Vol. 4, *I–Linder*. Project Runeberg, 2023. https://runeberg-org.translate.goog/smok/4/0464.html ?_x_tr_sch=http&_x_tr_sl=sv&_x_tr_tl=en&_x_tr_hl=en&_x_tr_pto=sc.

Thomas, Evan. *The Very Best Men: Four Who Dared*. New York: Touchstone, 1995.

Tinniswood, Adrian. *The Long Weekend: Life in the English Country House Between the Wars*. London: Jonathan Cape, 2016.

Tomes, Jason. *King Zog: Self-Made Monarch of Albania*. Gloucestershire: History Press, 2007.

Vanderbilt, Cornelius, Jr. *Queen of the Golden Age*. New York: McGraw-Hill, 1956.

Walzl, August. *Kärnten 1946. Vom NS-Regime zur Besatzungsherrschaft im Alpen-Adria-Raum*. Klagenfurt: Universitätsverlag Carinthia, 1985.

Wemyss, Lady. *A Family Record*. London: Curwen Press, 1932.

Wharton, Edith. *A Backward Glance*. New York: D. Appleton-Century, 1934.

Whiting, Lilian. *Italy, the Magic Land*. Glasgow: Good Press, 2019.

Who's Who in American Sports. Washington, DC: National Biographical Society, 1928.

Wilhelm II. *My Early Life*. London: Methuen, trans. ed. 1926.

Wilson, Tim. *Frontiers of Violence: Conflict and Identity in Ulster and Upper Silesia, 1918–1922*. Oxford: Oxford University Press, 2010.

PERIODICALS

Andalusia Star, Andalusia, AL. November 5, 1926.

Baltimore Sun, September 3, 1916.

———. August 21, 1923.

"The Baronial Busches." *Life* magazine, May 2, 1955.

Boston Globe, January 16, 1911.

Brooklyn Daily Eagle, May 29, 1938.

Butte Daily Post, March 9, 1909.

Capital Journal, Salem, OR. May 20, 1921.

Chicago Tribune, August 14, 1909.

Daily Globe, St. Paul, MN. February 1, 1889.

Daily Journal, Telluride, CO. "Muriel White Married to a German Count." April 28, 1909.

Daily Record, May 1, 1909.

Deutscher Reichsanzeiger und Preußischer Staatsanzeiger, Berlin. June 25, 1943.

East Liverpool Evening Review, March 19, 1909.

Evening World, March 8, 1909.

Irish Independent, June 7, 2008.

Los Angeles Herald, March 10, 1909.

———. April 29, 1909.

———. August 29, 1909.

Manchester (CT) Evening Herald, April 27, 1938.

Neenah Daily Times, Neenah, WI. July 30, 1914.

Neustädter Heimatbrief 11, no. 1 (January 1960).

New York Daily News, June 15, 1940.

New York Times.

———. "American A German Peeress." January 28, 1912.

———. "Americans Who Marry Italians." May 5, 1907.

———. September 19, 1880.

———. March 14, 1909.

———. April 18, 1909.

———. May 2, 1909.

———. April 3, 1910.

———. January 16, 1911.

———. September 3, 1916.

———. September 18, 1920.

———. November 4, 1920.

———. September 7, 1927.

———. April 4, 1937.

———. March 10, 1938.

———. April 17, 1938.

———. May 26, 1938.

———. June 26, 1938.

———. April 5, 1939.

———. April 15, 1939.

———. April 23, 1939.

———. October 22, 1939.

———. March 3, 1943.

———. March 1, 1947.

———. September 21, 1951.

———. November 29, 1952.

———. April 10, 1961.

New York World, July 16, 1903.

North American Review's War Weekly ("Harvey's Weekly") 1, no. 49 (December 7, 1918): 4.

Oshkosh Northwestern, March 9, 1909.

Pittsburgh Index 20, no. 14 (April 3, 1909): 5.

Pittsburgh Sun-Telegraph, February 11, 1939.

San Francisco Call, September 20, 1903.

———. March 10, 1909.

Sunday Pictorial, London. January 3, 1943. https://www.ucl.ac.uk/library/ssees-archives /nac3.htm.

Time magazine, August 22, 1932.

The Times, London. "Sex Scandal behind Brideshead Revisited." August 10, 2009.

"Verbunden mit der Annener Volkszeitung: Anzeigenblatt für Witten-Annen und die Stadtteile Rüdinghausen, Stockum und Düren." *Annener Zeitung.* July 14, 1925.

Washington Herald, March 21, 1909.

Wyoming Derrick 14, no. 23 (August 13, 1903).

INDEX

Page references for photos are italicized.

Baghy, Julia Geraldine de, 131, 168
Baghy, Virginia de. *See* Apponyi de Baghy
  Blackburn Máriássy de Márkus et
  Batizfalva, Virginia
Balfour, Arthur, 22, 46
Balhmann, Anna, 11
Bayard, Thomas F., 28
BDM. *See* Bund Deutscher Mädel
Beale, Harriett S. Blaine "Hattie," 33
Beatrice, Princess of the United Kingdom,
  32, 33
Beauchamp, William Lygon, Earl of,
  43–44
Bennett, Margaret Rutherfurd White
  "Lolly," 87, 92, 93–94, 164, 200, 218
Berlepsch, Caspar von, Baron, 163, 196
Berlepsch, Christof von, 198
Berlepsch, Nurmie von, 198
Berlin: British representation in, 99–100;
  dinners with Nazis in, 2, 110; Hitler
  assassination attempt, 204–5; Iron
  Curtain escapes, 218; Olympic
  Games in, 126, 128; Seherr-Thoss
  family in, 62, 64, 71, 75, 95, 98–99,
  100; US embassy in, 2, 89, 92–93,
  189; White–Seherr-Thoss courtship
  in, 50, 51
bisexuality, 43–44
Blackburn, Eleanor Virginia, 173
Blackburn, Joseph Apponyi, 173
Blackburn, Joseph B., 173
Blackburn, Virginia. *See* Apponyi de
  Baghy Blackburn Máriássy de
  Márkus et Batizfalva, Virginia
blackmail, 61
Blaine, James G., 18
Blaine Beale, Harriett S., 33
Blueberry Hill, 157–58, 210
Boebel, Elisabeth, 130
Boris III, King of Bulgaria, 183–84

Brambilla, Julia Meyer, 70–71
Braun, Eva, 130
British prisoners of war, 3, 185, 187, 218
Buckler, Eliza "Didy" Ridgely White, 6,
  8, 29
Buckler, Georgina Grenfell Walrond, 47,
  112
Buckler, Lucy, 54
Buckler, Thomas Hepburn, 6, 8, 29
Buckler, William Hepburn "Willie," 8, 30,
  53, 112
Budapest National Museum, 132
Bund Deutscher Mädel (BDM), 93–94
Busch, Adolphus, 211

Campbell, Jane (Princess di San
  Faustino), 39, 41–43, 47
Cannon, Adelaide, 145
Cannon Kingsland Duncan, Marian
  DeForest, 144
Canstatt, Susanne Schilling von, Baroness,
  212
Carroll de Kergorlay, Mary Louise,
  Countess, 69
Carroll de La Grange, Anita, Baroness, 69
Chamberlain, Austen, 44–48
Chamberlain, Joseph, 32, 44, 45–47
Chamberlain, Mary Crowninshield
  Endicott, 32
Chanler, Elizabeth Winthrop, 10
Chanler, John White, 10
Chanler, Mrs. William Astor, 68–69
Choate, Joseph H., 51
Church, Alanson, 189, 199, 202, 209, 212,
  213–14
Church, Alice Kennedy Sands, 30, 150
Church, Christopher, 212, 213
Church, Edgar M., Sr., 30, 149–50
Church, Edgar Moore "Ted," Jr.: CIA/
  OSS Zog surveillance, 175–76,

ABOUT THE AUTHOR

Richard Jay Hutto served as White House appointments secretary to the Carter family and was chairman of the Georgia Council for the Arts. A former attorney, he is an internationally recognized writer and lecturer and has been featured as an on-air historical expert. One of his books was adapted for television. Hutto has written extensively about the marriage of America's Gilded Age heiresses to titled husbands. See more info at www.TheCountess.net.